U0802050

名誉主编◎胡景平
策划统筹◎谢　玮

景德镇匠人志

匠心无迹

THE CRAFTSMEN OF JINGDEZHEN & ITS VANISHING FOLK CRAFTSMANSHIP

主编◎吴远征

江西高校出版社
JIANGXI UNIVERSITIES AND COLLEGES PRESS

图书在版编目(CIP)数据

景德镇匠人志：匠心无迹 / 吴远征主编 .--南昌：江西高校出版社，2019.11（2022.3 重印）

ISBN 978-7-5493-6656-9

Ⅰ.①景… Ⅱ.①吴… Ⅲ.①手工业工人—生平事迹—景德镇Ⅳ.① K825.72

中国版本图书馆 CIP 数据核字 (2017) 第 328262 号

JINGDEZHEN JIANGREN ZHI
JIANG XIN WU JI

出版发行	江西高校出版社
社　　址	江西省南昌市洪都北大道 96 号
总编室电话	(0791)88504319
销售电话	(0791)88522516
网　　址	www.juacp.com
印　　刷	天津画中画印刷有限公司
经　　销	全国新华书店
开　　本	787mm×1092mm　1/16
印　　张	15.75
字　　数	250 千字
版　　次	2019 年 11 月第 1 版 2022 年 3 月第 2 次印刷
书　　号	ISBN 978-7-5493-6656-9
定　　价	98.00 元

赣版权登字 -07-2017-1694

版权所有　侵权必究

图书若有印装问题，请随时向本社印制部（0791-88513257）退换

出 品 方　景德镇市古镇投资管理有限公司

Producer:Jingdezhen Ancient Town Investment Management
Co.,Ltd.

总 顾 问　王力农　陈雨前

General Consultant: Wang Linong Chen Yuqian

名誉主编　胡景平

Honorary Editor-in-Chief: Hu Jingping

策划统筹　谢　玮

Planned and coordinated by: Xie Wei

主　　编　吴远征

Editor-in-Chief: Wu Yuanzheng

学术指导　王安维　张德山　韩晓光

Academic Advisor：Wang Anwei Zhang Deshan Han Xiaoguang

编　　委　严　佳　徐慧文　肖瑞彬
黄　辉　汪春荣　蓝田玉（特邀）

Editorial Members：Yan Jia Xu Huiwen Xiao Ruibin
Huang Hui Wang Chunrong Lan Tianyu (Guest Editor)

翻译指导　朱练平

Translation Guidance：Zhu Lianping

翻　　译　景德镇学院　CI 译客工作室
戴洁霞　陈　堃　扬　扬

Translator：Jingdezhen University CI Translation Workshop
Dai Jiexia Chen Kun

编　　撰　景德镇学院老城文化研究课题组
景德镇学院文化遗产保护传承网络传播中心

Written by：Research Team for Old Town Culture of Jingdezhen University
Protection and Inheritance Internet Communication Center of
Cultural Heritage of Jingdezhen University

打造世界瓷都的“记忆之殿”（序一）

胡景平

如果说文化是一座城市的灵魂，老城文化则是一座城市的集体记忆和精神基因。

近年来，通过各种形式保护老城文化，变老城文化资源优势为旅游资源优势，将老城文化作为城市旅游产业的特色品牌，已成为当代城市管理者和建设者的共识。而出版专著，举办影展，拍摄专题片，创作民俗题材的文学作品、雕塑和风俗画，乃至创建老城文化博物馆，也成为一些城市收集、梳理老城文化，立体化打造“记忆之殿”，助推社会经济发展的重要战略。

作为蜚声中外的历史文化名城，景德镇具有两千多年的城市发展历史。在悠久的演变历程中，景德镇形成了特色鲜明的包括陶瓷文化在内的民俗文化、里弄文化、会馆文化、书院文化、匠人文化、名人文化、建筑文化、饮食文化、商贸文化和方言文化，由此汇聚成异彩纷呈的景德镇老城文化。

随着旧城改造脚步的日益加快和城市人口流动的日益频繁，以及现代城市文化的兴起，那些曾经如水和空气一般朝朝暮暮渗透于我们日常生活的老城文化正在逐渐稀释，在淡化，在异化，甚至在离我们远去。通过口述历史、底层叙事和影像写真等多元化方式，原生态地保存这座千年古镇的老城文化记忆，就是留住这座千年古镇的集体记忆和精神血脉，留住这座城市的根。

为了挖掘、保护和传承千年古镇的历史文脉，丰富老城博物馆的文化史料，忠实记录景德镇老城文化的原生态样本，景德镇市古镇投资管理有限公司携手景德镇学院历史文化研究学者和传播专家及社会力量，以编撰和出版老城文化保护与传播项目《景德镇老城记忆》系列读本为契机，着力打造功在当代、利在千秋的《景德镇老城记忆工程》。这套书以中英文双语版传播，借此创建相关数据库，以文字与影像为后人构筑一座宝贵的“记忆之殿”，为打造与世界对话城市战略提供文化软实力支撑，体现了一个国有企业的社会责任和时代担当，可谓功在当代、利在千秋。

此项计划启动以来，在合作双方的共同努力和社会各界的大力支持下，已经初见成效。今天，摆在大家面前的这部分量不轻的专著，就是我们呈献给这座历史文化名城的珍贵献礼。翻开这套图文并茂的专著，我们仿佛看到了一幅幅动态的良工百业风俗画，看到了曾经在这方水土歌于斯哭于斯而今已渐行渐远的先民群像，看到了这座文化名城历史河床堆积层中最鲜亮的多元化文化遗存，看到了江南雄镇气势恢宏的史诗与摇曳多姿的雕像，更看到了一个世界瓷都的文化自觉和文化自信。

“工匠来八方，器成天下走。”作为一座没有围墙的城市，素有“千猪万米”之誉的景德镇自古以来就物华天宝、人杰地灵。站在保护历史遗产与铸造城市形象的坐标上，多样化、多层次、多视觉地深入挖掘、记录和研究这座历史文化名城的老城文化形态特质，就是留住一座城市的集体记忆，守望一代人的集体乡愁。这一善莫大焉的义举，不仅有助于景德镇夯实城市文化内涵、塑造城市品牌形象，对于讲好中国故事、传播中国声音、大力弘扬优秀传统文化，乃至促进中华民族伟大复兴，也是一个值得借鉴的可贵样本。

希望有更多有识之士投身于《景德镇老城记忆工程》，与我们携手同行，为进一步挖掘、记录和研究这座历史文化名城的老城文化，留住我们的乡愁，并借此立体化打造千年雄镇的“记忆之殿”，助推社会经济发展的重要战略同心戮力，共襄盛举。

A "Memory Palace" for the Porcelain Capital of the World (Preface One)

Hu Jingping

If culture is the soul of a city, old city culture is the collective memory and spiritual gene of a city.

In recent years, protecting the old city culture memory, changing the old culture resources into tourism resources advantages, taking the old culture as special brand of urban tourism industry through various forms, has become the consensus of the contemporary urban managers and builders. Publishing monographs, organizing movie exhibitions, shooting feature films, creating folk literature, sculpture, theme and genre painting, and even establishing city culture museum, can also become important strategy of some cities collecting, combing old culture, three-dimensional building temple of "memory", boosting the social and economic development.

As a famous historical and cultural city at home and abroad, Jingdezhen has a history of more than 2000 years. In the long evolution, Jingdezhen has formed a distinctive culture, including ceramic culture, folk culture, lane culture, hall culture, academy culture, the builders culture, celebrity culture, architecture culture, food culture, business culture and dialect culture, thus all of this evolved different old city culture of Jingdezhen.

With the quickening of the old city reconstruction steps and the increasing flows of urban population, as well as the rise of modern urban culture, those who like water and air generally exist in our daily life of the old culture is gradually diluted, playing down, alienating, even is far away from us. Through oral history, understratum narration and image pictorial way and the other diversified methods, ecologically preserving the ancient old culture memory of this millennium city, is to keep the collective memory and spirit of this millennium city, and the root of the city.

To dig, protect and inherit the historical context of this millennium city, enrich the historical culture data of the old city museum, record the original samples of the Jingdezhen city culture, Jingdezhen Ancient Town Investment Management Co., LTD., join hands with the ancient historical and cultural scholars and experts of Jingdezhen University and social forces, taking the opportunity of compilation and publication of the old city culture protection and communication projects "Jingdezhen city memory" series of books, to make efforts to build "Jingdezhen city memory project" which will contribute to contemporary now and future. This set of book communicates through English and Chinese version, and creates the related database, with words and images to build a precious temple of "memory" for future generations. In order to provide cultural soft power support for building a city strategy of dialogue with the world, it reflects the social responsibility and era responsibility of a state-owned enterprise.

Since the launch of this program, with the joint efforts of both parties and the strong support from all sectors of society, the results have begun to be achieved. Today, in front of you, this important monograph is our precious gift to this historic and cultural city. Open this book with pictures, we seem to see the frame including the social customs, workers, industries, see the portraits of ancestors who lived and worked in Jingdezhen, see the diversified culture heritage of the historic city with rich accumulation and see the magnificent epic with glittering statues, even see the cultural consciousness and cultural self-confidence of this city.

"Artisans come from all over the world, porcelain is sold everywhere." As a city without walls, Jingdezhen, known as "thousands of pigs and tens of thousands of cereals", has been a precious treasure since ancient times. Standing on the place of protecting historical heritage and casting the city's image, diversifiedly, multi-levelly and visually deep dig, record and study the historical and cultural qualities of city, is to keep the collective memory of a city, watch the collective nostalgia of a generation. This altruistic act, not only helps Jingdezhen strengthen urban culture connotation, shape the city brand image, for speaking good Chinese story, communicating Chinese voice, vigorously devoloping the excellent traditional culture, and promoting the great rejuvenation of the Chinese nation, it is a worthy reference and valuable sample.

We hope more people devote to the Jingdezhen city memory project, together with our colleagues, in order to further excavate, record and study the old culture to retain our homesickness, and we should three-dimensionally build one temple of "memory", try our best to boost social and economic development.

留住一座城市的记忆（序二）

吴远征

景德镇，举世闻名的世界瓷都。人们津津乐道的，总是其巧夺天工的制瓷技艺、美轮美奂的瓷器精品和积淀深厚的陶瓷文化。

陶瓷及其衍生出来的千姿百态的文化，当然是景德镇无与伦比的地方特色文化，是千年瓷都的根与魂。

然而，作为一座没有围墙的城市，景德镇除了历史悠久的陶瓷文化，还有异彩纷呈的匠人文化值得我们观察、思考、记录和镌刻。如果说陶瓷文化是景德镇的根与魂，那么非陶瓷类的匠人文化则是她的血与肉——正是这些异彩纷呈的匠人文化，构成了景德镇老城文化的重要内涵，滋养了这座历史文化名城屹立千年而不衰的生命躯干。

随着城市化进程的加快，景德镇老城区的面貌发生了天翻地覆的变化：一些儿时熟悉的里弄老街不见了，一些令人魂牵梦萦的老屋被拆除了，一些先民们赖以生存的老行当消失了。取而代之的是时尚的商业街和鳞次栉比的高楼大厦。

“在山泉水清，出山泉水浊。”有朝一日，当这座以手工制瓷技艺名闻遐迩的城市成为摩天大厦林立的水泥森林，那将是景德镇的悲哀而不是荣光。唯其如此，在呼吁旧城改造者改造与保护并重的同时，通过口述历史和影像档案等多种形式，对这座城市的老城文化进行抢救性挖掘和保护，为后世留住一座城市的记忆，已经刻不容缓了。正是基于这样一种美好初衷，我们在景德镇市古镇投资管理有限公司的鼎力支持下，携手有关有识之士成立了景德镇学院老城文化研究课题组，启动了构架宏大的景德镇老城文化研究工程。“景德镇老城文化记忆书系”之一的《景德镇匠人志：匠心无迹》，正是这一浩大工程的奠基之作。

撰写这样一本记录地方文化的原创性专著，最大的困难是没有多少参考资料和对采访对象的寻找。为了找到那些具有代表性的匠人，在将近一年的时间里，我们在偏街陋巷寻寻觅觅，在烈日和暴雨下艰辛奔走。在结束一场采访的归途中，偶遇一个“打爆米花”的，我们欣喜若狂，尾随其后，递水敬烟，奉若神明；上班路上，意外邂逅一个“吹唢呐”的，我们喜出望外，千方百计要了他的手机号码；情人节之夜，年轻人卿卿我我陶醉在花前月下，我们却刚结束对“豆腐西施”的现场采访，饥肠辘辘、疲惫不堪地回到城区；为了采访纯手工榨油的师傅，我们不辞辛苦两上篁岭，终于不辱使命探骊得珠……

其实，最让我们心生感慨的不是课题组同志们含辛茹苦、煎精熬血的采写工作，而是对那些已经消失或者正在消失的老行当及其从业者生存状态的深深忧虑。曾几何时，在这座江南小镇的成长史上，这些老行当及其从业者犹如婴儿与生俱来的胎记，承载着这座城市个性鲜明的文化基因和生命密码。当胎记褪去，基因断链，后人还能认得清他们的先祖吗？正因如此，我们才深刻认识到课题组同仁们辛勤付出的重要意义。

写作永远是一项充满遗憾的工作。就在本书即将付梓出版之际，作为主编者，我不仅深深地感觉到其中一些篇目在选材和行文等方面存在的种种缺憾，也深深地感到一种无可奈何的遗珠之憾——景德镇匠人文化千姿百态，在短短一年时间内，靠课题组三五个热心的同仁，难免挂一漏万。因此，关于老城文化记忆工程的构筑依然任重道远。

2018年6月8日夏雨淅沥的黎明

（吴远征，又名吴维惠，景德镇学院海上丝绸之路研究院副院长，景德镇市作家协会副主席，南昌大学影视艺术研究中心兼职教授，联合国教科文组织“陶瓷文化保护与创新”教席专家）

Retain the Memory of a City (Preface Two)

Wu Yuanzheng

Jingdezhen, the world famous porcelain capital. People are fond of saying the skillful porcelain making artistry, beautiful porcelain products and profound ceramic culture.

Ceramics and the various forms of culture derived from them are, of course, the incomparable local characteristic culture of Jingdezhen, the root and soul of the porcelain capital for thousands of years.

However, as a city without walls, Jingdezhen has not only a long history of ceramic culture, but also a colorful craftsman culture which is worthy of our observation, thinking, recording and engraving. If is the root of Jingdezhen ceramic culture and the soul, so the craftsmen of the ceramic culture is her blood and flesh—it is these colorful craftsmen culture, constitutes the important connotation of Jingdezhen city culture, cultivation of the famous historical and cultural city stands one thousand torso and long life.

As the pace of urbanization quickes, the appearance of Jingdezhen city changed beyond recognition: some familiar lanes of the old street in childhood are missing, some obsession house dismantled, some people who live in old industry disappeared. In its place are fashionable high streets and tall buildings.

In mountain, the spring is clear, when the spring is out of mountain, it is cloudy. It will be a tragedy, not a glory, for Jingdezhen one day when the city, famed for its artisanal porcelain, becomes a concrete forest of skyscrapers. Only then, in the call for old city reconstruction of renovation and protection at the same time, through the oral history and a variety of forms such as image file, to search and protect the city' s old town culture , for later generations to retain the memory of a city, is urgent.Based on such a good original intention, under the support of the Research Team of Old Town Culture of Jingdezhen University, we launched the grand architecture of Jingdezhen city culture research project. As one of the "Jingdezhen old city cultural memory book system" ， "no craftsmanship" is the foundation work of this huge project.

The biggest difficulty in writing such an original monograph on local culture is not much reference material and the search for interviewees. In order to find those representative craftsmen，we have been searching in the narrow streets and alleys for nearly a year，running hard in the hot sun and rain. On the way home from an interview，we were overjoyed to see a "popcorn popper" ，followed by water，cigarettes and deities. On the way to work， we met a suona player by accident. On valentine' s day night，when the young people were so lovey-dovey and intoxicated，we had just finished our live interview with Tofuxishi. We came back to the city hungry and tired. In order to interview the master of pure manual oil pressing，we took pains to go twice on the Huangling mountain，and finally got the ball on the mission.

In fact, the most regrets let us mind are not write work of team comrades endure all kinds of hardships，but deep concern of living condition for the old business and its practitioners which are disappearing or have disappeared.Once upon a time, in the growth history of the jiangnan town，the old business and its practitioners like babies born birthmark，are bearing the distinct culture genes and life password of the city. When the birthmarks are removed and the genes are broken，will future generations recognize their ancestors？ Because of this，we have realized the importance of hard work of our team members.

Writing is always a regrettable job. Before the book was published，as the main editor，I not only deeply feel some articles with regrets in the material and style，etc，also deeply feel a kind of helpless regret of pearl—Jingdezhen craftsmen cultural differences，in a short span of a year，by team enthusiastic colleagues，it is hard to avoid exhaustive. So there is still a long way to go in constructing the cultural memory project of the old city.

The rainy summer dawns on June 8, 2018

（Wu Yuanzheng, also known as Wu Weihui，deputy director of Maritime Silk Road Institute of Jingdezhen University，vice chairman of Jingdezhen Writers Association，guest professor of Film & Television Arts Research Center of Nanchang University，chair expert of UNESCO "Ceramic Culture:Preservation and Creativity" ）

目录

雅　艺

手　艺

CONTENTS

Elegant Art

Handicraft Art

Food Processing Art

雅艺
Elegant Art
高志山／摄影

漆画师刘寒：
苦寒造就“漆彩人生”

【老手艺项目】 漆艺（漆画）

漆艺（漆画）表现出中华民族深厚的文化底蕴和文明历史，是中国艺术史上的瑰宝。从河姆渡发掘的朱漆碗有7000年的历史。唐代的漆艺达到鼎盛并传播到日本。中国近代漆画是在传统漆艺基础上逐渐发展而成的一个独立的艺术门类。漆画技艺包容性强，融合了油画、版画、雕刻等门类艺术表现形式，有很高的艺术性与欣赏性。漆画是传统技艺和绘画艺术的结合。

【匠人小传】

刘寒，男，江西都昌人，南昌大学油画硕士研究生毕业，长期致力于油画及漆画工艺创作与形式语言研究，曾师从福建省工艺美术大师、福州大学美术系主任吴嘉诠教授和陈立德等漆画名家，练就了扎实的基本功。作品《鄱湖岸边是我家》被江西工艺美术馆收藏，并被评为馆藏一等奖；漆画《鄱湖情》获“中国工艺美术百花奖”铜奖，《夕阳·诗境篇》获江西工艺美术展金奖，《秋歌》《家园》《田园曲》等作品在江西省宣传部，江西省文化厅、文联、美协等的艺术展上获奖。

2017年创作的漆画《数字体育》入选全国第九届体育美展。

【匠心之路】

偶一遇见终成痴迷

刘寒学的是油画专业，谈起与漆画的结缘，他颇有感慨：当年画展一偶遇，此生执着莫它属。1998年在北京学习期间，刘寒参观全国美展，被漆画艺术展区的漆画深深吸引。他第一次受到一种艺术震撼，漆画的颜色绚丽大气、沉稳厚重，兼具“鲜活”与“朝气”，色彩的视觉效果有一种气势袭人，同时又不艳俗、不张扬的内敛美。他在漆画前忘情欣赏的同时，也在内心坚定了要从事漆画创作的志向。

默默创作忍受艰辛

迷上漆画后，刘寒业余时间都扑在对漆画的研究与探索上了。从选材、制作到成为一位漆画家，其中经受的磨难、付出的艰辛与努力，无以言述，只凭着对漆画的一片痴心，他一头扎进去就是20年。从最初对各种漆的性能摸索到技法上的突破，不是一蹴而就的，而是经过了漫长的探索和师友的指点的。从江西漆画最常用的聚氨酯漆入手，再到腰果漆，最后到传统大漆的运用，每次运用不同材质，都必须通过长期实践完成感性经验的积

累，才能系统地了解不同漆的特性，才能下笔与漆进行愉悦的对话，收获意外惊喜。

与传统大漆（生漆）的磨合过程，更是无比艰辛。谈起自己与大漆的磨合经历，刘寒有太多感受。他说："一个真正的漆画家，只有继承与发挥传统大漆的特性优势，其作品方有经久不凋的价值。用传统大漆创作出的漆画色彩高贵典雅、沉稳古朴，特有的经久不退的宝石般的光泽胜过世间所有化学合成漆。大漆也是目前世界上最环保的无化学添加剂的材质。具备如此优势的大漆，却有一点让创作者深感无奈——生漆会'咬人'，很多人一接触就过敏，全身红肿，皮肤上突起一个个水泡，痒得难受，就是俗称的'漆疮'。"谈起自己受漆"咬"之苦的经历，他依然心有戚戚。2016 年，正当他全身心沉浸在一幅大型画的创作中，他的手上脸上就开始红肿起泡，且奇痒难耐，最后他不得不丢下正在进行的创作，到皮肤病医院住院治疗两个礼拜。除了身体的痒，一个画家还得忍受内心的痒，创作到一半的画被迫搁置，那种灵感涌动而画笔不在的感受，确实很无奈。

"漆彩"人生创新突破

漆画强调材质和工艺，所以在艺术的表现上常会受到限制，难以表达广博深厚的题材，同时也制约了漆画艺术的创新。作为扎根在瓷都景德镇的艺术家，刘寒在漆画艺术上一直寻求一种地域性的艺术表现形式，将本地艺术风格与漆画工艺结合，将现代意识与传统材质完美融合，尝试着运用新的漆画语言阐述自己对世界的认识与思考。刘寒认为，漆画所用材料是漆，但漆画是画，定位应注重艺术，而非传统工艺；再加上创新，才能使漆画成为独一无二的艺术。

在创作题材上，他热衷于表现瓷都特色及身边的日常景物。他创作的漆画《草鞋》，主题寓意深刻。景德镇过去被称为“草鞋码头”，一代代窑工穿着草鞋创造了景德镇的陶瓷文明。如今，伟大的共产党继承了当年红军的“草鞋精神”，使中华民族走向了繁荣富强。刘寒很善于用大漆的原色表现身边富有生命力的风景。他的作品《柿子红了》《高原的沸腾》就是运用黑、红、白三色表现生命的张力与山河的壮美的：大漆黑得极致，给人以无限的想象；大漆的朱红，妍丽而不艳俗，沉稳古朴，故有“质有余者不受饰也”之说。简单的色调最能表现丰富的质感。

【匠人心语】

刘寒表示，在艰苦的艺术探求和成长过程中，他一路耕耘，一路享受着创作的快乐。今后他将更深入地去探求漆画艺术领域的新工艺，把漆画与景德镇陶瓷绘画艺术融合在一起，创造出富有瓷都特色的漆画、陶瓷作品。刘寒相信，漆画艺术将会如同漆的本性一样历久弥新。

（蓝田玉 / 撰文　刘寒 / 画图）

Liu Han, a Lacquer Painter : Bitter Cold Makes the Lacquer Colors Life

The Ancient Craft: Lacquer Art （Lacquer Painting）

The lacquer art （lacquer painting） is a treasure in Chinese art history, reflecting well the profound culture and civilization of Chinese nation. The painted bowl unearthed in Hemudu has a history of 7, 000 years. The lacquer art reached its peak during Tang dynasty and then spread to Japan. Chinese modern lacquer painting is a kind of independent art which was gradually developed from the traditional lacquer art. The art of lacquer painting is inclusive, it combines oil painting, blockprinting, engraving and other forms of artistic expression with a high degree of artistry and appreciation. it is a combination of traditional art and painting art.

The Brief Biography of the Craftsman

Liu Han, male, from Jiangxi Duchang, a master of oil painting, graduated from Nanchang University and was long-term committed to process creation and formal language study in oil and lacquer painting. He has ever learned after Professor Chen Lide, Wu Jiaquan（a craft master and director of Fine Arts Department of Fuzhou University） and so on, which gave him a solid foundation of basic skills. His work "The Shore of Poyang Lake is My Home" was collected and won the first place in Jiangxi Craft Art Museum; his lacquer painting " Feeling for Poyang Lake" won Chinese Arts and Crafts Baihua awards—bronze medal; his "Sunset and Poetry" won the gold medal of Jiangxi arts and crafts exhibition; "Song of Autumn", "Homeland", "Idyll" and other works have won prizes at many art exhibitions. His lacquer painting Digital Sport created in 2017 was selected for the 9th national sports show.

The Growth of the Craftsman

Once Meeting Leads to Obsession

Liu' s major is oil painting, when talking about lacquer painting, he sighed: he just came across it by accident, and it became a pursuit of his life. During his study in Beijing in 1998, he visited the national exhibition and was fascinated by the lacquer paintings of the art exhibition area. He was amazed the first time at the art of lacquer painting. While he was enjoying himself in front of the painting, he was also determined to pursue his ambition of lacquer painting.

Quietly Creating and Enduring Hardships

Having been obsessed with lacquer painting, Liu spent all his spare time in studying and researching it. From material selection and painting creation to being a professional lacquer painter, the hardships he has endured defied description. He threw himself into lacquer painting for as long as 20 years, who was lived just with his passion for the lacquer painting. From researching the function at the beginning to the breakthrough in the skills of various lacquers was not achieved overnight, it requires a long exploration and guidance from teachers and friends. To master the characteristics of different painting material and harvest surprises, he practiced each various lacquer a very long period, such as the polyurethane coating that is commonly used in Jiangxi lacquer painting, the cashew lacquer and the traditional Chinese lacquer.

The traditional Chinese lacquer (raw lacquer) is especially difficult to handle. Regarding his experience with this lacquer, Liu feels too much.He said: "As a true lacquer painter, to maintain the value of his works, he has to inherit and give play of the advantages of the traditional Chinese lacquer. The color painted in this lacquer has the most elegtant gloss that no synthetic one could present. Besides, such lacquer, without any chemical additive, is the most eco–friendly lacquer in the current world. Though with so many advantages, it still has one flaw that many lacqerpainter can't bear: it may 'bite'. many people are allergic to it. Once they touch it, their skin would break out in a rash, which is extremely itchy." When talking about it, Liu still feels the pain. In 2016, as he was fully immersed in the creation of a large painting, his face became red and swollen and grew many bubbles intolerablly itching. Due to this, he had to give up his ongoing creation, and seek treatment in a skin hospital for two weeks. Apart from the tickling of the body, he also has to endure the itch of the heart. When the painting is put on hold and the inspiration surging, but the paintbrush is not present, it is unbearable and really helpless.

The Breakthrough of the "Paint Color" Life

Because lacquer painting relies heavily on the painting material and the processing of it, the performance of art is often restricted, and also it constrains the innovation of the art. As an artist rooted in Jindezhen, Liu Han has been pursuing the regional art forms. By combining the local art style with lacquer painting techniques and integrating the modern ideas and traditional subjects, he tries to use new lacquer painting language to expound hisunderstanding of the world. Liu Han holds that different from the lacquer that is used in lacquer painting, lacquer painting is a painting in itself, so we must pay more attention to the art, instead of the traditional process, adding innovation, lacquer painting could become a unique art.

As to the subject matter, he likes to use the common things that could reflect the features of the porcelain captital. His painting Straw Sandals has rich implications. It implies the city of Jingdezhen, called Wharf of Straw Sandal in the past, because the ceramics culture of Jingdezhen was created by the kilnmen wearing the straw sandals.Our Party inherited from the red army the "Straw–Sandal Spirit", which made our nation prosperous and strong. Liu Han is very good at using the original color of the traditional Chinese lacquer to express the vitality of the common scenery.His work "Persimmons Are Red" and "Snow Mountain" used only three colors: black, red, white. But it demostrates obviously the tenaciousness life and the beauty of the mountains and rivers. The blackness the traditional Chinese lacquer provides is quite perfect. It gives infinite imagination. And also the scarlet of this lacquer is of the primitive simplicity, beautiful and not gaudy. Simple color can demonstrate the rich sense.

The Innermost Words of the Craftsman

Liu said that along the road of his arduous artistic exploration and growth process, he works all the way and enjoys his creations all the way. In the future, he will probe further into the new lacquer painting art, absorbing intensively the ceramic painting art to create more lacquer paintings with features of the Porcelain Captial. Liu Han believes that the art of lacquer painting will be permanent as the same as the lacquer itself.

(Written by Lan Tianyu, photographed and drawn by Liu Han)

假山园艺师郭应强：
时光艺术的创造者

【老手艺项目】假山盆景艺术

中国传统园林艺术有着几千年的辉煌历史，造园须有山，无山难成园，园中必放盆景。从皇家的御花园到达官贵人的后花园，以及平民百姓的小院，都是靠假山与盆景的点缀来增添雅趣与生机的。假山、盆景在园林艺术中占据着独特地位，在园艺领域中已自成体系，是中华民族的一种雅文化。盆景艺术被称为缩小的园林，从古至今，为我们的生活营造出一种清幽典雅的意境。尤其在当今社会，人们被拘囿于水泥森林中，越来越渴望在宅前屋后或是方寸阳台之上弄点假山盆景，以养心养性。

【匠人小传】

郭应强，45 岁，江西乐平人，现居景德镇。他在父亲的影响下，自幼喜欢花草树木，热爱石艺，现已从事假山盆景造型艺术二十余年，主要业务是承接酒店、别墅私宅的假山盆景营造。他在老年大学边的园林花卉市场开门店，经营自制假山盆景。

【匠心之路】

舍与得的艺术悖论

一个冬日午后，我们如约来到坐落在景德镇老年大学对面的“瓷都园艺”。走进郭应强陈设假山盆景的院子，是一种美的享受。咫尺盆盎间，凝天缩地赏山水，青苔花木郁葱茏，草棚石桥添野趣，犹如一幅微缩版山水画。置身于淡淡冬阳中的山石盆景天地里，可以使人走出日常的纷扰喧嚣，做一下深呼吸，仿佛空气中弥漫着山野的味道。走进院子的时候，主人正在对着一盆古松斟酌怎么剪枝造型。笔者穿行园中，先把精致美丽的假山盆景细细赏玩一番，然后再与主人对话采访。

笔者走近前，指着他正摆弄的松树问他要如何给它“动手术”，主人滔滔不绝叙述起他的思路：“如果取文人盆景的逸趣，就必须剪掉它的主枝干，往旁枝造型，松树的造型精妙之处在于苍、虬、斜、逸。盆景树形要有变化，要形、景、意结合，才能耐看，这就需要利用技艺处理蟠扎、修剪，布局，塑造树形、树干，进行老态处理，再经过长时间的培育。这个过程体现的是园艺师的功力与技艺，达到人工胜天然，也就耐看了。”

他的审美与造型构思确实非常专业，但笔者还是觉得挺可惜，长势那么茂盛、

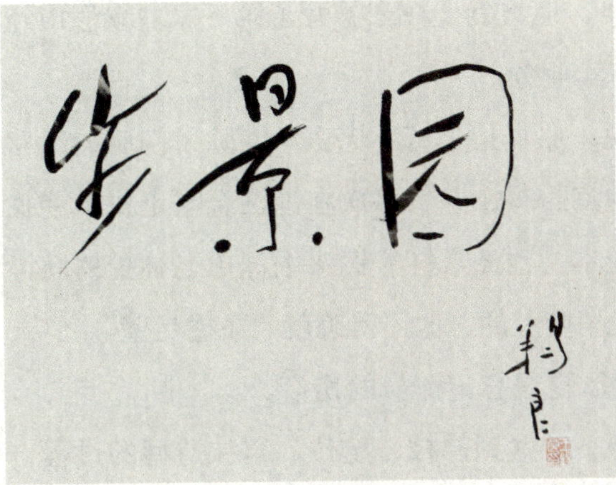

那么粗壮的主干却要被活活“截肢”。郭应强说，制作盆景最适合套用的一句话就是“舍得，有舍才有得”，盆景制作是一门减法艺术，删繁就简，确定树势之后就需要大刀阔斧地修剪枝条，只有舍得剪掉在你看来很可惜的枝与叶，才会得到美的艺术造型。

家学熏陶终成一生挚爱

高中毕业后，郭应强落榜回家，出外打工几年后，觉得还是应回家做一份属于自己的事业。由于自幼对盆景造型痴迷，他很快明确了自己的创业路要怎么走——制造假山盆景。这个想法理所当然得到了父亲的大力支持。

虽然郭应强自小对盆景有着浓厚的兴趣爱好，有一点粗浅的底子，但要以此为职业谋生，毕竟还不能成气候。在父亲的引荐下，他来到湖北武汉，跟随一个假山盆景造诣颇深的师傅学习。从区分太湖石、英石、吸水石、石笋石等不同类型石头的结构与硬度，到研究每一种用于造型的植物的生长规律与枝条可塑性，然后到怎样将树与石完美缔结成盆景艺术，这不是一蹴而就的，而需要艰辛探索。在那个年代关于盆景制作的专业书籍也不多，郭应强只能自己摸索尝试。盆景的气韵和制作也本无定法，全凭造型者对于美学的认识与把握。在工作的间隙，郭应强也常常会看一些美术类书籍，增强自己的美学素养。

经过两三年的积累与锤炼，2003 年，他与妻子在豪德开了第一家盆景假山经营店，承接一些假山堆叠造型、盆景售卖业务。

回忆起创业阶段的生活，郭应强说，那真是“苦不堪言”，除了门店的经营管理与盆景假山制作，还要经常去外地淘石头，并曾多次在浙江金华走村串巷找好树胚。开店最初时，为了节约经营成本，他经常扛着锄头去深山老林挖树胚，形状有些特色的树苗一般都是长在悬崖峭壁上的，他还得练就“飞檐走壁”之功，攀上悬崖去挖树，挖回来几棵好苗常常欣喜得忘记浑身的伤痕。

对于制作盆景来说，从选苗、育胚、上盆到修枝、定位、蓄枝造型的过程，可说是漫长的，既充满着期待和希望，又充满着艰辛和乐趣，可以使人得到精神的慰藉。“一寸枝条生数载，佳景方成已十秋。”经过年复一年的修剪塑形，一棵不起眼的小树长成一盆层次分明、枝似虬龙、雄浑苍劲的独特盆景，体现的正是对生命艺术的塑造。郭应强向笔者介绍他那棵黄杨木盆景，说已有百年树龄了，在他手上已有近二十年，价值估算近十万。不是真正热爱盆景艺术的人很难体会到盆景艺术的丰富内涵和真谛，更无法体会园艺师制作过程的艰辛与乐趣。

【匠人心语】

“对我们做假山盆景的匠人来说，在咫尺之地，创造出多方胜景，带给人审美愉悦，就是对至高境界的追求。”郭应强说，他也希望中国盆景艺术能得到更好的发展与传承。他愿意不遗余力地将自己二十年积累的经验传授下去，让景德镇的盆景艺术发扬光大。

（蓝田玉 / 撰文　丰月 / 摄影）

Guo Yingqiang, a Rockery Gardener : A Creator of the Art of Time

The Ancient Craft: The Rockery Bonsai

Chinese traditional landscape art has a history of thousands years. If you want to build a garden, there must be a rockery in it; otherwise it will be never regarded as a garden. Besides, there must be a potted plant there. From the Imperial Garden to the garden of the cabinet minister and the courtyard of ordinary people, all of them are embellished by rockery and bonsai which are used to add elegance and vitality. Rockery and bonsai have occupied a special position, and it has been formed its own unique system in the field of gardening, which has become a kind of Chinese elegant culture. The rockery bonsai is named as a miniature garden. From ancient times to the present, it creates an artistic conception for our life: quiet and elegant. Especially in modern society, people, who live in modern buildings, are increasingly longing for putting rockery and bonsai around their house or the small balcony to improve their character.

The Brief Biography of the Craftsman

Guo Yingqiang, coming from Leping, Jiangxi Province, is 45 years old and now lives in Jingdezhen. Under the influence of his father, Mr. Guo has a preference for flowers, trees and stonework. He has engaged in the pose art of rockery bonsai for more than twenty years and now he is specialized in the creativity of rockery bonsai for hotels and villas. He sets up his workshop in garden and flower market which is near to Jingdezhen University of the Elderly, dealing in self-made rockery bonsai.

The Growth of the Craftsman

The Art Paradox: Lose and Get

A winter afternoon, we came to the "Cidu Gardening" opposite to Jingdezhen University of the Elderly and walked into the courtyard of Guo Yingqiang's furnished rockery and bonsai, which was like a miniature mountains–and–waters painting and brought us aesthetic enjoyment. Staying in the mountain and bonsai world under the light winter sun, you might smell the flavor of the wild forest by taking a deep breath, it is a simple way to get rid of all your worries. When we stepped into the yard, the owner was thinking how to form a basin of pine pruning. Walking through the garden, we had a chance to appreciate the exquisite beauty of the rockery bonsai. After that, we began an interview with the master.

We approached, pointed the pine tree he was working on and asked him how he was "operating" on it. The master narrated his train of thought off the reel: "if taking the refined interests of literatus bonsai, you have to cut off its main branch and model the side branches. The essence of the modelling of pine trees is the dark green, curling, tilt and extension. There must be changes in the shape of the bonsai, and you have to combine the form, view and meaning, so the bonsai can make a feast for the eyes, it needs the skill to deal with bind, trim, overall arrangement, model the shape of tree, make the tree trunks look very old, after a long period of cultivation. The process embodies the gardener' s skills. When man–made prevail over the nature, the bonsai is worth appreciating ."

His aesthetic and modelling design is extremely professional indeed, but what the trunk that is thickset need to be trimmed makes me feel pity. Guo Yingqiang said, When people are making bonsai, they should remember a motto that anything you gain requires something you pay. Bonsai production is an art about subtraction, deleting complex things and making it easy. When you recognize the tree potential, you need to trim the branches radically. Only you can make up your mind to trim off them you will get a pretty artistic modeling.

A Lifelong Love Grown from the Family Tradition

After graduating from high school, Guo Yingqiang failed and returned home. Having worked outside for a few years, he thought he should set up a business of his own at home. Because of his obsession with bonsai modeling since childhood, he knew clearly the direction he should take on the entrepreneurial way: making bonsai rockery. Certainly, his idea was greatly supported by his father.

Although being interested in bonsai since childhood and having learned a little about it, he still had some difficulties to start his own business. Later his father introduced him a master in bonsai building and thus he came to Wuhan in Hubei Province to learn after the master. From distinguishing the structure and hardness of different types of stone, such as Taihu Lake stone, Absorbent stone and Stalagmite, etc. to the study of the growing rules of every plant and of the plasticity of every branch used for making modeling, and to how to combine trees and stones perfectly into bonsai art, the whole process cannot be acquired overnight. It needs a long practicing and experimenting. At that time , there were not many books about bonsai making , so Guo could only grope and try by himself . There is no fixed mode for the artistic conception and production of bonsai. It depends entirely on the creator' s understanding of the beauty. In his spare time, he often read some art books to enhance his aesthetic quality.

After two or three years of practicing and experience accumulating, he, with the help of his wife, ran a bonsai rockery store in Haode Square in 2003, undertaking some rockery modelling and bonsai selling business.

Reminding of the life of starting the enterprise, Guo Yingqiang said that was really a course of "suffering untold misery". Apart from running the enterprise and making bonsai, he had to travel extensively to collect the stones. He has gone to Jinhua of Zhejiang Province many times to look for good saplings from village to village. At the beginning of this business, to save the cost, he always took hoe to the deep mountains and forests to dig saplings. Saplings with special shapes always grow on cliffs, so he needs to learn the kung fu of "flying over the eaves and running on the wall". Whenever he climbed to the cliff and got back some good saplings, he would be so delighted and forget all the pains over his body.

The process of making bonsai may be very long. The procedures include from sapling selecting, sapling nursing, potting, pruning, positioning, branch cultivating and shaping etc. The work is hard, but full of fun and hope, which is a great consolation for us. "An inch of branch needs several years, but the wonderful scenery it present may last ten years." After years and years of pruning, a humble little tree may grow into a distinctive bonsai with layers of branches, which seems like a vigorous dragon. It is really the shaping art of life. When introducing the boxwood bonsai tree, Guo Yingqiang said it might be more than one hundred years old now and it has been with him for nearly 20 years. And maybe it deserves nearly 100 thousand yuan. It is difficult for those who do not truly love the bonsai art to appreciate the rich connotation and true meaning of bonsai. And it is impossible for them to understand the difficulties and fun of the gardening process.

The Innermost Words of the Craftsman

"For the craftsmen engaged in making rockery and bonsai, creating various fantastic scenery in a limited place which brings aesthetic pleasure to people is just like pursuing the supreme realm." Guo Yingqiang said. He hopes that the Chinese bonsai industry can get a better development and inheritance. Moreover, in order to develop and expand the Chinese bonsai industry, he is willing to pass on his experience and the skills he has acquired over the twenty years.

(Written by Lan Tianyu, photographed by Feng Yue)

玉石雕刻匠余宝泉：
不忘初心守玉心

【老手艺项目】玉石雕刻技艺

玉石雕刻技艺是中国最古老的手工艺之一。早在商周时期，制玉便成为一种专业，祖先们就用制成的玉器作为礼仪用具和装饰佩件。在漫长的文化沉淀中，玉器逐渐成为王公贵族、寻常百姓家藏身佩戴与案头、书桌陈列的珍宝，也因象征美好和君子风范而备受推崇，古有“君子如玉”一说。玉雕文化传承是一部内涵深厚的史书，承载着几千年的中国历史文化和祥瑞美好的记忆。自古至今，琢玉匠就是一种塑造美好、赋予吉祥的职业。

【匠人小传】

余宝泉，45岁，景德镇市乐平人，现在乐平市奇石一条街开玉石雕刻店铺。他初中毕业后即拜师学艺，学习玉石雕刻手艺，立志用一辈子把玉石雕刻手艺做精。其玉石雕刻作品雕工精细，在设计上注重体现玉石的天然之美，花鸟鱼虫题材的雕刻作品更是如此。他从事玉石雕刻二十多年来，雕刻作品深受顾主的喜爱。

【匠心之路】

桐城学艺结玉缘

在乐平奇石一条街上的一个店铺里，我们慕名寻到余宝泉。店铺不大，整洁敞亮，博古架、玻璃柜里摆满精雕细刻的玉石物件。初见余师傅，第一感觉是淳朴、憨厚，随着采访的深入，我们发现他极其诚恳务实，身上透露出一个琢玉匠人的沉静与严谨。听我们说明来意，他很热情地把他所有的雕刻作品都搬出来排放在桌上，并讲述他从事玉石雕刻的经历。

余宝泉与玉石结缘，要从一封家书说起。余宝泉出生在乐平一个小山村，因家境比较贫困，初中毕业后他就辍学回家。母亲是安徽桐城人氏，桐城是一个深有文化底蕴的城市，20世纪90年代初，玉器产业就很发达。外公听说他辍学在家，就从桐城寄来一封信，让余宝泉去桐城学玉雕手艺。当时18岁的余宝泉对玉知之甚少，可以说只知道“珍贵”二字。

到了桐城，外公介绍余宝泉进入玉雕厂学习玉雕技艺。为了练习余宝泉的基本功，师傅起初让他用石头废料练手，雕刻一些简单的寿桃之类的物件。入门学艺，师傅只是在旁边稍加点拨，具体操作还得靠自己慢慢摸索。为了提高雕刻造型能力，没有经过美术训练的余宝泉，经常买书自学绘画，刻苦临摹；雕刻实践时，他再从实物中揣摩造型。比如雕刻“年年有鱼”时，他就在工作台前放一条鲤鱼照着画照着刻。

凭借着对玉石天生的悟性，加上自己的努力和师傅们的口传心授，余宝泉量材取料、因材施艺的琢玉技巧越来越娴熟，为他日后成为一个职业琢玉匠人打下了坚实的基础。

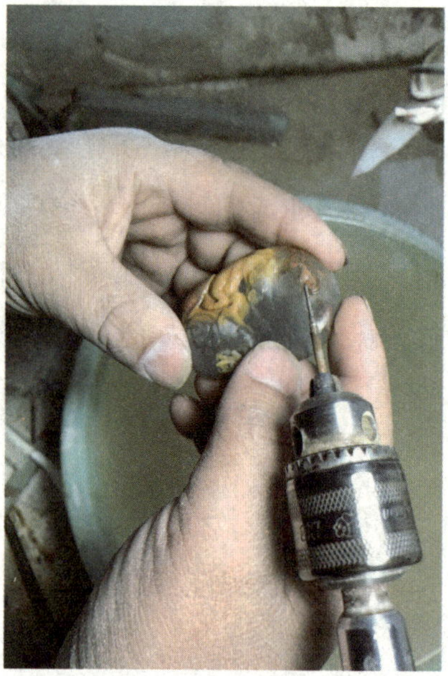

物尽其用运匠心

桐城学艺三年出师，1993 年，余宝泉来到苏州一个玉器厂做琢玉匠。钟灵毓秀的东吴之地，吴人巧治，高手云集。几年间，余宝泉遍访名师，玉石雕刻技艺日臻成熟，从雕刻到设计、绘图，无所不通。在苏州期间，他还得到一代玉雕名家范同生的悉心指点。

余宝泉当初主攻的是花鸟虫鱼类圆雕技艺，也是传统玉雕中吉祥文化表现最多的形式，如“年年有鱼”“富贵牡丹”“喜上眉梢”“瑞兽貔貅”等纹饰的雕刻。但世间没有两块相同的玉，玉石上的颜色纹理构造多姿多彩，一位高超的琢玉师，应懂得如何利用玉石上的天然色彩来发挥自己的想象空间，赋予玉器一定的文化内涵。玉石历经亿万年才来到匠人手中，玉石变成玉器的过程，正是玉石新生的过程。匠人需穷尽一生磨炼技能，才不会辜负这一段缘分，才能匠心独运地为每块玉石添上最华丽的一笔。

余宝泉说，玉雕技术是做减法的艺术，一刀下去就没有回头路，不可能再改弦易辙，一刀不成功就有可能废掉一块好玉。一件玉器不仅玉料宝贵，而雕琢之功更是难能可贵。因此，玉雕工艺水平的高低是决定玉器品位的重要因素，好的玉器需要构图精美和谐、工艺精雕细琢。

余宝泉说：“玉雕艺术常局限于原材料，在雕琢过程中，需把材料的毛病处理掉，比如利用色块、避开裂纹、掩盖瑕疵，都需要匠心巧运，细节处理需灵活。”

为此，客户每拿来一块原料，他都会根据玉石的大小、材质、纹路、色变来为其量身设计最适合的造型与画面，绝对不浪费一小片材质，不错用每一块玉石的纹理，真正使玉石物尽其用。

恪守节操守玉心

“人有善愿，天必佑之。”回到家乡开起作坊后，余宝泉对玉石雕刻技艺更加精益求精，吃住都在店铺，为顾客雕刻玉石器从来不偷工减料、唯利是图。因为他雕刻技艺精湛，加上为人厚道，朋友间口碑相传，他很快打开了市场，上门加工玉石器的人日益增多，许多景德镇的人也开车来乐平找他加工玉器。

匠心是一种品质，是一份专注，是一份严谨，更是一种态度。开店铺十多年，余宝泉拒绝过许多送上门的生意。前几年，一些玉石爱好者将自己看走眼买的玉石送到他店铺来雕刻，余宝泉一看是没多大价值的玉石，就建议顾客别在他这花冤枉钱了，雕出来也没任何保存价值，而多半客人会很不高兴他这样说自己的东西不值钱，为此他还得罪了不少来给他送生意的顾客。

对于做玉石加工的匠人来说，顾客的信任最重要。前年，有一个顾客拿着一块玉石来他店里要求雕刻一块玉如意，由于这一块玉石的纹路表里不一，加工雕刻打磨后改变了原来的纹理，顾客取件时，坚决不相信这一块就是自己的玉石，怀疑被琢玉者换掉了他的好玉。一向为人正直坦荡的余宝泉为了证明自己的清白，爽快地对客人说：“你若不相信是你的玉，那就按你当初的估价把这块玉抵给我好了。”就这样他花高价买下了顾客不要的那块玉如意，宁愿损失金钱也不愿贬损一个匠人的信誉品格。

【匠人心语】

一流的匠人，必有一流的技术，更要有一流的心性，人品比技术更重要。我不是大师，但我的作品一定要对得起我的手艺，对得起顾客付出的价钱，对得起这份职业。

（蓝田玉 / 撰文　黄辉 / 摄影）

Yu Baoquan，a Jade Carver：Remaining True to Our Original Aspiration and the Soul of Jade

The Ancient Craft: The Jade Carving

Jade carving is one of the oldest handicraft in China. Early in the Shang and Zhou dynasties，the jade making became a professional，and the ancestors used the jade articles as the ceremonial utensils and ornaments. In the long cultural precipitation，jade articles have gradually become the treasures of the princes and common people. They symbolize beautiful symbols and gentlemanly demeanor. Jade culture is a profound connotation of history，carrying thousands of years of Chinese history and culture and auspicious memories. Since ancient times，the jade craftsman is a kind of career to create good luck.

The Brief Biography of the Craftsman

Yu Baoquan，45 years old，a person in Leping，Jingdezhen，now opens a jade carving shop on a street in Leping. After graduating from middle school，he learned jade carving from teacher，and engaged in jade carving craft in his all lifetime to do fine. His jade carving works which were carved meticulously，embody the natural beauty in design，especially in the design of carving flowers，birds，worms and fishes. More than 20 years engaged in jade carving，his sculpture are deeply fond by the customers.

The Growth of the Craftsman

Studied Art in Tongcheng and Affiliated with Jade

In a shop on a stone street in Leping，we came to find Yu Baoquan. The shop is small，neat and bright，full of carved jade objects in the glass shelf cabinet. The initial Master Yu，the first impression is simple and honest，with in-depth interviews，we found that he was sincere and pragmatic，who revealed a jade carving craftsmen’s calm and rigorous. Listening to our business，he is very enthusiastic to move all of his works on the table，and talk unceasingly about jade carving skills with experience.

The relation of Yu Baoquan and jade, must start with a letter. Yu Baoquan was born in a small mountain village in Leping. Because his family was poor, he dropped out of school after he graduated from junior high school. His mother is a native of Tongcheng Anhui, Tongcheng is a deep cultural heritage of the city, at the beginning of 1990s, jade industry is very developed. The grandfather heard that he dropped out of school and then sent a letter from Tongcheng to let Yu Baoquan go to Tongcheng to learn the art of jade carving. Yu Baoquan, 18 years old at that time, knew little about jade. It can be said that only "precious" two words are known.

In Tongcheng, the grandfather introduced Yu Baoquan to the jade carving factory to learn the art of jade carving. In order to practice basic skills, master first let him practice with stone carving waste, to carve some simple items such as Peach-Shaped objects. Introduction to arts, master just provide suggestions, specific operations have to rely on their own way. In order to improve the ability of sculpting and model, although he had never been trained by the fine arts, he often bought books to teach himself to paint and took pains to copy. When he practiced the sculpture, he tried to figure out the shape from the real thing. For example, when he carved "fish every year", he put a carp in front of the work bench and carve it on the picture.

With his natural understanding of jade, coupled with his own efforts and the teacher's oral teaching, Yu Baoquan's skill of selecting material and the skill of teaching the talented person become more and more familiar, it lays a foundation for him to become a professional jade carving craftsman.

Make Full Use of Each Piece of Jades

Yu Baoquan studied art in Tongcheng for three years. In 1993, Yu Baoquan went to a jade factory in Suzhou to work as a jade craftsman. This place nurtures great talents, many master gathered at here. In a few years, Yu Baoquan visited famous teachers, jade carving techniques are getting more and more mature, from carving to design, drawing, he knew all of this well. During his time in Suzhou, he also received the careful guidance of a generation of famous jade master Fan Tongsheng.

Yu Baoquan's main focus was on flower, bird and insect fish sculpture techniques, and it is also the most expression of traditional auspicious culture in jade carvings. For example, "Every Year There Are Fish" "Wealthy Peony" "Happy" "Brave Troops, the Auspicious Beast" and other decorative carvings. However, there are no two identical jades in the world. The color textures on jade are colorful. A super jade carver should understand how to use natural colors on jade to exert his imagination and give jade a certain cultural connotation. After millions of years of condensing, jade came to the hands of the craftsmen. The process of turning jade stone into a jade is the process of a new life of jade. The craftsmen need to exhaust their life to hone their skills and they will not live up to the fate of this period. They will be able to add the most magnificent piece of jade to each stone.

Yu Baoquan said that the art of jade carving is an art of subtraction. There is no turning back when it comes down to a knife, and it is impossible to change its course. If it is unsuccessful, it may destroy a good jade. A piece of jade is not only valuable for jade, the power of carving is even more valuable. Therefore, the level of jade craftsmanship is an important factor in determining the quality of jade products. Good jades require exquisite and harmonious composition and craftsmanship.

Yu Baoquan said： “the jade carving art is often limited to raw materials， in the process of carving， we need to get rid of the wrong material， such as the use of color， avoiding cracks， concealing blemishes， all of this require ingenuity skillfully， using details should be flexible.”

So， when a customer brings a raw material， he will tailor the most suitable form and picture according to the size， texture， line and color change of jade， and never waste a small piece of material， he always uses the texture of jade correctly and makes full use of each piece of jade.

Soul of Honesty

“People have good wishes， and heaven will bless.” After returning to their hometown to open a workshop， Yu Baoquan made more and more refinement of jade carving technology， eating and living in shops， carving jade objects for customers， never cutting corners and making mercenaries. Because of his exquisite carving skills and his kindness to people， his friends passed word of mouth. He soon opened the market， and the number of people who came to process jade objects increased. Many people in Jingdezhen drove to Leping to find jade articles.

Originality is a kind of quality， is a focus， is a rigorous， is also a kind of attitude. After opening the store for more than a decade， Yu Baoquan refused to go through many business operations. In the past few years， some jade enthusiasts sent their own jades that they bought for sale to his shop to sculpt. Yu Baoquan saw that there was not much valuable jade. He advised the customers not to spend money on the jades， and there was no preservation value for them. Most of the guests were very unhappy because he said that their own things are worthless， so he also offended many customers who came to send him business.

For processing jade craftsmen， customer trust is the most important. Two years ago， a customer with a piece of jade went to his shop and required carving a piece of jade， because this piece of jade carving lines are quite different， the original texture changed after grinding， when the customer picked it up， he do not believe this one is his own jade， jade carving are suspected of being stealthily replaced his good jade. In order to prove his innocence， Yu Baoquan， who has always been honest and magnanimous， said to the guests readily: “If you don’t believe it’s your jade， please give me the jade according to your original estimate.” So he bought the jade that the customers didn’t believe， would rather lose money do not want to disparage an artisan’s reputation character.

The Innermost Words of the Craftsman

First-rate craftsmen must have first-rate technology， and they must have first-rate convictions. Character is more important than technology. I am not a master， but my work must be worthy of my craft， worthy of the price paid by the customer， and worthy of the profession.

（Written by Lan Tianyu， photographed by Huang Hui）

胡琴制作师程国祥：一曲心弦向谁诉

【老手艺项目】胡琴制作

二胡始于唐朝，至今已有一千多年的历史。它最早发源于我国古代北部地区的一个少数民族，那时叫“奚琴”。到了宋代，胡琴又被称为“嵇琴”。一直到近代，胡琴才被称为“二胡”。

【匠人小传】

66岁的程国祥老人，自小就跟随父亲程树民学习手工制作二胡、京胡等民族乐器的技艺。据程国祥老人回忆，1952年其父从老家安徽来景德镇开了这红光乐器店。

程师傅说，手工制作二胡、京胡程序复杂，许多环节“只可意会，无法言传”。程师傅不仅会木艺，更懂音律，从选材、构件制作到组装、调音，他都进行了细致研究。

【匠心之路】

寻访：闹市一隅觅琴师

在江家上弄的弄口，有一家红光乐器店。这家乐器店只有10平方米左右，但在柜台上方的招牌下，一排二胡特别引人注目。笔者走进这家老店，探寻它的前世今生。

据店主程国祥师傅介绍，其父在新中国成立初期就开了这家店，当年在镇上乐器店也就只此一家。当年南昌、九江、鄱阳等地的乐器店也就一两家，在“文革”前期，江苏扬州人王湘昌在九江开了一家乐器店，后来他下放到农村，当时九江就没有了乐器店。鄱阳也有一家，后来也没有了。这些附近邻市、邻县的店主都是程师傅父亲的师兄弟，现在那些店早已经不存在了，只有这家红光乐器店一直开到了现在。

传艺：子继父业

“我今年快70岁了，从小就跟着父亲学做二胡的手艺。”初见程师傅，他边摩挲着心爱的二胡边说。20世纪50年代到80年代，景德镇京剧团、各个学校、其他大小文艺团体都跑到江家弄口的这间小店订制乐器。不过，最近几年，纯手工制作的二胡也开始遇冷了。店面后面隔了一间储物室，货架上许多制作二胡的工具都布满了灰尘。

坚守：做好琴，做好人

“父亲在世的时候，经常告诫我，做琴要一心一意。”程师傅说，“我这辈子谨遵父训，一辈子做琴，虽然生意越做越清淡，但我的手艺可以说是越做越精。”

程师傅说，从外表看，二胡结构简单，但其复杂的手工制作工艺考验着工人师傅的功夫，单说一节檀木，就需要砍、锯、刨、铲、削、锉、镂、钻、铰、磨、光等多道工序，每一道工序都决定着乐器的质量，不能马虎。其中又以“锉”这道工序用工最多，费力最大，耗时最长，二胡每个部件都少不了一个“锉”字。在操

作使用“锉”方面以六个字概括：平、直、匀、精、准、光。而这些需要多年的基本功。二胡不仅制作工艺复杂，而且要求制作者既要会木艺，也要懂音律。

心愿：开店传艺

“二胡制作周期长，成本高，收益小，年轻人愿意学的不多，我的儿子和孙子对这个也不感兴趣。”程国祥老人叹了口气。虽然这十几年中也陆续来过一些二胡爱好者愿拜他为师学做二胡，但由于家中店面小，地方窄小，实在无法教学，他只能婉拒。

“我年纪大了，现在就是怕二胡制作的手艺绝了后。现在市里的琴行很多，但二胡基本上是从外地买来的，我真想将这个手艺传承下去。如果有人想学，我愿意免费教他。”

【匠人心语】

“二胡这东西是有灵性的，每一把都不一样。”

“如果有一天二胡制作的技艺消失，那将会是世人的巨大损失。”

（黄辉撰文 / 摄影）

Cheng Guoxiang, an Erhu Maker: To Whom the Heartstrings were Played

The Ancient Craft: Huqin Making

Dated back from Tang Dynasty, the musical instrument, Erhu, has a history as long as a thousand years. It originated from an ethnic minority in the north of ancient China, and it was called "Xiqin" then. When it came to Song Dynasty, huqin was named as "Jiqin". And not until the modern times was huqin renamed as "Erhu".

The Brief Biography of the Craftsman

The 66-year-old craftsman, Cheng Guoxiang, followed his father Cheng Shumin to learn the skill of making folk musical instruments like erhu, jinghu and etc. when he was a child. According to his recall, his father came to Jingdezhen from the hometown in Anhui and opened Hongguang Musical Instrument Shop in 1952.

Master Cheng said that the procedure to manually make erhu and jinghu was complicated, and a lot of steps are hard to explain in words and people could only imagine them. Master Cheng doesn't only know the wood art, but also understand the rhyme, and he studied in details from the selection of material and production of structural components to configuration and tone tuning.

The Growth of the Craftsman

Seek the Erhu Maker in a Corner of the Downtown

At the mouth of Jiangjia Up Lane lies the Hongguang Musical Instrument Shop. The shop is only around 10 square meters but a row of erhu hanged on the counter under the signboard is especially arresting. The writer stepped into the old shop, explored its past and present stories.

According the shop owner Master Cheng's introduction, his father came to open this shop in the early years of the People's Republic of China, which was the only one musical instrument shop in the town. And there were only one or two musical instrument shops in Nanchang, Jiujiang, Poyang and etc. In the early years of Cultural Revolution, Wang Xiangchang from Yangzhou of Jiangsu opened a musical instrument shop in Jiujiang, but it was closed after he was sent to the village, so was the shop in Poyang. The shopkeepers in cities and counties in vicinity all apprenticed the same master as Master Cheng' s father, and all those shops have been closed for long, while only the Hongguang Musical Instrument Shop is still being opened right up to today.

The Son Follows in His Father' s Steps to Inherit the Crafts

"I am around 70 years old this year, and followed my father to learn the crafts of making erhu in childhood." Master Cheng said while rubbing his beloved erhu when the writer saw him for the first time. From the 1950s to the 1980s, the Peking Opera troupes, all schools and other literature and art groups of all sizes in Jingdezhen went to this shop at the mouth of Jiangjia Lane to customize the musical instruments. However, the purely handmade erhu began to cool down in recent years. Inside the storage room segregated behind the shop, there were many tools for making erhu and they were covered by dusts.

Perseverance in Making Good Erhu and Being a Nice Person

"When my father was alive, he always admonished me to put thorough concentration when making erhus." Master Cheng said, "I strictly followed my father' s instruction to make erhus in my whole life. Although, the business is getting worse, but my skills are getting more proficient."

Master Cheng said that the erhu was simple in structure if seen externally, but the complex production technique by hand is a test to the craftsman' s skill. It started from a length of sandalwood, and would go through multiple processes like cutting, sawing, planning, shoveling, peeling, filing, carving, drilling, reaming, polishing, buffing and so on, of which each step would affect the quality of erhu, so no carelessness was allowed. Of all these processes, only filing is the most employed, laborious and time-consuming, as every single piece of the component in an erhu needs to be filed. The operation by using files could be concluded into six characteristics, and they are flatness, straightness, evenness, preciseness, accuracy and smoothness, which required years of basic skills. Due to the complexity of the production technique, the craftsmen must know not only the wood art, but also the rhyme.

Wish to Keep the Shop Open and Pass Down the Skill

"The cycle time for making erhu is long with high cost and low earnings, so there are few young people willing to learn the skill, and neither my son nor the grandson is interested in this." Master Cheng sighed and said. Although some of amateurs were willing to apprentice him to learn the skill to make erhu in the past ten years and more continuously, but he had declined for the shop is too small to teach them.

"I am old now, so my greatest concern is that the skill to make erhu will fail to be handed down. Even though there are many shops selling erhu in the city now, yet most of them are bought from outside, so I do hope to pass down my crafts. And if there were anyone who wants to learn the crafts, I am willing to teach him for free."

The Innermost Words of the Craftsman

"Erhu is a spiritual object, and each is different."

"If the skill for making erhu vanishes someday later, it will be an immense loss to people."

(Written and photographed by Huang Hui)

裱画师茆家东：
补悬便可起云烟

【老手艺项目】裱画

装裱是一门高雅、复杂、精致的技艺，是极具我国民族传统特色的艺术之一。裱画师的工作就是在画像或图画完成之后，为了更好地保存以及观赏，通过糨糊等制作工艺把画装裱起来。“三分画七分裱”，装裱是一门历史悠久而高雅精致的技艺，经过装裱的书画更加美观且能更长久地收藏传世。

【匠人小传】

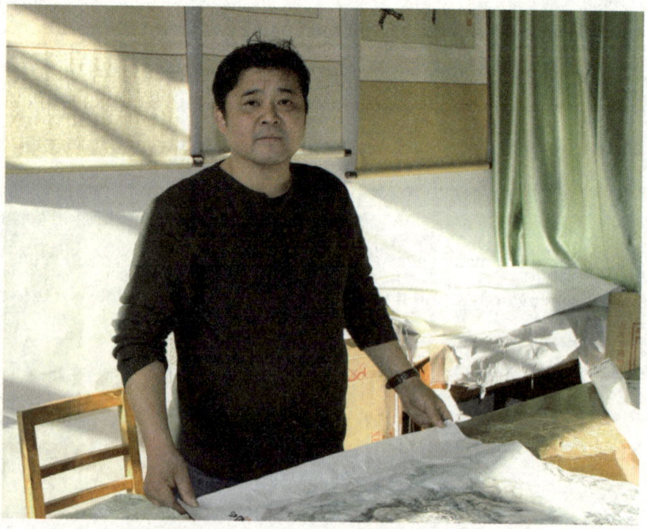

茆家东，47岁，景德画院裱画师，从1991年开始，就在工人文化宫开设佛印社裱画室，从事裱画工作近30年。作为景德镇少数坚持传统手工裱画工艺的裱画师，他用心装饰

和保护景德镇书画家们的艺术珍品，装裱了大量的留在景德镇的历史及现代名人字画，使之成为这座城市的历史珍藏品。

【匠心之路】

机缘巧合：从老家到瓷都裱字画

据茆师傅介绍，他从小就跟着安徽省博物馆荣宝斋高级书画装裱师黄秋生学裱画手艺。茆师傅曾在合肥市文化馆、黄山书院等单位从事书画装裱工作。谈及在景德镇从事装裱这一行，茆师傅感慨万分。20 世纪 90 年代初，景德镇部分知名陶艺家在创作纸质书画时，苦于没有让人满意的裱画师傅对其作品进行装裱，只能把字画托运到合肥请茆师傅装裱，很不方便。也就在那时，景德镇陶瓷历史博物馆和龙珠阁等文物部门因要抢救一批文史性古旧字画，决定由当时的景德画院出面专程到安徽聘请茆师傅到景德镇裱画。

手工裱画：传承工匠精神

谈及装裱字画的工艺，茆师傅说，一幅字画不论大小，装裱都要经过九大步骤：熬好浓度合适的糨糊，再刷浆、托芯、上墙、下墙、镶活、腹背、绷背板、装框。

其中最耗时的是上墙后风干的过程。茆师傅说，春秋之时是最适合裱画的季节，湿度大的天气风干程度就要靠裱画师自己掌控。茆师傅介绍，最初，古老的裱画工艺要经历一年的时间，经历春夏秋冬四个季节空气湿度的变化。要想装裱一幅好的作品，细心和耐心非常重要。

茆师傅说，手工装裱字画虽然耗时耗力，但是装裱出来的作品禁得住时间的考验。在他看来，很多传统的工艺没办法用科学技术来代替，机械装裱虽然很快捷，但是用到的胶膜没有办法溶解；而手工装裱用的是糨糊，就算过了几百年以后，还可以再次“翻新”装裱。

淡泊名利：甘为书画做嫁衣

谈到装裱书画的宗旨，茆师傅脸上露出了笑容：“我们就是为书画家服务的，我们服务的目的就是推动文化的进步。当年市文联拿我裱的画到南昌去参展，专家们一致认可我裱画的工艺，这就是对我最高的奖赏。”

茆师傅告诉笔者，他在年轻的时候认为装裱字画是一门技术活，所以只管裱画；而他现在的感觉是，每一张字画都不容易。一名裱画师，首先要读懂每一幅拿来裱的画，要对得起每一幅画，而不是对得起裱画的工钱。

【匠人心语】

“我做这一行，可以说是感觉越做越难，应该说是越追求完美就越难。一幅画，画得再好，裱得不好，也显示不出作品的审美情趣。”

（黄辉撰文 / 摄影）

Mao Jiadong, a Painting Framer: To Vitalize the Paintings Through Framing

The Ancient Craft: Painting Frame

Framing is an elegant, intricate and delicate skill, and it is one of the traditional arts in our nation. Painting framer’s main job is to frame the painting by pasting and skills alike after the portraits or paintings are finished so as to better preserve the painting for appreciation. Framing even plays a more important role than the painting itself, so it is a time-honored delicate skill, the calligraphy and painting through framing appears more artistic and can be preserved for longer.

The Brief Biography of the Craftsman

The 47-year-old painting framer, Mao Jiadong, in Jingde Art Institute has spent around 30 years in painting framing since 1991 when his Fo Yin Studio was opened up at Workers’ Palace of Culture. As a rare craftsman persisting in the traditional technique to frame the painting, he heartedly decorates and preserves the artistic treasures from the calligraphers and painters in Jingdezhen, mounting a great number of paintings and calligraphies either handed down in the history of Jingdezhen or created by the modern famous artists and making them as the precious historical collections in this city.

The Growth of the Craftsman

Come to Frame Painting in Jingdezhen from the Hometown

According to Master Mao’s introduction, he started to learn the skill of painting framing from the advanced framer, Huang Qiusheng, in Rongbaozhai of Anhui Provincial Museum when he was a child. After that Master Mao worked in units like Hefei Cultural Center, Cultural Academy of Huangshan and so on embarking on painting framing. Referred to the reason for coming to Jingdezhen, Master Mao felt with emotion. In the 1990s, many of famous ceramic artists suffered from unsatisfactory mounting by the local painting framers on their paper artworks, so they had to send their paintings and calligraphies to Hefei and invite Master Mao to frame their works, which was pretty inconvenient at that time. Just then the Culture Sectors like Jingdezhen Ceramic Historical Museum, Dragon Pearl Pavilion and so on were rescuing a collection of ancient literary and historical calligraphies and paintings, thus they made the determination and assigned Jingde Art Institute to pay a special visit to Anhui to hire and invite Master Mao to Jingdezhen for painting framing.

Manual Painting Framing, an Inheritance of Craftsmen' s Spirits

Referred to the technique of painting framing, Mao said the mounting could be divided into nine main steps in spite of the size of the calligraphies and paintings, they were boiling the paste to a proper density, then brushing the paste, foiling the paper, pasting the upper, pasting the bottom, mounting, paving the plate on the back, fastening the back place and framing.

Master Mao said that the air drying of the paste on the upside was the most time–consuming step and the most suitable seasons for painting framing were spring and autumn. In humid climate, the framers need to control the time length based on their experience. According to Mao' s introduction, the painting framing by the ancient technique would take a cycle time as long as one whole year after it was exposed to the variation of humidity in all seasons. In a word, it is very important to keep patient and prudent to frame the painting well.

Master Mao said the painting framing by hand withstood the test of time although he needed to spend more time and energy. In his opinion, lots of traditional technique could not be replaced by the modern science and technology. The framing by machine is more efficient, but the adhesive film was unable to dissolve thoroughly. Instead, the painting framing by hand took use of the paste, so the artworks could be re–framed after stored for hundreds of years.

Be Indifferent to Fame and Wealth, and Willing to Foil the Calligraphies and Paintings

Referred to the purpose of painting framing, Master Mao smiled and said, "we offer the service to the calligraphers and painters, and our service mains to promote the progress of the culture. The Municipal Literary Federation once took the painting framed by me to Nanchang for an exhibition, and all the experts admired my skill in the painting framing, which was the highest reward to me."

Master Mao told the writer that he regarded the painting framing was merely a skill when he was young, so he would focus on the framing. But the feeling changed now as it was not easy to create even a single piece of the calligraphic and painting artwork. As a framer, he must apprehend the innermost meaning in each artwork to be framed, an then he could treat the artwork fairly instead of being worthy of the payment for the framing.

The Innermost Words of the Craftsman

"It feels more difficult if you worked in this industry for longer, in another word, it' s harder if you pursue more perfection. The artwork can' t display its aesthetic taste if the framing is bad no matter how excellent the painting is."

(Written and photographed by Huang Hui)

驯鸟师黄国和：
一生心系人鸟情

【老手艺项目】驯鸟

驯鸟自古有之，主要是消除鸟的野性，使鸟初步伏笼；而要真正使鸟不怕人和物，自然鸣唱，则需要一个很漫长的过程。鸟养熟了自然就会起性，性足则能鸣善斗。

遛鸟可增加鸟的稳定性。遛鸟可以利用早晨、黄昏之时，拿着鸟笼到外面走走。到鸟场野外公园林地，将鸟笼挂在树上，一则使鸟儿习惯变换环境，二来在鸟类众多的地方，可以使鸟儿领略、学习善鸣鸟的鸣声，时间久了之后，鸟自然就会学会善鸣鸟的鸣音，唱出悦耳的曲子。

【匠人小传】

家住茶山的养鸟老人黄

国和，年轻时就以养鸟为乐。据说，在他十几岁时，有位老人给了他两只画眉，他就玩上了鸟，也就是这样玩起瘾了，鸟人痴心，一玩就是50多年。此外，黄国和老人还精于各种鸟笼的整修，曾在石开有一间鸟笼店，名曰“昌南第一笼”。他加工的鸟食料更是受到养鸟同行的交口称赞。

【匠心之路】

养鸟：万般宠爱于鸟身

据黄师傅介绍，鸟一般是群居的，但一座山头一般只有一只雄鸟。雄鸟占雌鸟，靠的是争斗。两只雄鸟争斗，败的一方就要飞走，另寻巢穴；胜的一方就在此地“占山为王”，繁衍下一代。

制作鸟食很有讲究。鸟过冬后，春天的鸟食中要配胡萝卜、西红柿、红枣、玉米、蚕蛹、鸡蛋、牛肉等。因为鸟刚过冬，身体娇弱，要吃好些。夏天就不能这样，如果再吃这些食物鸟就会掉鸟毛。所以夏天鸟食中配枸杞子、菊花等。

鸟笼：个中情趣“鸟人”自知

谈及鸟笼，黄师傅又打开了话匣子。他说，江浙一带人比较喜欢方笼，景德镇叫草笼，制作较为简单，基本上没有什么工艺可言，是驯鸟时用的，这种笼子好打扫卫生。这种鸟笼，笼子里有槽子，鸟进去吃食后，头部就不会乱甩，这样就节约了鸟食。

黄师傅拿出一只工艺考究的鸟笼说：“这个笼子是景德镇一位制笼前辈的作品，叫百鸟笼。笼上包括笼钩雕了98只鸟，再加上笼布上的绣花鸟和笼中的活鸟，共100只鸟。景德镇目前仅存两只这样的鸟笼，是仿照安徽黟县鸟笼制作的，选用的材料是五年以上的黑檀木。”

黄师傅在景德镇的养鸟界小有名气，不仅得益于其养鸟方法得当，更得益于他加工整修和装潢鸟笼的技艺。他向笔者展示了制作鸟笼的工具：篾刀、刮刀、雕刀、手锯、手钻、拉条板、钢圈模、钢锉、老虎钳、木凿、小台钳等。他在网上把半成品鸟笼买来，再进行加工。比如云南金竹笼质地细腻，竹皮黄色，在加工的过程中抹上香油，鸟笼就呈枣红色，纯朴自然，这样收藏价值便极高。

“笼衣也有讲究，更有学问。”黄师傅如是说，“四川一带以红笼衣为主，其目的是养鸟而斗；北京一带以绸缎笼衣为主，以示皇宫贵族之气；而我们景德镇一带则以黑笼衣为主。”

【匠人心语】

“我们养鸟人也有自己的规矩。鸟有三不捉：幼鸟不捉，因为难以养活；母鸟不捉，因为它要在大自然中繁殖下一代；开春不捉鸟，因为这个季节的鸟刚过完冬，身子弱，难养。”

是的，无论是人，还是鸟，都是大自然的一部分。回归自然，才是生物的共性。

（黄辉撰文 / 摄影）

Huang Guohe, a Bird Trainer: A Passion for Birds Lasted a Lifetime

The Ancient Craft: Training Birds

Since ancient times, there was the business of training bird. The main intention of training bird is to remove the wild nature of the bird and make the bird willing to stay in the cage. Generally, it takes a long time to fully get the birds being used to the human environment, and achieve the natural singing from them. But once the birds are familiar with you, it will feel attached to you and sing to you joyfully.

Walking bird can calm down the bird' s emotions. The best time for walking bird is in the morning and evening. You may take your bird to the fields or to the public park. Hang the cage on one branch of a tree. By this way, your bird may enjoy the new environment and the tuneful warbling songs from other birds in the trees. A long time later, your bird will become a good singer, and give you quite sweet songs.

The Brief Biography of the Craftsman

Huang Guohe, the old man who lives in the Tea Mountain, enjoys keeping birds when he was young. It is said that when he was a teenager, an old man gave him two thrushes, and since then he fell in love with the birds and got addicted to playing with the bird. Till now, he has been keeping birds for more than 50 years. In addition, Huang Guohe is good at repairing the bird cages. So he has once a cage store in Shikai, known as "The First Cage of Changnan" . The foodstuff he made for the bird has received good reviews from his peers.

The Growth of the Craftsman

Bird Keeping: The Deepest Love for the Bird

Huang told us that birds belong to the gregarious animal and in one mountain there is usually one male bird. For a nest of female birds, the male has to fight with each other. The winner stays and establishes a kingdom of the birds in the mountain for reproducing next generations, and the loser has to leave immediately.

Also there are strict principles for making birdseed. For instance, in spring, the bird food should contain carrots, tomatoes, red dates, corn, pupa, eggs, beef, etc. Because the bird has just lived through the winter and so need more nourishing food to build up their body. In summer, however, if you feed them this food, you will get your bird lose hair. At this time, the food should be blended with some Chinese wolfberry and chrysanthemum.

Birdcage: the Joy of Keeping Bird Belongs Only to the "Birdman"

When it comes to the cage, Huang' s words poured out again. He said that the people of Jiangsu Province and Zhejiang Province prefer the square cage, which is called straw cage in Jingdezhen. The square cage is very easy to make. The making process contains no artistic element. It is usually used during the training period. This kind of cage is more convenient for cleaning, because there is a food slot in the cage. With this slot, the bird cannot shake its head when eating, and also that can save a lot of birdseed.

Master Huang took out a bird cage, which bore some artistic attributes, and said, This cage is a work of a senior cage maker in Jingdezhen. It is called Hundred-bird Cage. There were carved 98 various birds over the cage, including the cage hook. Plus the living bird in the cage and the bird pattern embroidered on the cage garment, there were 100 birds in all. Currently, there are only two such cages in Jingdezhen, which are designed after the works of Yixian county of Anhui Province. Besides, the basic material of making such birdcage is the high-quality ebony of five years old at least.

Mr. Huang won much fame due to his proper method of training birds and his skillful renovation and exquisite decoration for the cages. He showed us his tools of making birdcage: the slabs, the scraper, the carving knife, the hand saw, the hand drill, the strip board, the steel ring, the steel file, the vise, the wood chisel, the small tongs, etc. Often, he buys some semi-finished products online for his processing and creation. Take the Yunnan Golden Bamboo Cage for example. It has a fine texture and the bamboo stick is yellow. When processing this kind of cage, dab on it some sesame oil and the cage may take on the purplish red, which may get the cage appear more natural and simpler, and make it much more collectible.

"As mentioned above, there are more principles for the cage clothes" Huang said, "In Sichuan, the cage clothes are mainly red, which implies the purpose of keeping bird is just for fighting. And in Beijing, the clothes are mainly made of silk and satin, which showed the nobility of the imperial palace. And here Jingdezhen was dominated by the black clothes."

The Innermost Words of the Craftsman

"There are many rules we 'the birdman' have to obey. For example, there are three kinds of birds we can not capture: the young birds, which are difficult to raise; the female birds, which give birth to the next generations; the birds that have just lived through the winter and would not be easy to raise due to a long time of coldness they have endured."

Yes, both humans and birds are part of nature. Returning to nature is the commonality of all the living beings.

(Written and photographed by Huang Hui)

照相师曹开琪：
让美的瞬间化为永恒

【老手艺项目】照相

胶卷时代，摄影是一门纯粹的技术活，拍摄一张照片要仔细斟酌才能按下快门，经过暗房处理、修片着色之后才算完成。照相馆也因此分出四个全手工工种：照相、暗房、修片、着色。曹开琪涉猎颇广，四项技艺融会贯通，尤精照相。到现在人人摄影的数码时代，他仍然保持着胶卷照相时代养成的严谨摄影态度。对自己的拍摄对象，他一定做到主题突出、用光讲究、构图新颖等，用一

丝不苟的精神体现一个老照相师对待摄影事业的匠人匠心。

【匠人小传】

曹开琪，男，1963 年生，1982 年毕业于江西省赣州商业学校摄影班，曾几度师从于名家，毕业后进入景德镇百年老店受之照相馆专事人像摄影，是景德镇颇有影响的照相师。

【匠心之路】

旧时照相馆

曹开琪回忆，旧时照相是一门技术活，不像现在，人手一个手机，无论游山玩水，还是遇到突发事件，随时可以拍摄。在受之照相馆工作时，他每次拍摄之前，都要根据顾客的高矮胖瘦及肤色差异选定适合的灯光，而取光由于受到设备落后等因素的约束，照相师往往要用黑纸板和锡箔纸制作专门的打光灯，再选定合适的角度以求拍出最美的照片。拍集体照往往又比拍证件照难得多，照相师指挥拍照对象找好位置以后，要捕捉到人们不眨眼的一瞬间按下快门，这十分考验一个照相师的水平。所以他们往往也只能连续拍摄两三张照片以求选出最好的那张。

那个时代的照相情结

20 世纪照相机还是稀罕物，所以节假日去照相馆照相成为一种时尚。当时景德镇居民为了拍出一张好照片，往往打早便穿戴整齐去往照相馆照个相，节假日还需排队等候。父亲想用照片定格儿女满月时的模样，夫妻想用照片保存结婚时的美好瞬间，少女也期盼用照片博意中人一笑……其时乡下人家进城一趟路途遥远且交通不便，特意去镇上照相馆拍照的更是少之又少。

曹开琪曾经遇到一位垂垂老矣的耄耋老翁，老翁拿着一张已经泛黄的婴儿满月纪念照，请他翻拍放大。交谈中得知，照片中的婴儿是老人的儿子，照片是60年前的旧照。前几年儿子因病去世，留下风烛残年的老父苟延残喘孤独度日。逝者如斯，想起一个甲子前儿子满月酒的情景和一家人其乐融融幸福美好的日子，老人哀叹有恍如隔世之感。此情此景，令人动容。曹开琪了解情况后，为之动容，放下手中所有活计，优先为老人翻拍儿子的照片，了却了老人的美好心愿，而且分文未收。

再先进的设备也无法取代匠心

“虽然我们现在摄影的设备全部都在更新，但是我们的照片，说实在的，退步了。”曹师傅语重心长道，“我还记得十多年前我有幸看过一位景德镇陶瓷大师父亲的一张人像照片，那是20世纪30年代的照相馆拍摄的，从照片上就能看出照相师在拍照时对用光和抓拍人物表情的瞬间是多么的讲究，直到现在我都还在感叹自己远远不如。因为那个时候的人都很认真地对待每一次拍摄。”

曹师傅这些追忆的话语不免透着些遗憾，但他对于摄影的执着和追求可见一斑。对于摄影，他永远怀着一颗在路上的朝圣之心。

【匠人心语】

“一生只做一件事，足矣。我此生最大的梦想和幸福是让美的瞬间化为永恒。”说起从业感想，曹开琪如是说。

是的，一生只要做好一件事，这种认真，不正是对匠心的最好诠释吗？

（继鹏 / 撰文　曹开琪 / 摄影）

Cao Kaiqi, a Photographer : To Eternalize the Moment of Beauty

The Ancient Craft: Taking Photos

In the film age, photography is a pure technical work. A good picture needs careful study before pressing the shutter. And it can't be finished without the darkroom treatment and the film repairing and coloring. The work in the studio is divided into four manual steps: picture taking, darkroom treatment, film patching and coloring. Cao Kaiqi integrated in himself all the four techniques, especially the picture taking. Now in the digital age, he still maintains the rigorous attitude. Any subject in his pictures is presented well with proper light in a unique composition, which shows an old photographer's craftsmanship with meticulous spirit.

The Brief Biography of the Craftsman

Cao Kaiqi, male, born in 1963, graduated from Jiangxi Ganzhou Business School in 1982, majored in photography, and has been apprentice to several masters before. After graduation, he began his work in a photography studio renowned in Jingdezhen, and then developed into a famous cameraman in this city.

The Growth of the Craftsman

The Old Photo Studio

Cao Kaiqi recalls that photography was a technical work in the past, unlike the mobile phone which every person could have one and shoot at any time. When working in the Shouzhi Photo Shop, each time before filming, he had to judge the light according to the customers' size and color. And due to the poor equipment and so on, he had to use black cardboard and foil to get special light and then choose an appropriate angle in order to make the most beautiful picture. Group photo was much more demanding than ID photo. Because when taking a group photo, the cameraman had to choose a perfect location, and shoot it without anyone in the group blinking the eye. That was very testing.

The Photographic Complex of That Era

In the last century, cameras were still a rarity, so it was a fashion to take photos on holidays. In order to get a good picture, the people often dressed up before going to the photo studio, and had to wait in line for the holidays. Fathers wanted to use the photograph to fix the appearance of children when they are one month old, husbands and wifes wanted to use the photo to save the beautiful moment of marriage, young girls also looked forward to using the photograph to win a smile of the person in their heart... At that time, the rural people had no the luck to take photoes in town due to the inconvenient traffic.

Cao Kaiqi once met an old man, holding a photo of a baby, and asking him for reproducing. The baby in the picture was the old man' s son, the photo was taken 60 years ago. His son died a few years ago, leaving him unhelpful in the world. Thinking of the happy life before with his young baby, and touched by this scene, Cao Kaiqi put down all his work at hand, gave him priority and remade his son' s portrait free of charge, fulfilling the wishes of the old man.

No Equipment Can Replace Ingenuity

"Though all the equipments are being updated, our photoes' quality is declining." Cao said seriously, "I remember that ten years ago I saw a photo of a ceramic master' s father. It was taken in a photo studio in 1930s. From the photograph, it could be seen that the cameraman had devote particular care to the light and expression at the moment of shooting. Until now, I still can' t feel equal to that. People at that time were all very serious about each shot."

A deep pity could be felt in Mr. Cao' s reminiscing words, and his persistence and pursuit of photography can be seen. For photography, he has always been on the road with a pilgrim heart.

The Innermost Words of the Craftsman

"One thing just doing in a life, that' s enough. My greatest dream and happiness in this life is to make beautiful moments permanent." Cao Kaiqi said, when speaking of his feeling about his career.

Yes, indeed. One thing in a life is enough. Such earnest attitude in him is just the best interpretation of a craftsmanship, isn' t it?

(Written by Ji Peng, Photographed by Cao Kaiqi)

刻章匠胡庆华：
方寸之间写春秋

【老手艺项目】刻章

印章，是我国特有的历史文化产物，古代主要用作身份凭证和行使职权的工具。它的出现，是基于社会生活的实际需要。早在商周时代，印章就已经产生。如今的印章，已成为一种独特的、融实用性和艺术性为一体的艺术瑰宝。

【匠人小传】

年近七旬的胡庆华老人，从事手工刻章已近50年。1971年，年仅16岁的他进入景德镇工艺雕刻原子印章厂（原景德镇刊刻社）学徒。据胡庆华老人回忆，厂里的刻印师傅的手法都各有特点，只要拿出印章，他就知道是哪位师傅刻的。

现在，他在原服装一厂对面开了昌江印章雕刻厂。前来刻印章的顾客大部分都要求用机械刻制。胡师傅说，他是一个很安静的人，尽管如今要求手工刻章的顾客不多了，但自己还是会经常手工刻一些印章。他深情地说："几十年做下来了，我已经离不开这一行了。"

【匠心之路】

回忆：一块铺板吃三年

据胡师傅回忆，厂里当年有 40 多人，刻章工种大致分为两种：一种是专门写字的，一种为刻字的。当时，刻公章的有 11 人，刻私章的有 6 人。刻公章的人工资是按字数算的。厂里共有雕刻和材料两个车间，车间下面有木刻班、刻橡皮班、刻皮花印班、刻牛角公章班和私章班。当年的二级工，每天的工作任务是刻私章 16 个，完成了基本任务就拿基本工资。胡庆华老人说，他当年的师傅是当时最高的七级工，是专门写反字的。

胡师傅笑侃道："当年手工雕刻印章的行当有一种说法，叫'一块铺板吃三年'，也就是说手工印章起初的材料只有木头，材料的成本低，后来才有了其他材料。"

1998 年，厂子解散了，从那以后，从事这一行的人就不多了。

技法：过"五关"印章方成

手工刻章看起来容易，做起来就难了。胡师傅说，这功夫没有几年学不来，我当学徒就干了三年。一方戳料，刻了磨平，磨平了又刻，日久天长大拇指上都磨出了厚厚的茧子。

胡师傅介绍，手刻印章要过五道关。这第一道关，就是在纸上正手练反着写字。练到熟练时，师傅才让在章料上学下刀。

刻章第二道关，就是练腕力。刻章时，手握刀要不颤不抖，下刀力道要恰到火候。没有很好的腕力做支撑，就根本没法下刀刻，即便刻出来也是白费劲，还瞎了料。当初，师傅要求特别严格。到了冬季冰天雪地时，他就按照师傅的要求蹲在雪窝里，手拿刻刀，在雪地上练习刻字。

刻章第三道关，就是心有章法。刻章，讲究的是章法。印文章法就是字与字、行与行之间的位置安排和整体布局的方法。章法的基本要求是平衡、老实、大方、端正。在此基础上，再追求自然生动、别饶情趣和玩味。

刻章第四道关，就是练气功。刻章在用气上讲究气随意行，以刀为笔，一气呵成。刻制一枚印章，从下刀到刻制完活，中间运刀如行云流水，不做停顿。胡师傅取出一方石料介绍说，这个就得一口气刻下来，至多用两口气，这样才能保证笔势贯通，首尾一气。

【匠人心语】

“我带了两个徒弟，都是自己的女儿，胡丽婷和胡丽萍。她们现在雕刻的技术已经很好了，我希望自己干了一辈子的行当能在她们手上得到传承。”胡师傅深情地说道。

（昌南一芥撰文 / 摄影）

Hu Qinghua, a Stamp Maker : Carving the History into a Small Size

The Ancient Craft: Seal Carving

A seal is a unique product of the historical culture in our country, and the main function in the ancient times was a person's identity credential and a tool to discharge the duties. It originated from the actual demand in social life. As early as Shang and Zhou Dynasties, the seal had come into being. The current seal has become a peculiar art treasure compounded with practicability and artistry.

The Brief Biography of the Craftsman

The old man, Hu Qinghua, who is nearly 70 years old, has been working on seal carving for approximately 50 years. In 1971, he entered into Jingdezhen Technical Carving Atomic Seal Factory (the old Print Carving Association) as an apprentice at the age of 16. Hu Qinghua recalled, each seal carving master had his own characteristic, and he could identify the ownership of the seal when it was showed to him.

Now he established Changjiang Seal Carving Factory opposite to the former No. 1 Garment Factory. Master Hu said, he was a very quiet person, although few customers asked for seals carved by hands nowadays, he often carved some seals manually. He said with deep affection, "I can't leave this industry after having been working on it for decades."

The Growth of the Craftsman

Memory:Practice Carving on a Plank for Three Years

Master Hu recalled there were more than 40 workers in the factory, and seal carving workers were mainly classified into two groups, one group specialized in writing and the other carving. 11 workers worked on carving official seals and 6 worked on personal seals. The salary of the workers carving official seals was calculated by the amount of the carved characters. There were two workshops in the factory, one for carving and the other for seal material, and inside the workshop there were wood carving team, rubber carving team, decorative leather carving team, xo horn official seal team and personal seal team. The daily task for 2nd rank workers was to carve 16 personal seals, and they could get the basic wage when the basic assignment was completed. The old Hu said that his master was the highest 7th rank worker at that time, and he was specialized in writing in an opposite way.

Master Hu said with a smile, "There was an old proverb in our industry at that time, and it was 'Practice carving on a plank for three years'. That is to say, the manual seal could only be carved on wood initially for the cost of the material was low, and we had other materials later."

In 1998, the factory disbanded, and then, people engaged in this industry were less.

Technique:Pass Five Hurdles to Complete a Seal

The manual carving seal looks easy, but it's hard to do. Master Hu said that it would take years before mastering the skill, and he had apprenticed for three years. A seal material was carved and rubbed down over and over again, and the thick callous rubbed out on the thumb after a long time.

Master Hu said that an apprentice must pass five hurdles before manually carving the seal. And the first hurdle was to use the right hand to write the Chinese characters reversely on the paper. When the apprentice was able to write proficiently, the master would allow him to learn to write on the seal material with a knife.

The second hurdle of the seal carving was exercising the wrist. When carving the seals, the knife held by the hand should neither tremble nor shake, and the strength must be controlled to an appropriate degree. Without the forceful wrist, it was impossible to carve with the knife, and even if the seal was carved out, it was vain and a waste of material. At the beginning, the master was particularly rigorous. When it came into chill and the frozen winter came, he followed the master's requirement to squat in the snow hollow practicing carving the Chinese characters on the snowfield with the knife on hand.

The third hurdle was bearing order in mind. Seal carving emphasized the order. The order to carve onto the seal is the arrangement of the position between characters and between rows as well as the method of the integral layout. The basic requirement for the order is to keep balanced, frank, generous and upright. Mastering this basis, the apprentice could further pursue the nature, vividness, humor and wit.

The fourth hurdle to seal carving was to exercise breathing. The breath in and out followed the will, and knife replaced the pen to write smoothly for one time on the seal. When carving a seal, the knife would not stop and move smoothly like floating clouds and flowing water from the start to the end when a seal was achieved. Master Hu took out a stone material and said carving must be completed within one breath or two breaths at most, and only in this way the coherence of the characters at the head and end on the seal could be guaranteed.

The Innermost Words of the Craftsman

"I taught two apprentices, and both were my daughters, Hu Liting and Hu Liping. Their skill to carve the seal is pretty proficient now, and I hope the industry I worked for my whole life could be passed down to my daughters." Master Hu said with deep affection.

(Written and photographed by Changnanyijie)

木雕匠朱伟海：精雕细镂几度秋

【老手艺项目】木雕

建筑装饰木雕，一般分为大木雕刻和小木雕刻两类。大木雕刻主要是指梁、枋、斗拱等构件上的装饰雕刻，小木雕刻则是指包括家具在内的细木工装饰雕刻。传统建筑以木为材，强调构架的组合方式，使每一个部位都成为雕刻的场所，无论是梁、枋、檩、柱等大构架，还是天棚、栏杆、门窗等，甚至门簪、牙子等小部件，都有雕刻装饰。由于各木构件位置、功能、形状有差异，雕刻手法与题材内容也有所不同。时至今日，那些散落在乡野城镇的巧构奇筑、巧夺天工的木雕，融历史文化、建筑艺术、工艺美术于一身，或古朴端庄，或华美巍峨，风格迥异，绚丽多姿。她们有如一颗颗熠熠生辉的明珠，镶嵌在景德镇的大地上，构成了世间罕

见的人文景观，被誉为“中国历史文化瑰宝”和“江西最有特色的文化遗产”。

【匠人小传】

30岁的木雕匠朱伟海是乐平人，从16岁开始拜潘建斌为师学徒。名师出高徒，经过三年的刻苦学艺，他逐渐学会了木雕的精雕细法。历史的厚重，沧桑的演变，乡土的富庶，不仅造就了乐平悠久灿烂的农耕文明，而且造就了乐平独具特色的建筑传统文化。朱伟海在乐平如鱼得水，11年里参加过多座古戏台、古祠堂、古建筑的修复工作。

【匠心之路】

他，对木材材质要求很高

秋天的一个日子，我们有幸认识了木雕匠朱伟海先生，并参观了他的雕刻工坊。我们采访他时，他首先为我们讲述了木材材质对木雕的重要性。

木雕艺术和工艺对于木材材质的要求很高。古代遗留的木雕，如家具、陈设观赏用品、佛教用品以及规模较大的建筑木雕，首选的材料大都是质地较硬的名贵木材，包括紫檀、樟木、花梨木、楠木、黄杨木等。紫檀，也称“青龙木”，切面呈棕紫色，坚硬细致，深沉古雅，是木雕的珍贵材料。樟木，也叫“香樟”，分黄樟、红樟、灰白樟、乌肚樟四种，尤以黄樟最适合用于木雕，其木质坚韧细腻，纹理清晰，不变形，不受虫蛀，所以也是木雕的好材料。花梨木，又称“花榈”“降香黄檀”，俗称“黄花梨”，与紫檀相似，色似琥珀，现已不多见。它质地坚硬，纹理细密，适合做家具小件。楠木，分水楠木、香楠、金丝楠三种，尤以金丝楠最为名贵，木质坚硬，不受虫蛀，不易腐蚀。黄杨木，也称“瓜子黄杨”，木质坚韧细密，色泽纯正。在古代建筑用料中，也能见到这些木材。由于建筑中使用的木材体量较大，而上述木材较为稀有，且生长缓慢，所以在建筑中并不普遍采用。人们在建筑时一般会根据不同的位置用料，同时也考虑装饰雕刻的需要。人们最常用的是硬杂木以及木质略松软的木材，如樟木、榆木、柞木、楸木、红松、椴木、杉木等，既符合建筑力学要求，又易于进行建筑中的木雕装饰。

他，已掌握十多种雕刻手法

朱伟海在十多年的雕刻实践中，积累了丰富经验，掌握了十多种雕刻手法，包括浮雕、镂空雕、圆雕、半圆雕、透空双面雕、锯空雕、阴雕等，并能根据雕刻对象的实用性、艺术性特征来运用技法。雕刻刀具他也用得得心应手，包括平凿、三角凿、雕刀以及蝴蝶凿、翅头凿等。

他，修复古戏台如鱼得水

乐平人建戏台，似乎有一股遏制不住的狂热：一村建台，四邻攀比，风起云涌，势不可遏，以至出现一村两三台、四五台的壮观景象。建戏台时，各种人才大显身手，充分展示各自才华，使戏台最终集建筑、雕刻、工艺、文学、美术于一体，从而成为一座艺术殿堂。随着时间的推移，有些古戏台已经破落，如不及时修复，就有倒塌的危险。

浒崦地处乐平镇桥镇北一公里许，其戏台建于清同治十三年（1872 年），因年久失修，显得有些破烂不堪，后在浒崦乡贤的大力支持下得以重修。朱伟海有幸和几位雕匠前辈一起参与了修复古戏台的木雕工作，历经两年而竣工。修整一新后的浒崦古戏台，远看重檐翘角，华丽壮观。屋脊中央竖一硕大彩釉瓷瓶，瓶中插一铁叉，直指云天，瓶颈以四根铁链系住屋檐四角。檐下悬挂铁马风铃，风起铃响，清脆悦耳。台高14米，宽25米，深12米，正中以木质雕的屏风横向隔开，使之成为相互背依、紧密相连的晴、雨双面的戏台。晴台面北，是全台的主体，雕工精美，气势恢宏。台顶上有三口藻井。中间一口为螺纹斗拱式，稍前两侧各有一口轿顶式藻井。后壁上端悬着一块镂有十八罗汉衬底的镀金匾额，上书“久看愈好”四个苍劲大字。台前四根漆黑锃亮的顶梁大柱上，挂着当地名儒手写的楹联，字迹潇洒俊逸。戏台两侧各一厢房，与雨台相通，供演员进、出场。台上雕梁画栋，遍布戏剧人物浮雕，密密麻麻不下百余处，人物千姿百态，栩栩如生。

他，不断追求雕梁画栋的艺术

朱伟海建筑木雕的工艺水平和艺术水平都很高，表现题材多是人物、山水、花鸟、鱼虫、祥禽瑞兽等。特别是戏曲、历史传统中的情节是他建筑木雕的特色。那些构图完整、雕刻精致的人物场景木雕，以人物为主，注重相互间的呼应和联系，把不同人物的衣着、体态、神情刻画得生动传神，再衬以亭台楼榭与山水林木，人景相融，呈现出一派和谐完美的生活场景。精细部分的雕刻可谓“鬼斧神工”，缕缕须发、片片瓦砾、花之脉络、兽之鳞甲都清晰可见，令人惊叹。

【匠人心语】

“建筑是大工艺，工艺是小建筑。小者是在手上使用、把玩；大者是人在其中活动。”

“不论木雕、砖雕还是石雕，表现在建筑上，都成为建筑结构中不可分割的一部分，从大型的公共建筑到各式各样的民间建筑，从大门、屋脊到梁柱、窗牖，或多或少都要有一点雕刻。有人说这是有意的点缀，我倒觉得它恰似一部乐章的旋律，生活乐曲中不可缺少的旋律。”

（汪春荣撰文 / 摄影）

Zhu Weihai,a Wood Carver : How Many Years Have Passed Through Finest Carving and Cutting

The Ancient Craft: Woodcarving

The decorative woodcarving on architecture is generally divided into two types based on its dimension. The big woodcarvings are mainly the decorative carvings on the beam, architrave, bucket arch and other construction parts, and the small woodcarving refers to decorative carving on joinery including the furniture. The traditional architecture with wood as material emphasizes the compound mode of the framework, making each part to be the place for carving, such as the big framework like the beam, architrave, purlin, pillar and etc., and small parts like ceiling, rail window, door, even gate hairpin and others, they all could be decorated by the carving. Due to the distinction in position, function and shape of each wooden component, the carving technique, subject and content will also be different. Right up to today, those oddly shaped and marvelous woodcarving scattering in the countryside and town, combining the historical culture, architectural art and industrial art, are either simple and demure, or magnificent. Being diversified in style and color, they are like sparkling pearls mounting on the earth of Jingdezhen and constituting the rare human landscape, which is renowned as "the historical and cultural treasure in China" and "The most distinctive cultural heritage in Jiangxi".

The Brief Biography of the Craftsman

Zhu Weihai is a 30-year-old woodcarving craftsman in Leping city, he started to learn from Pan Jianbin as an apprentice at the age of 16. Thanks to the demanding teacher, Zhu gradually mastered the method of carving the wood ingeniously after studying hard for three years. The rich history, epochal transition and fertile soil contribute to not only the centuried and gorgeous agricultural civilization but also the traditional culture of the unique architecture in Leping. In Leping, Zhu Weihai feels like fish in water, he participated in the renovation of many ancient stages, ancestral hall and ancient construction in the past 11 years.

The Growth of the Craftsman

He Has a High Demand on the Texture of Timbers

On an autumn day, we fortunately got acquainted with Mr. Zhu Weihai who is a woodcarving craftsman, and visited his woodcarving workshop. When we started the interview, he firstly told us the importance of the texture of the timber to the woodcarving.

The demand on the texture of the timber is pretty high for the woodcarving art and technique. The remaining woodcarving articles from the ancient times, such as the furniture, ornamental articles, Buddhist articles and big scaled or sized architectural woodcarvings, were mainly made out of the valuable timbers whose texture was comparatively harder, including red sandalwood, camphorwood, palisander, nanmu, boxwood and son on. The sandalwood with another name as "cyan dragon wood" is brown and purple in section, hard and subtle in texture, and deep and elegance in quality, and it is the valuable timber for woodcarving. The camphorwood with another name as "fragrant camphorwood" can be divided into four types as yellow camphorwood, red camphorwood, grey camphorwood and black belly camphorwood, of which the yellow camphorwood is the most suitable timber for woodcarving as it's durable in texture, clear in vein, non-deformable and mothproof. Palisander, also called "Ormosia henryi" "Dalbergia odorifera" or commonly known as "pear wood", is similar as red sandalwood with the color as the amber, which is rare nowadays. It's also hard in texture and tiny in vein, which is appropriate for small pieces of furniture. Nanmu is divided into three types as water nanmu, fragrant nanmu and phoebe nanmu, of which the last type is the most valuable. It features the harness, and non-deformation and non-rottenness. Boxwood, also called as "seed boxwood", is also durable in texture and pure in color. These timbers were common in the ancient construction. However, they are not widely used in the modern construction for the big demand in volume and slow growth of these rare timbers. So we will select the timber generally according to the different position on the construction, and also consider the requirement of the decorative carving at the same time. We often use some hardwood and some timbers which are soft in texture, such as camphorwood, elm, xylosma, catalpa wood, pine wood, basswood, fir and etc., which are both in compliance with the requirement in architectural mechanics and easy for making the woodcarving decoration in the construction.

He Has Mastered More Than Ten Types of Carving Skills

In more than ten years' dedication to the woodcarving industry, Zhu Weihai accumulated the rich experience and mastered more than ten types of woodcarving skills, and he would utilize the skill according to the practicability, artistic characteristic and position of the carving object. He is also very skilled with carving tools, including flat chisels, triangular chisels, carving knifes, butterfly chisels, wing-tip chisels, etc..

He Repairs the Ancient Stage Like Ducks in Water

People in Leping were endlessly crazy for building the stage, and if one village built up a stage, all the villages in neighborhood would follow the trend and made comparisons mutually, which was like storming sweeping the ground and unstoppable, so it contributed to the spectacular scenes in which more than one stages were built in a single village. In building the stages, all kinds of talents fully revealed their ability to build up a stage which was a compound of skills in architecture, carving, technique, literature and art and made it an art hall. As the time elapsed, some of the ancient stages were shabby. If they couldn't be repaired timely, there will be a danger of collapse.

Huyan is one mile away to the north of Qiao Town in Leping, the ancient stage was built in the 13th year of Tongzhi reign in Qing Dynasty (in 1872 A.D.), which looked kind of tattered for being out of repair for a long time. Under the great support of the sages in Huyan Village, funds were raised for renovation. The ancient Huyan stage is gorgeous and spectacular with layers of roofs and lifted corners if seen remotely. In the middle of the ridge stands a big color glaze ceramic vase where an iron fork is inserted with the blade pointing to the sky, and four strings of iron chains are stretched from the neck of the vase to the four corners on the eave. The bells hang below the eave, and they sound clear and melodic when blown by the wind. The stage is 14 meters in height, 25 meters in width and 12 meters in depth. The center is horizontally segregated by a woodcarving screen which closely connected sunny and rainy stages back to back. The sunny stage facing the north is the main body of the whole stage, which is full of exquisite carving and magnificent. On the roof of the stage there are three sunk panels. The panel in the middle is of the spiral arch style, and the other two on laterals slightly in front are panels of the sedan roof style. On the back wall hang a gold plating board engraved with a picture of eighteen arhats as the background, and four forcefully written characters "Jiu kan Yu Hao" are on it. On four big pillars which are pitch-black and shiny hang the couplets handwritten by the famous local scholars with natural and unrestrained script. There is one room on both ends of the stage, which is connected to the rainy stage, and it serves as the entrance and exit for the actors. The beam and rafters on the stage are all carved fully with the characters in dramas, they are all in different poses and expressions, which look alive.

He Has the Pursuit for the Art on Carved Beams and Painted Rafters

Zhu Weihai' s technological level and artistic level have reached a very high degree, and the main subjects in his artworks are figures, landscapes, birds and flowers, fishes and insects, and other animal symbols of auspiciousness. Especially the plots in the traditional operas and history, they are the main features of his architectural woodcarving. Those integrally composite and exquisite woodcarvings with the characters as the main body, focusing on the mutual relationship, depict vividly the various costumes, postures, expressions of them who were backgrounded and perfectly matched with the pavilions, buildings, forests and landscapes, those woodcarvings present a harmonious life scene. The exquisite section in the woodcarving is extremely skillful, and the tiny parts like beards, hairs, tiles, veins and scales of beasts can be clearly figured out, which is pretty astonishing.

The Innermost Words of the Craftsman

"The architecture is a big industrial art, while the industrial art is a small architecture. It' s small as it' s played on hands. While it' s big as it' s moving among people."

"Regardless of the woodcarving, brick carving and stone carving, applied to the construction, they are all indispensable parts of the architectural structure, from the large-scale public facilities to various folk construction, from the gate and ridge to the beam column and lattice window, they are more or less carved with some patterns, and someone said they were the deliberate decoration, but I think it is like the melody in the music, an indispensable melody in the music of life."

(Written and photographed by Wang Chunrong)

剪纸艺人许书亮：
匠心独妙裁云锦

【老手艺项目】民间剪纸

我国的民间剪纸是一门源远流长的手工艺术，最早发源于西汉时代，近年被列入国家第一批非物质文化遗产名录。剪纸有祈祥美化的传统意义，担任着教化礼仪、宣传美德、歌颂生活的传媒作用。在许多隆重场合和喜庆日子，象征着吉祥如意的剪纸艺术品，扮演着不可或缺的重要角色。

【匠人小传】

55 岁的许书亮一米多的个头，小时候的一场大病让他的身高停留在七八岁的年龄段。但这并没有动摇他自强不息的心，他坚信自己可以用双手改变命运。读中学时，他便跟随李世信老师学起了剪纸。在李老师的教导下，他基本掌握了雕、镂、剔、刻、剪等剪纸的多种基本技法。中学毕业后，他在家务农，又以自然为师，无论是花树瓜果还是蝴蝶、蜜蜂、螳螂等昆虫，都成了他剪纸的艺术造型素材。他用剪纸艺术形式表现了对生活真谛的追求，用剪纸艺术创造人生价值。

【匠心之路】

回忆：自小身体残疾，情系剪纸艺术

在中学读书时许书亮就意识到自己个子小，但并没有屈服于命运。他从小就喜欢绘画，特别是图案设计。学校教美术的李世信老师剪纸技艺颇佳，手把手地教许书亮剪纸。

中学毕业后，他就回乡务农。在生产队工作时，他随身带着剪刀。他一边帮生产队守秧苗，一边剪地上的树叶，剪出蝴蝶、蜜蜂等昆虫的造型，田埂上、河岸边随处可见他的“杰作”。他就这样以大自然为师，田里的西瓜、田边的柳树、池塘里的蜻蜓点水等都成了他剪纸的造型图案。有时他看见翩翩飞舞的蝴蝶，就捉来做标本，然后作为剪纸创作的造型图案。后来他创作《百蝶图》用的就是这期间获得的创作素材。

剪纸：用心灵与艺术对话

许书亮身材矮小，活动范围受到一定限制，但创作给他带来了更广阔的精神世界。

21 世纪初，许书亮到村办石岭瓷厂搞图案设计。他也参照瓷器上的图案，将其用到剪纸上来。20 世纪 80 年代，结婚时用“喜”字很流行，许书亮在这一带的十里八村小有名气，甚至九江、南昌等地的人都慕名到他这里来买剪纸作品。

在他灵动的剪刀下，一幅幅融思想性、观赏性、趣味性和地方性的剪纸艺术作品源源不断诞生，花、鸟、虫、鱼、人物、建筑、民俗，内容丰富，题材广泛，想象丰富，技法朴实，秀气与大气并重，技法与想象齐飞。在他双手的不断翻飞

中，一个个栩栩如生的形象被他创造出来，对于这些从自己手中诞生的可爱形象，他格外爱惜。也许正是身体矮小的缘故，他可以不被外面的世界打扰，沉浸于自己的剪纸世界中，用心灵与艺术展开对话。

故事：剪纸的生涯像首歌

1996 年，一次偶然的机会，观音阁的住持找到他，说寺庙重新修缮，有十几个蒲墩上面需要设计荷叶、莲子的图案。许书亮花了几个晚上进行创作，剪了十几个不同的莲花荷叶图案。住持看后非常满意，连声说：“善哉，善哉！多谢，多谢！”

“别的地方剪纸好多是拼剪，我是一剪一个图，一个完整的图，而且这个图玲珑剔透，紧密连接，没有一点断的地方，每一个图都是紧密连接为一个整体的，这是我剪纸的特点。”许书亮脸上略显自豪。一次，一位年轻人慕名而来，说家人九十大寿，请他剪一张八仙桌大小的繁体“寿”字。许书亮当晚进行创作，“寿”字在红纸中间，四个角为四个寿桃，整幅图案没有拼剪之处。顾客十分满意，连声说谢。

【匠人心语】

“对我来说，生活就是剪纸，剪纸就是艺术，即使生活百般为难，我也永不放弃剪纸。”

（黄辉撰文 / 摄影）

Xu Shuliang, a Paper Cutting Artist: The Beauty Cut out with the Hands

The Ancient Craft: the Folk Paper-cut

The folk paper-cut in China is a long-standing handicraft, which originated from the Western Han Dynasty, and it was listed into the first batch of Intangible Cultural Heritage by the nation in recent years. Paper-cut, as a tradition praying for auspices, takes on a media role to teach etiquette, advocate virtue and praise life. And the paper-cut artworks which token the good luck and happiness are indispensable in some solemn occasions and celebration days.

The Brief Biography of the Craftsman

The 55-year-old man, Xu Shuliang, is only around one meter in height due to a serious sickness in the childhood which stops him from growing up and keeps his stature at the age of seven or eight. However, the misfortune never shook his strong heart, and he firmly believed that his fate could be altered by his hands. In middle school, he followed his teacher Li Shixin to learn paper-cut art. Under Professor Li' s guidance, he basically mastered multiple fundamental skills for paper-cut such as turning, hollowing, trimming, engraving, cutting and etc.. After graduation from the middle school, he was farming at home, and learnt from the nature to cut the paper artwork into the shapes of the insects and plants around him. He expressed his pursuit of the truth of life in the form of paper cutting, and created the value of life by the art of paper-cut.

The Growth of the Craftsman

A Memory in Which He Fell in Love With the Paper-cut Art Regardless the Physical Disability in Childhood

Xu Shuliang realized his short stature when he studied in middle school, but never surrendered to the fate. He loved drawing when he was a child, especially the pattern design. The art teacher Li Shixin at the school was very skilled in the paper-cut art, and he taught Xu the paper cut by himself.

Later he farmed at home after graduation. When working in the production team, he took the scissors along with him. So he cut the leaves on the ground into the shapes of the butterfly, bees and other insects while looking after rice seedling, and his masterpieces were everywhere on the ridges of the farmland and banks of the river. He followed the nature as his teacher like this, and the watermelons in the fields, willows beside the fields, dragonflies skimming on the pool all became the patterns for him to create the paper–cut artworks. Sometimes when he saw the dancing butterflies, he would seize and make them into specimens, which became the patterns for his creation then. And the material for his subsequent creation of Picture of Hundreds of Butterflies was collected at that time.

Paper–cut, a Talk Between the Heart and Art

Xu Shuliang' s range of activities was restrained by his short stature to some extent, while the creation brought him a broader spiritual world.

At the beginning of the 21th century, Xu Shuliang went to Shiling Ceramic Factory run by the village to design the patterns. He also referred to the pattern on the ceramics and copied them onto the paper–cut artworks. In the 1980s, the hand–cut paper for wedding was quite popular, so Xu Shuliang was kind of famous around the regions nearby, and even someone came to buy his paper–cut artworks after hearing his fame from Jiujiang, Nanchang and other cities.

By his smart scissors, the paper–cut artworks with ideology, ornamental value, interestingness and regionalism were created one after another continuously. Blossoms, birds, insects, fishes, figures, architectures, folks are all the subjects for his creation which is rich in content and imagination, skill is plain , and it' s also a combination of elegance and grandness. When his hands were moving up and down, one and another lively image was made out, and he cherished all these lovely images created by his hands in particular. Maybe it was his stature that isolated him from the disturbance out of his real world, so he could immerse in his own paper–cut world and talk with the art spiritually.

The Paper–cut Career Feels Like a Song

In 1996, the abbot of Guanyin Pavilion found him by accident and requested for some lotus leaf and lotus seed patterns designed on a dozens of cushions when the temple needed to be revamped. Xu Shuliang spent several nights on the creation, cutting out a dozen of various lotus and leaf patterns. The abbot was very satisfied after seeing the patterns, and repeated his gratitude for his benignity.

"Most of the paper–cuts made in other places are spliced after each parts are cut out, while mine is cut one paper sheet, so it' s an integral paper–cut. In this way, the paper–cut works are more exquisitely carved and cohesive without any cutting points. And this is the features of my paper–cut artworks." Xu Shuliang said a little bit proudly. Once a young man visited Xu after hearing his fame and invited him to cut an old–fashioned–square–table sized Chinese character "Shou" for the young man' s family member' s 90 years' birthday. Xu Shuliang created out the paper–cut on just one piece of paper sheet without splicing that night, and the character was positioned in the center of the red sheet with one peach in each of the four corners. The customer was quite satisfied with the artwork, and appreciated him repeatedly.

The Innermost Words of the Craftsman

"For me, life is paper–cut and vice versa, although, the life is hard, I will never forgo the paper–cut."

(Written and photographed by Huang Hui)

糖画师翁金生：
酸楚里面透着甜

【老手艺项目】糖画

手艺人制作糖画，以糖为材料，以勺子为“笔”，以糖稀为“墨”，在石板上飞快地来回浇铸画出造型，各种生动的图案造型便在手艺人的手下跃然纸上。画造型，民间手艺人的手上功夫是关键。造型完成后，手艺人随即用小铲刀将糖画铲起，粘上竹签。

在景德镇，不管是“老崽里仔”还是“小崽里仔”，心中的糖画情结都是永久的童年记忆与情趣。那些游走在街头巷尾的小摊的糖画，是当年孩子们最爱的零食；曾游走在大街小巷的糖画老人是他们每天的期盼。

【匠人小传】

今年 67 岁的翁金生做了 35 年的“糖人”。早先，他家附近住着一位叫涂春英的糖画老艺人，自幼爱绘画的翁金生跟随这位老艺人学糖画。后来，在乐平桃酥厂里熬糖的舅舅帮助他改进了熬糖的技术。翁师傅以“勺作笔、糖为墨、腕走笔”的糖画，线条匀称、形态饱满，形成了独有的风格样式，给人以美的享受。

【匠心之路】

现场授艺赠送糖画

笔者见到翁金生老人时，他正在人民公园摆摊。两个学生模样的女孩正认真地听着翁师傅讲解制作糖画的过程。翁师傅边搅拌糖料边说：“绘画，讲究的是眼明手快、全神贯注，力求一气呵成；同时还必须保证每一根线条都是连上的，要不然粘竹签的时候就容易变形。像这些兔子、金鱼都非常简单，用一勺半糖就够，最难的就是画龙和虎，得两三勺糖……如果你能画得来，我就送你一个糖画。”

“你是想让我们传承你的手艺吧！”女孩会心地笑了。

“对，对，对！”翁师傅也笑了起来。

两个女孩很感兴趣，在翁师傅的指导下现场学画。翁师傅对她们的“作品”并不满意，于是让自己 10 多岁的孙女再演示一遍。只见他的孙女把糖料搅拌均匀，然后就神情专注地开始画起山雀来。他的孙女动作娴熟，手腕的运行忽快忽慢，手中的勺子忽高忽低，不一会儿工夫，“笔下”的山雀就呈现在人们眼前。旁边驻足而立的人们不禁点头，微笑着称赞，两个女孩更是拍手叫好。

翁师傅随手又做了两个笑脸男娃糖画送给两个女孩，以表示对她们的鼓励。

师傅领进门，修行在个人

翁师傅制作糖画使用的工具很简单：一个加热糖料的炉具、一块光滑的大理石板、一把钢铲和一个自制的小勺，勺子的另一端还安有一根筷子。他说，制作糖画除了需要控制手劲儿，还需控制熬糖的火候，火太大糖就容易变稀走形，火小了糖又会太硬，无法成形。“每天早上五六点钟，我就起来熬，用慢火熬一个多钟头才行。”他接着说道，“熔化糖要用小火，火大了糖就会焦。用温火将糖慢慢熔解，糖完全熔解后就可以用来绘画了。”

回忆起从事这一行当的原因，翁师傅很是感慨：“我小时候的年代是加工食品稀少的年代，糖画是我童年最爱的零食。记得我读小学的时候，有个叫‘麻子’的糖画匠，我很喜欢他的糖画，放学后就站在他的摊子前看他画糖画。现在我画糖画有很多就是画他的图案。后来，我家附近住着一位叫涂春英的糖画老手艺人，我也跟他学过画糖画。”

一条龙的故事

2012 年是龙年，翁师傅想把自己内心深处的东西通过糖画表现出来。当时他用了 20 多天的时间，创作了一条长 4 米、高 1 米的糖龙。“从用铁丝扎架子

到熬糖制作，我花去了130多斤糖，只用了70多斤，还浪费了好几十斤糖，熬了两个通宵，那条糖龙才做好。”谈起当年制作糖龙，翁师傅显得很兴奋，“我是从年前就开始做，正月初十10点我把它扛出来了，算是希望十全十美吧！”翁师傅告诉笔者，他做的龙连龙角都是糖做的，不仔细看会以为是树根哩。

据翁师傅介绍，当初他的家人不太看好他做大糖龙。翁师傅是在空调房间里做好的，平常不让自己的家人看到。他家人不赞成他画糖龙是因为做糖龙有危险，熬糖时糖如果滴到手上，就会烫到甚至掀掉皮肤。但功夫不负有心人，糖龙终于做出来了。

不吃我的糖画真遗憾

翁金生老人的儿子和孙女都会做糖画。但翁师傅坦言，他们只会将其作为业余爱好。翁师傅认为，糖画手艺人慢慢减少是有原因的。糖画工艺受季节影响很大，由于糖画绘制成形后，需要冷却凝固，酷暑季节糖画不容易定形，不适宜销售。此外，糖画销售时间也很固定，主要就是学生上学、放学时间以及节假日，手艺人难以维生。现在的糖画市场并不景气，随着物质生活的丰富，购买的人慢慢减少，导致很多糖画手艺人为了生计纷纷转行。在景德镇，现在摆糖画摊子的没有几个人。

【匠人心语】

“糖画的弱点就是不能保存，如果能保存，我会把自己精心制作的糖画全部捐给国家。国家给了我许多，我已经是买了社保的，应该说是老有所养了。我想把景德镇的陶瓷文化与糖画文化结合起来。”

这时，翁师傅的电话铃声响起：“都说冰糖葫芦酸，酸里面它透着甜……”

（昌南一芥 / 撰文　丰月 / 摄影）

Weng Jinsheng, a Sugar Painter : Sweetness Hidden in the Sour and Bitter

The Ancient Craft: Sugar Painting

Sugar painting, is a drawing on the slab with sugar as the material, quickly made by an craftsman using a spoon as his pen and the diluted sugar as his ink. All sorts of vivid patterns may appear on the slab from the hands of the craftsman. For the pattern modelling, the hand work of the craftsman is very crucial. When the painting is finished, it would be scooped up with a bamboo stick onto it.

In Jingdezhen, people whether is "old pup" or "little pup", the sugar picture complex is a permanent childhood memory and interest for them. Previously, the sugar paintings on the streets and alleys were their favorite snacks and the children looked forward every day to the coming of the old sugar painter.

The Brief Biography of the Craftsman

Weng Jinsheng, 67 years old, has been a "sugar man" for 35 years. Earlier, there was an old sugar craftsman named Tu Chunying lived near his home. Weng, interested in drawing since childhood, learned it from him. Later, his uncle, who was the sugar cooker in Leping' s Taosu Pastry Factory, helped him improve his sugar-cooking technology. Weng, taking the spoon as pen and the sugar as ink, has made many sugar paintings, of which the lines were symmetrical and the forms were full, and which presented a unqie style and offering some aesthetic feeling.

The Growth of the Craftsman

Skills Imparting and Sugar Painting Giving

When I saw Mr. Weng, he was in the People' s Park. Two girls, who looked like students, were listening carefully to Weng' s explanation of the process of sugar painting. While stirring the sugar, Weng said, "During painting, your hands must be quite nimble, and all your attention should be focused. Try to make it at one stretch. At the same time, you have to guarantee that all lines are linked. If not, the shape may be distorted when sticking the bamboo stick. These rabbits and goldfish are easy to make. For them, a half teaspoon of sugar is enough. The hardest is to draw the dragon and the tiger, which may require two or three spoonfuls of sugar... if you can paint successfully, I will give you one for free."

"You want us to carry on your craft!" The girl smiled.

"Yes, you' re right." Mr. Weng also laughed.

The two girls were quite interested. Under the guidance of Mr. Weng, they began to make painting on the slab. Not content with their work, Weng asked his 10-year-old granddaught to demonstrate the painting work again. The little girl stirred the sugar up first, and then got her attention focused. With dexterous movements of her wrist, sometimes held high and sometimes very low, she began her drawing. After a short while, a lifelike titmouse appeared on the slab. The people standing nearby nodded, smiled and praised, and the two girls applauded.

Mr. Weng made two smiling child figures and gave them to the two girls for encouragement.

The Master is for Ushering You in, and You Are for Deciding Your Achievement

Weng' s tool of making sugar painting is simple: a stove for heating sugar, a piece of smooth marble slab, a steel scoop and a special small spoon with a stick on the other end. In addition to a good control of the hands, you have to take care of the heat control when cooking sugar. If over heated, the sugar is easy to be distorted, if heated less than enough, the sugar cannot take shape. "Every morning at five or six o' clock, I get up to cook sugar, boiling it with slow fire for about one hour."

Recalling the reason of enter the sugar painting area, Mr. Weng was very emotional: "When I was a child, it was a time when processed food was scarce, and sugar painting was my favorite childhood snack. I remember when I went to elementary school, there was a sugar painter called "Mazi". I loved his sugar painting. Every time when the school was over, I would go to his store to watch him painting. Now many of the patterns I paint are those he had painted. Later, my master Tu Chunying settled down near my home and I began to learn after him.

A Story about a Dragon

The year of 2012 is the dragon year in Chinese culture. Mr. Weng wanted to show his innermost feelings through the sugar paintings. So in that year, he created a sugar dragon that was 4 meters long and 1 meter high, which took him more than 20 days. "From the frame making with iron wire to sugar cooking, it cost him more than 65 kg of sugar. But the sugar on the dragon was only 35 kg; the rest was simply wasted. In addition, to make it, I had got two nights unsleeping." When talking about the production of the sugar dragon, Weng looked very excited. "I started to do it before the Chinese New Year, and I carried it out in January 10th in the lunar calendar. I hope everything is perfect!" Master Weng told me that the dragon' s horn he made was sugar too, which might be taken as a tree root.

According to Weng, his family didn' t like him to do the big sugar dragon. Weng had no choice but to do it in the air-conditioned room, without been found by his family. The main reason for his family' s disaproval was that sugar dragon making was too dangerous. If the boiling sugar dripped onto the hand, it would lift off the skin. But his hard work paid off finally, the sugar dragon was completed later.

The Firm Idea: Pityful Is Not Having Tasted My Sugar Painting

Weng Jinsheng' s son and granddaughter are both proficient in making sugar paintings. But Mr Weng admited that they will only use it as a hobby. Weng suggested that there were grounds for reduction in the number of sugar painting craftsman. Sugar painting process may be greatly affected by the seasons, because when the sugar painting is finished, it needs cooling and solidification, which would not occur in the hot summer. So the summer is not a good season for selling sugar painting. Besides, its sales time is also very limited, which is mainly when the students go to school or go back from the school and holidays. Therefore, it is very difficult for the sugar painting craftsman to earn a living from it. Now the sugar painting market is in depression. With the abundance of material life, fewer and fewer people like to eat sugar, which prompt the sugar painting craftsman to change into other businesses. In today' s Jingdezhen, few people would set up a stall making sugar paintings.

The Innermost Words of the Craftsman

"The weakness of sugar paintings is that it cannot be preserved. If it can be preserved, I will donate all my carefully crafted sugar paintings to our nation. Our nation gave me a lot. I have bought social security and so I won' t be worried about my living in my later years. In addition, I want to integrate the ceramic culture of Jingdezhen with the sugar painting culture.

At this moment, the telephone of Weng rang: "All people say candied haws are sour, but they are sweet inside..."

(Written by Changnanyijie, photographed by Feng Yue)

制香匠陈砚：
在静穆岁月里燃一炷心香

【老工艺项目】制香

香在中国有6000多年历史，最早是用来敬鬼神、清净身心的，古人视为神物。佛教传入后，燃香成为佛教仪式中的一种形式，佛教徒用以表达虔诚的宗教信仰。香被誉为连接天界和尘世、生者与冥界的媒介，它穿越时空传递世人的信念。除了作为宗教信仰的媒质，在传统文化中，燃香也是古人一大雅好。古书中曾列举了十几种人生乐事：酌酒、试茶、阅书、临帖、诵经、焚香、莳花……

【匠人小传】

陈砚，46岁，江西都昌人，手工制香传承人，矢志不渝地从事手工制香20多年。景德镇地区大多数零售香行里的香及寺庙用香都出自他的制香作坊。

【匠心之路】

香烟袅袅，心似明镜

我们多方打探，终于打听到在浮梁县洋湖村尚有一处艰苦坚守着的制香作坊。在一个暖融融的冬日，我们驱车进洋湖村，找到了手工制香传承人陈砚。

陈砚小时候就有几分佛性。外婆家后面有一家做香的人家，每次去外婆家，他都会跑到那户人家去看他们制香，渐渐地，每一道工序他都熟稔于心。母亲是一个虔诚的佛教徒，家里常年供着佛灯敬着香，自家也开了一片香铺卖香烛之类。在家风熏陶下，陈砚日渐对佛教有所启悟，对与佛教有关的香事也有了浓厚兴趣。

1996 年，成家后的陈砚，在选择创业方向时，竟毫不犹豫地选了制香业，爱人也开了一家香烛铺，夫妻两个组合成一个产业链。

心香一炷，燃起向往

别看香只是小小的一根，制作的工序却有十几道。普通的大众用香，原材料还算简单点，如果要制作高端点的檀香熏香，材料复杂，工艺更精细。普通香的原材料主要是榆木粉、锯末屑、玫瑰精等。制作香时，每道工序都得把握好，不然做出的香不是燃不着就是燃烧的时间短。

榆木粉为黏性料，要占到用料的 30%，锯木屑等原料占到 70%。100 克香粉（含榆木粉）用 50 摄氏度左右的温水约 70 克和拌即可。和出来的香泥是松散的，放置半个小时左右即可开始制作。水不能多了，水放多了一是不好脱模，二是做出来的香晾干后收缩得会太紧实，点不燃。装模的时候压的力度要合适，太紧或太松都会导致断火。

最后，把做好的香大把大把放进木桶中，来回滚动木桶，使香与香之间互相摩擦，这叫“抛光”。抛光到位的香光滑紧密，燃烧时间长，一般这道工序要费时半小时左右，偷懒不得，否则做出的香就略显粗糙。一根做工精细的香拿取时应不掉香粉，不沾手，香脚细且直。按标准，香的燃烧时间要达到古人说的一炷香时间，也就是要达到 1 个小时（半个时辰）。

香飘四季，执着一生

做香 20 多年，陈砚苦过，累过，在困境中挣扎过。虽然制香算不上什么了不起的事业，也赚不了多少钱，之前没买车时，还得风里雨里骑着三轮车送货，但陈砚从没有想过放弃。

在困境中坚守，陈砚也显出一丝无奈。现在一把香（20 支）的批发价不到一块钱，一天做不了一千把，除去阴雨天，一年能生产的时间也只有八九个月，刨除 3 个工人工资及原料费也没多少钱赚，去年一场大水淹了作坊，让他受到不小的损失。因为这样一些缘故，老婆一直叫他关停这边的制香厂。但想到一旦停下来，景德镇也就少有制香的人了，一些老主顾得从外地渠道进货了，他还是坚持了下来，凭着自己 20 年的制香手艺支撑着厂子。不过，现在制香的主要工序已换成机器操作了，如果仅靠纯手工已赚不到饭吃的。

【匠人心语】

"我会一直坚守在传统制香这个行业里，不管社会如何变化发展，祖宗留下来的好东西不能丢，多一个人制香，就多一个人传承，也就少一分遗忘。"香火不断，陈砚与香为伴的人生还在继续。

（蓝田玉 / 撰文　丰月 / 摄影）

Chen Yan, an Incense Maker: Enjoying the Quiet While Burning Incense in the Heart

The Ancient Craft： Making Incense

Incense has a history of more than 6，000 years in China. It was first used to honor ghosts and spirits， and the ancients regard it as a fetish. After Buddhism was introduced， burning incense became a form of Buddhist ritual and Buddhists used it to express their religious beliefs. The incense is hailed as the medium that connects heaven and earth， the living and the underworld， and it conveys the belief of the world through time and space. In addition to serving as a medium for religious beliefs， in the traditional culture， burning incense is also an ancient and elegant interest， Ancient books have listed dozens of happiness: drinking wine， testing tea， reading books， practicing calligraphy， reading cripture， burning incense， flowering...

The Brief Biography of the Craftsman

Chen Yan， 46 years old， was a native of Duchang in Jiangxi Province. He inherited the hand-made incense and was committed to making hand-made incense for more than 20 years. Most of the incense in most retail incense shops and the temple in Jingdezhen came from his incense-making workshop.

The Growth of the Craftsman

The Smoke of the Incense Rising， the Heart Likes a Mirror

We inquired in many ways and finally heard that there was still a incense-making workshop in Yanghu Village， Fuliang County. On a warm winter day， we drove into Yanghu Village and found Chen Yan， the inheritor of hand-made incense.

Chen Yan had a little bit of buddhahood as a child. Behind the grandmother' s house， there is a family who makes incense. Every time he goes to the grandmother' s house， he will go to see them making incense. Gradually， every process is familiar to him. The mother is a devout Buddhist. The family is always dedicated to the Buddha light to incense， and her family has also opened a fragrant shop selling incense and the like. Under the sway of home-breathing， Chen Yan gradually became enlightened about Buddhism and had a keen interest in

Buddhist-related incense.

In 1996, after getting married, Chen Yan did not hesitate to choose the incense industry when he chose to start a business. His wife also opened a incense shop, Chen Yan and his wife combined into an industrial chain.

The Heart Incense Burns up the Hope

Don't look that incense is only a small one, but there are dozens of production processes. Ordinary people use incense, its raw materials are still simple, if you want to make high-end sandalwood incense, the material is complex, the process is more sophisticated. The raw materials for ordinary incense are mainly eucalyptus powder, sawdust and rose essence. When making incense, each process must be handled well, otherwise the incense made is either not burning or burning for a short time.

Eucalyptus powder is viscous material, accounting for 30% of the materials used, and sawdust and other raw materials accounted for 70%. 100 grams of fragrant powder (including eucalyptus powder) can be stirred with about 70 grams of warm water at about 50 degrees Celsius. The agitated mud is loose, and it takes about half an hour to start making. Water can not be too much, it the water is too much, it is not good for demoulding, and the second , if the incense after drying shrinks too tightly, if is not burning well. The force of pressing should be appropriate when loading the mold. Too tight or too loose can cause a fire.

Finally, put a lot of good incense into the barrel, rolling the barrel back and forth, so that the incense and incense rub between each other, which is called "polishing". The incense that is polished well is smooth and tight, and it takes a long time to burn. Generally, this process takes about half an hour, and it is not allowed to be lazy. Otherwise, the incense is slightly rough. A fragrant workman should not lose the fragrant powder, not touch his hands, and have a delicate and straight foot. According to the standard, the burning time of the incense must reach the time of the incense that the ancients said, that is, the burning time should reach 1 hour.

Fragrant for Seasons, Insist on a Lifetime

After more than 20 years of making incense, Chen Yan suffered and tired and struggled in difficulties. Although making incense is not a great cause, it can't make much money. When I didn't buy a car before, I had to ride a tricycle to deliver goods in the rain, but Chen Yan never wanted to give up.

In the predicament, Chen Yan also showed a hint of helplessness. Now, the wholesale price of one incense (20 sticks) is less than one yuan, and it cannot be done for one thousand a day. In the rainy days, production could go on for only 8 to 9 months each year, and the three workers' wages and raw materials are eliminated. there is not much money left, a flood last year flooded the workshop, causing him to suffer big losses. For some reason, his wife has been calling him to shut down the incense factory. However, once he thought of stopping, Jingdezhen would have few people who had made incense. Some old customers had to purchase goods from foreign channels. He persisted and supported the factory with his 20 years of fragrant craftsmanship. However, the main process of making incense has been replaced by machine operation. If you rely on pure handcraft, you cannot earn money.

The Innermost Words of the Craftsman

"I will always stick to the traditional incense-making industry. No matter how the society changes and develops, the good things that ancestors have left cannot be lost. If one person makes incense, one more person will inherit it and less oblivion." the burning of incense is continuing, Chen Yan's life with incense is continuing.

(Written by Lan Tianyu, photographed by Feng Yue)

手艺

Handicraft Art

邹锡进／摄影

Zouxijin \ photo

银匠栗晗曦：
特立独行的寻梦者

【老手艺项目】手工银器

中国手工打制银器传统技艺历史非常悠久，与先民的日常生活和审美需求密不可分。手工银饰工序繁杂，打制流程包括熔炼、制条、拉丝、压片、裁剪、焊接、打磨、抛光等。整个制作过程枯燥乏味。一件银冠、银锁或者雕花之类的手工银饰品，往往需要半个多月的时间，甚至更久。传统银饰一般以鱼、团花、万字符、甲骨文等为设计元素，体现中国风格。

【匠人小传】

栗晗曦，女，原籍山东临沂，27岁，手工制作银饰传统工艺传承人。大学学的是会展专业，毕业后开过设计工作室，最终选择的却是手工银饰传统工艺。近年来，她不仅以美妙绝伦的银饰佳品赢得了广泛粉丝，还通过开办手工制作银器体验传习班的方式推广传统工艺，受到好评。

【匠心之路】

特立独行的女银匠

生长于山东临沂的小栗，没有山东女汉子的豪爽，却有几分江南女子的婉约与秀逸。其大学攻读的专业为中国传媒大学南京分校会展专业。有一次，喜欢天马行空游山玩水的小栗偶然到贵州苗寨一游，被当地银饰品深深地吸引了，继而爱上了手工制作银器传统工艺，渴望掌握手工打造银饰技艺，做出自己喜爱的银饰品。她放弃了原本不错的设计工作，跑到贵州凯里拜中国工艺美术大师、非物质文化遗产传承人李正云大师学艺。

宝剑锋从磨砺出

刚到苗寨时，小栗遇到不少问题。首先是饮食生活上的不适应。其次是语言沟通上的困难。老师和工坊里的其他人员聊天时，基本都说苗语，小栗一点都听不懂，只有单独和她说话时，老师才会说普通话。这没有影响小栗留下来耐心学艺的决心。

手工打制银饰品，除了熔炼、制条、拉丝、压片，造型和焊接是两个关键技术。小栗学过绘画，造型不成问题，最难的是各个部件的焊接。很长一段时间，要么焊接点过于粗陋，要么因温度过高，花了好几天时间制作出来的花样部件被烧坏了甚至熔化了，让她懊恼不已。

还有一次，焊枪把一件刚买不久的外套烧出一个大洞，让她心疼得几晚没睡。

更有甚者，有时因为火力太猛，会把手指烧伤，疼得她好几天都没法干活。

有时，由于神情专注，手指头会被锋利的刀片割出很深的口子，殷红的血

滴在洁白的银器上，犹如绽开的花朵。每当此时，也只能用创可贴包扎一下，接着干。

苦心人，天不负。就是如此近乎苛刻的磨砺，使她手艺日益精进，望着自己亲手制作出来的一个个精美的银饰品，小栗倍感欣慰。

老手艺承载着特殊情怀

景德镇系蜚声中外的瓷都，陶瓷文化底蕴深厚，这也为小栗的银饰题材和工艺创新提供了广阔的空间。2017 年的一个秋日，独行侠一般的小栗只身来到手工艺之都景德镇，经朋友介绍，在一幢景漂公寓住下来，期望在这座传统文化底蕴深厚的城市书写一个银匠的传奇。

有个女子把爸爸当年送给妈妈的银镯子弄丢了，心里面一直很内疚，看到小栗工坊开设手工制作银饰品体验课程的消息，也了解到小栗老师手工制作银饰品的技艺娴熟，喜出望外，兴冲冲地登门学艺。在小栗老师的精心指导下，她亲手制作了一件与原物一样的手镯送给妈妈，圆了一个美好心愿。

传统工艺的布道者

非物质文化遗产的生命在于活态化传承。为此，小栗不仅利用微信公众号等新媒体推介手工制作银饰传统手工艺，还在工作室推出了形式多样的银饰手工制作传习班。爱好者可选择自己喜爱的饰品样式来工作室亲手制作。在小栗师傅的指点下，他们就能做出一件颇具纪念意义的银饰。因为小栗的手工艺过硬，为人又古道热肠，为了圆梦而前来小栗小作坊的银饰制作体验者越来越多了。也许，这正是传统老手艺的魅力所在吧。

【匠人心语】

一件手工银饰品，由银条变成银丝，继而在手艺人耐心细致的打造和烈火高温的焊接下成为传世物件。银饰品制作，考验的不仅是手艺人的眼力和体力，还有耐力和创造力。我愿意像一块银子，在岁月的淬炼和打磨下，绽放生命的光华。

（陶阳客 / 撰文　吴雨霏 / 摄影）

Li Hanxi, a Silversmith : A Maverick Dream Cather

The Ancient Craft: Handcrafted Silverwar

The history of Chinese handmade silveware are time–honored, and it is inseparable from ancients' aesthetics and their daily life.The process of making silverwork is extremely complex, which includes smelting, slivering, redrawing, preforming, tailoring, soldering, polishing and so on.The whole process is very boring. For instance, a silver ornament like sliver crown, sliver lock or carving technique, may often take half a month or longer to be completed.The traditional silver ornament generally use designs such as fish, flowers, swastikas and oracle–bone inscriptions, etc.. It embodies the Chinese style.

The Brief Biography of the Craftsman

Li HanXi, 27 years old and a female whose native place is Linyi in Shandong Province, is a successor of traditional crafts which is relative to hand–made silverware. She majored in exhibition in university and opened a design studio after graduation. However, she finally chose the traditional crafts of hand–made silverware. In recent years, her wonderful silver ornaments win a large number of fans but she was well and widely recieved for holding classes providing opportunities of experiencing making silverware.

The Growth of the Craftsman

A Maverick Female Silversmith

Grown in Linyi, Shandong, the girl has no the generosity of Shandong women;she is more like a woman from south China, she seems to be graceful and excellent. She majored in the exhibition in Nanjing branch campus of Communication University of China. She likes to go sightseeing in a wild and unrestrained way.Once she visited Miao of Guizhou, she was deeply attracted by the local silver jewelry. Then she fell in love with traditional crafts of handmade silverware.She was eager to master the art of hand–crafted silver and made her favorite silver jewelry.When she came back to Nanjing, she gave up her graphic design company which was a good business.She went to Kaili in Guizhou to learn from intangible cultural inheritor Li Zhengyun, who was called the Chinese master of arts and crafts.

Honing Gives a Sharp Edge to a Sword

When she first came to the Miao, she met a lot of problems. The first is the inadaptation in diet. And the second is the difficulty of language communication. The teacher and the other people in the workshop talked about the Miao language basically, and Li didn't understand at all. Only the teachers speak to her alone, they could speak mandarin. This does not affect the determination of staying and learning the craft patiently.

The procedures of making handmade sliver ornaments includes smelting, slivering, drawbench and tabletting etc. of which sculpt and welding are two key technologies. Li studied painting, so sculpt is out of question, but the best hard is welding of inderidual parts.In a long time, either the point of weld is too rash, or the special parts made for several day suffer accidental burnout, this made she feel remorseful and angry.

Once, welding gun burned a big hole in a newly bought coat. And it made her stay up for a few nights.

What's worse, because the fire was too strong, she burned her finger, the pain kept her from working for a few days.

Sometimes, because she was so focused, the finger were cut deeply by the sharp blade, and the red blood was dripping on the white silver, just like a bursting flower. At such times, she just bounded up by band aid, and went on with her work.

All your hard work will pay off. It is such an almost strict training that she has gradually become a skillful silversmith. Whenever looking at these exquisite silver ornaments made by herself, she feels a great relief.

The Old Craft Carrys Special Feelings

Jingdezhen is a world-famous porcelain capital with ceramic culture in deep inside, which also provides a broad space for Xiao Li's silver decorative themes and technical innovation. In the autumn of 2017, Xiao Li who likes a individualist came to Jingdezhen, the Handicraft capital. Due to a friend's introduction, she joined the group of people living in Jingdezhen, expecting to write a legend of a silversmith in this city which owns profound traditional culture.

Once there was a sad-faced young woman, who lost the jade bracelet which was a love token her father gave her mother fifty years ago. She knew Xiao Li was a skillful silver maker and got news of opening experience course for silver making, so she visited excitedly and learned the skills. After Xiao Li's careful guidance, she made a bracelet as the same as the original one and her wish came true.

Evangelist of Traditional Skills

Intangible cultural heritage's life is in inheriting flexibly. Because of this, Xiao Li not only promotes the traditional handicraft of handmade silver ornaments by new media, such as the WeChat, but also launches a variety of silver handmade training class in the studio. The enthusiasts can choose their favorite ornament and make them by hand. Under the guidance of Xiao Li, they can make a very memorable silver ornament. Because Xiao Li has a perfect mastery of handicraft and is very warmhearted, more and more people come to Xiao Li' workshop to strike for dreams. Maybe this is the charm of traditional art.

The Innermost Words of the Craftsman

A piece of hand-made silver ornament is made from silver bar into silver filament. Then after craftsman's patient creation and the welding of fire and high temperature, it becomes an individual which will be inherited over centuries. The manufacture of silver ornaments is not only a test of the skill and strength, but also a test of the endurance and creativity. I want to be like a silver, under the quenching and grinding of the time, blooming the glory of life.

(Written by Tao Yangke, photographed by Wu Yufei)

铜匠萧成武：
“屠龙之技”写新篇

【老手艺项目】铜匠

旧时，手工匠作行当有“九佬十八匠”之说，其中铜匠就占有一席之位。铜匠作业，之所以称之为“打制”或“打”，是因为铜匠并不炼铜，只是以铜板或铜片为原材料，用锤子之类工具敲打出诸如铜壶、铜锅、铜瓢、铜铲、铜锣、铜茶盘、铜锁之类的器皿来。一个铜匠的手艺好不好，就要看他的敲打功夫到不到位。

【匠人小传】

萧成武，原籍江西省新建县，祖祖辈辈为铜匠。父亲萧仁和打铜的手艺好，在豫章城（南昌市）开的“萧仁和铜号”颇有名气，还在附近县城开了分号。许多官僚和大老板都慕名找他打制铜制品。

抗战时期，他逃难到景德镇，在公馆岭附近开铜号小店，从此在古镇以铜匠为业。解放后公私合作联社，老爷子以15担紫铜入社，成为古镇当时一大趣谈。

萧成武出生于景德镇，13岁即跟随其父进社学徒，苦练三年方学成满师，继承了家族所有手工制铜技艺。但是，随着铜原料的日渐枯竭和铝制品的兴起，手

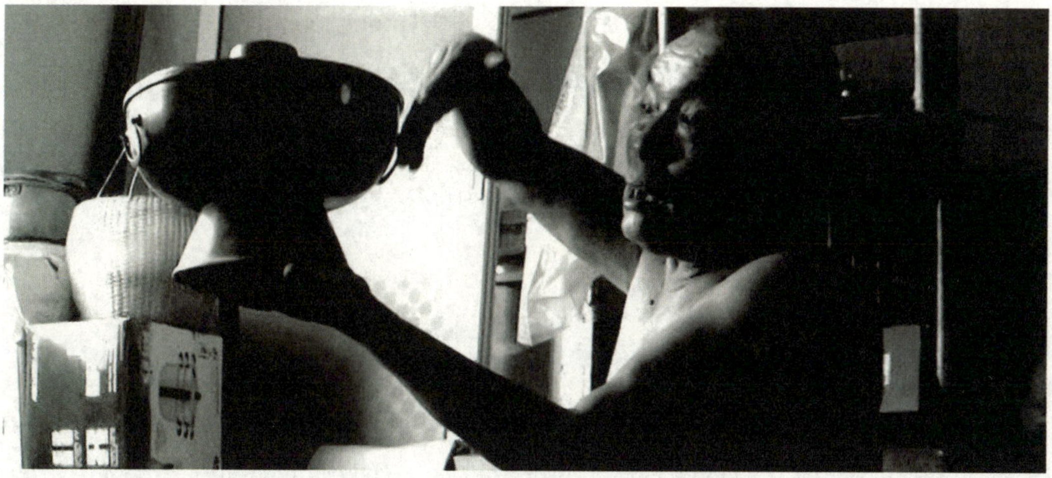

工制铜遂成“屠龙之技”，萧成武之后改弦易辙做起了制瓷模具的手艺和钣金工，一辈子与金属工艺打交道将近 50 年。

【匠心之路】

铜匠世家的艰辛之路

铜匠不仅是一个体力活，其技艺含金量也非常高。

萧师傅介绍，为了谋生，他 13 岁就开始跟着父亲学艺。头一年整整烧了一年的炭。当时他对于烧炭这件事是比较抵触的，不过也只有沉住气，第二年开始打铜条。敲是铜匠入门的必修课，而这也是一个优秀铜匠必须掌握的技艺，落锤重容易将铜打破，落锤轻打出物件的形状就难以保证。在近一年的时间里，少年萧成武都是在单调枯燥又累又苦的敲打中度过的。寒来暑往，朝朝暮暮，伴随他的只有作坊里叮叮当当的敲打声。在父亲严厉的管束下，夏天，双手磨出了血泡；冬日，双手冻开了口子，也不能懈怠。

苦心人，天不负。萧师傅夜以继日的勤学苦练，练就了扎实的基本功。打了一年多的铜条，他终于能够把一块厚重的铜打成薄如蝉翼的铜片。父亲开始让他打制一些锅碗瓢盆等最基本的东西。

学成后，父亲就让他协助自己做一些庙堂委托打制的法器、灯具等寺院用品。

这些法具都是靠铜匠纯手工来制作完成的，这对铜匠的绘画、刻花技艺有着很大的考验。在萧师傅的记忆中，当时，除了每天白天要学习敲打外，夜间还要学习绘画、刻花等传统绘画图案，学习过程非常复杂。这种经过苦练掌握的造型技艺，让萧师傅一辈子受用不尽，也使他成为一个出类拔萃的铜匠。从合作社到钣金厂，直到退休，他一直是单位上的业务能手。

“屠龙之技”的转型发展

随着铝制品的大量出现和铜材料的日渐枯竭，许多铜匠的老手艺成了屠龙之技，找不到用武之地。有的改行做了金匠或铁匠，有的则干脆彻底离开城市，回家种田谋生。萧成武似乎总是技高一筹，善于应变。他根据市场要求转型升级，运用铜匠技术做起了工艺品雕刻手艺。

此外，因为陶瓷火锅经不住高温的持久炙烤，容易炸掉，不如铜的耐用，所以一些顾客慕名找到萧师傅定制铜质材料的火锅。“一个上好的铜器火锅可以用一百多年！”萧师傅一边敲打着一个铜器火锅，一边介绍，话语中充满执着和自信。看来好的传统工艺永远都有传承价值。

【匠人心语】

好几千年以前，我们的祖先就开始铸铜。作为日用品的铜制品已经被铝制品和其他工艺取代了。但是，手工制作铜器的技艺永远是中国人的宝贵遗产，从许多博物馆收藏的铜器古董上可以看出，铜匠那种吃苦耐劳的意志和精雕细琢的匠心永远不会过时。

（陶阳客 / 撰文　徐胜男 / 摄影）

Xiao Chengwu, a Coppersmith: A New Page Written with the "Dragon-slaying Skills"

The Ancient Craft: Copper Craftsman

In the old days, there were "nine men and eighteen artisans" in the craftsman' s work. Coppersmith occupies a space among different kinds of industries. Coppersmith homework is also called "making" or "play" , because coppersmith do not smelt copper, only make copper plate or copper sheet as raw materials, use tools such as a hammer to knock out such as copper pot, copper pan, copper gourd ladle, copper shovel, tea tray, copper locks and other similar vessels. Whether a coppersmith is good or not depends on his skill in beating.

The Brief Biography of the Craftsman

Xiao Chengwu, originally from Jiangxi province, Xinjian county, the ancestral generation are bronze craftsman. His father, Xiao Renhe, was a good copper-maker. He was well known for his "Xiao Renhe Copper" in the city of Yuzhang (Nanchang). Many bureaucrats and big bosses turned to him to make copper products.

During the war of resistance, he fled to Jingdezhen and opened a small shop near Gongguan Mountiain. After the liberation, the public-private partnership opened, the old man took 15 bundles of coppers to join the community, it became a great fun.

Xiao Chengwu was born in Jingdezhen. At the age of 13, he joined his father as an apprentice in the community. Afer 3 years of hard training, he became a skillful coppersmith. But with the dwindling of copper raw material and the rise of aluminum products, hand-made copper became "dragon-slaying skill" , Xiao Chengwu later reversed course and started a craft of making porcelain mold and became a sheet metal worker, he dealed with metal craft for almost 50 years.

The Growth of the Craftsman

The Hard Road of the Coppersmith Family

The coppersmith is not only a manual labor， but also a skill with high technology.

In order to earn a living， Xiao said he began to learn from his father at the age of 13. The first year was a year of burning coal. At that time， there was resistance to the burning of charcoal， but what he could do was only to calm down， in the next year， he began to beat copper. Percussion is a compulsory course for a copper craftsman to get started. It is also a skill that a good copper craftsman must master. In the past year， Xiao Chengwu， a young boy， was in a monotonous， boring， tired and bitter beating. All that accompanied him every day were the beating sounds in the mill. Under his father' s strict control， his hands were frothing in the summer. In the winter， hands frozen with open mouth， he also did not slack off.

Hard work pays off. After diligent study and hard training day by day， Xiao mastered solid skills. After more than a year' s beating， he was finally able to beat a thick piece of copper into a thin piece of copper as thin as a cicada feather. His father asked him to make some basic things， such as pots and pans.

After studying well， his father asked him to help him make some temple artifacts， lamps and lanterns and other temple supplies. These tools are all hand-made by the coppersmith， which is a great test to the skill of the coppersmith in painting and carving flowers. In the memory of Master Xiao， at that time， in addition to learning to knock in the daytime， he had to learn painting， carving flowers and other traditional painting patterns at night. The learning process was very complicated. This kind of modeling skills mastered after hard training， let Xiao benefit for a lifetime， also make him be an outstanding coppersmith. He was a professional expert from the cooperative to the sheet metal factory until his retirement.

The Transformation and Development of the Dragon-slaying Technique

With the presence of a large number of aluminum products and the gradual exhaustion of copper materials， many coppersmiths' old skills have become the skills of slaying dragons. Some went on to become goldsmiths or blacksmiths， others simply left the city and went home to work. Xiao Chengwu always seems to be better at responding. He transformed and upgraded according to the market demand， using the copper craftsman technology to start the carving craft.

Besides， because the ceramic hotpot can' t stand the constant baking of high temperature， it is easy to blow up， and it is not as durable as copper， so some customers ordered the hot pot made of copper by Mr. Xiao. "A good copper hot pot can last more than a hundred years! Master Xiao banged on a copper hot pot while introducing it， his words were full of persistence and confidence." It seems that a good traditional craft will always be of great value.

The Innermost Words of the Craftsman

Our ancestors began to cast copper thousands of years ago. As a commodity， the copper products have been replaced by aluminum and other processes. However， hand-made art of the bronze is the priceless heritage of the Chinese people forever， from many bronze antiques of museum， you can see that the persistent minds and exquisite originality will be everlasting.

（Written by Tao Yangke， photographed by Xu Shengnan）

锔瓷匠江朝文：
着手成春显慧心

【老手艺项目】锔瓷

景德镇是瓷器的故乡，自然就有锔补修复瓷器这一行当，世人所知道的“没有金刚钻，就别揽瓷器活”这句歇后语就是从锔瓷这一行当里出来的。锔瓷是中国最古老的瓷器修复技艺，行当经历了从宋代到当今中国的不同时期，跨越了一千多年的历程，影响了中国多少代人的生活。

【匠人小传】

80后的江朝文，13岁就开始跟随爷爷学锔瓷的手艺。他的祖籍在安徽，早在清朝的乾隆后期，其家族沿昌江河而下迁徙，后在鄱阳古县渡定居。江师傅把锔瓷手艺与景德镇陶瓷完美地结合起来，在不同器物上修饰不同的锔子，锔上合适的图案，这完全就是一种艺术再创作的过程，巧妙运用冲线或残缺，创造出更美的艺术。

【匠心之路】

记忆：镇上的“街挑子”

瓷器坚硬耐磨，更可持久使用，可瓷器的致命弱点是易碎。每当一件瓷器破碎后，便无计可施，留着无用，弃之可惜。匠人们便开始琢磨如何将破碎的瓷器修补好，经过了艰苦的摸索实践，在实践中总结、理顺、规范出一套合理的锔瓷技艺，其中最大的贡献就是发明了独一无二的“金刚钻”和“锔钉”，继而便产生了锔补修复瓷器这一行当。而这一行当的出现，很快就被老百姓接纳，破碎的瓷器得到了再生，拥有者减少了购买新瓷器的费用，同时让锔瓷匠人得到了劳动报酬。

学徒：儿时练得“童子功”

江朝文从小就耳闻目染了祖传的锔瓷技艺。据他回忆，自己刚开始学徒的时候，先要学打铁锤，这道工序要先学半年。在下雨天时，家人就让他把铁砧放在老家的青石板上用人力去拖，以便把铁砧磨平。

谈到学习醮火这道工序，江师傅仍然记忆犹新。他说，当年也没有现在的先进工具，完全是采用最原始的办法。把煤油灯和白炭放在面前学习醮火工艺，主要是学怎么换气。刚开始学的时候，由于没有掌握好换气的方法，煤油灯的煤烟倒吹回口腔。

工序：用锔钉缝补生命

江朝文师傅一再跟笔者强调，用锔钉修补瓷器，就是告诉人们：瓷器坏了就是坏了，就像人与人之间免不了都有裂痕在，我们坦然接受，精心修补，而并非掩盖。

锔瓷第一步就是找碴、对缝，对破损的瓷器恢复原状，准备修补。

第二步是定位点记，根据瓷器的纹饰结构以及样式张合位置和位点，确定锔钉数量和位置。

第三步就是打孔，用金刚钻打孔。打孔也是对锔瓷人的一大考验，有些瓷器厚度就几毫米，打孔时都是毫厘之差。一是手要拿得稳，对得准，不能打穿；二是孔要对称，不能有一点偏差。

第四步是制作锔钉，锔钉制作体现手艺人的水平，锔钉的韧性和制作锔钉的水平也决定着锔补器皿的使用寿命。锔钉分为金钉、铜钉、花钉。锔钉的大小得根据器物的大小以及破损程度来计算。这样，器物修复后不仅盛水不易漏，而且还给器物本身增添了几分韵味。

第五步是用鸡蛋清和瓷粉调和补漏，防止瓷器漏水，这样完整的锔瓷就完成了。

意义：将历史和文化延续

传统的锔瓷技艺在传承与表现这一类题材时，可以说只有原汁原味地保留了古代匠人那种虔诚专注、活计至上的谦卑思想，才可能将题材中所蕴含的寓意与风俗情趣充分地释放和传达到手中的器物上，使观者能够清晰充分地体悟到从锔瓷技艺中弥散开来的民俗大美与绝伦技艺。

江师傅拿起一只残缺的花瓶向笔者介绍，这个瓷瓶是一位客户的父母当年结婚的纪念品，瓷瓶上除了有腊梅等吉祥图案，还有其父母的名字和赠瓶人的祝辞和名字。对这位客户来讲，这只瓶子对主人的纪念意义远远超出了其经济意义。江师傅说，这几天他都在琢磨怎样使这只瓶子既保留原物的残缺之美，又要给予它第二次生命。

【匠人心语】

“锔瓷的时候是在修复器皿，同时也在修复生命。在修复生命的同时，也在修炼自己。让自己沉下来，静下来，去把活儿做好。你静不下来，活儿就做不好。”

（黄辉撰文 / 摄影）

Jiang Chaowen, a Ceramics Mender: Wisdom Contained in the Mended Ceramics

The Ancient Craft: Ceramics Mending

Jingdezhen City is the place where the ceramics were invented, and naturally the industry to repair the broken ceramics came into being here, from which the old widespread proverb "Don't work on ceramic if you don't have the adamant drill" came. Ceramic repairing is the most ancient repairing technique, and it went through the different times from Song Dynasty to the modern China. The industry with a history spanning more than a thousand years has influenced generations' lives in China.

The Brief Biography of the Craftsman

Jiang Chaowen, the post-80s, started to follow his grandfather to learn the skill to repair the ceramic at the age of 13. His ancestral home was in Anhui, while his ancestors migrated down the Changjiang River and later dwelt in Guxian Town of Poyang County as early as late Qianlong in Qing Dynasty. Master Jiang faultlessly combines his repairing skill with the ceramic made in Jingdezhen, selects diverse staples to decorate the different ceramic ware and makes them into the appropriate patterns, which is utterly an artistic recreation process by utilizing the cracks and fragments to create a more beautiful art.

The Growth of the Craftsman

Memory, the Craftsmen Shoulder Carried Loads on Streets of the Town

The ceramic ware is hard, lasting well and more durable, but the fata weakness is fragileness. Every time when the ceramic ware was broken, the users could do nothing on it, and the ceramic ware was useless if kept but wasteful if discarded. The craftsmen started pondering how to repair the broken ceramic ware, and after the tough grope and practice, the craftsmen summed up, disentangled and standardized a set of reasonable ceramic repairing technique in which the greatest contribution was the invention of the adamant drill and repairing staple, and the industry of ceramic repairing came into being afterwards. The emergence of the ceramic repairing industry was soon accepted by the people, the broken ceramic ware was reproduced which reduced the consumers' expenditure spent on the new ones, and the ceramic repairmen also got the payment for their labor.

Apprentice Must Learn Kung Fu in Childhood

Jiang Chaowen witnessed the ancestral ceramic repairing technique when he was a kid. He recalled that it was the first step to learn hammering when he started to apprentice, which lasted as long as half a year. When it rained, his family members would ask him to put the anvil onto the green slate and drag it by manpower till the anvil was planished.

Referred to the step of quenching, Master Jiang's memory was still fresh. He said that there were no advanced tools in the past as today so they were utterly taking the most primitive methods. Put the kerosene lamp and white carbon in front to learn the skill of quenching, and it's mainly about the way to take the breath. At the beginning, as Jiang didn't master the method to breathe, the soot was even blown back into the mouth from the kerosene lamp.

Process, the Use of Staples to Sew and Mend the Life

Master Jiang reiterated to the writer that the ceramic ware repairing told the people that the broken ceramic ware was irrevocable as the crack would permanently be on it, which was the same as the inevitable fissure in the interpersonal relationship. We should frankly accept and elaborately make up for it instead of covering up the crack.

The first step for repairing the ceramic is to find the correct position, match the fragments and restore the original state of the damaged ceramic ware so as to be prepared for the repairing.

The second step is to mark the position, fix the point and confirm the quantity of the staples according to the structure and style of the decoration on the ceramic ware.

The third step is to punch holes by using the adamant drill. Punching is another great test to the craftsmen as some ceramic ware is only a few millimeters in thickness, so deviation is as subtle as inches. Firstly, the hand must hold the articles stably, and then the craftsmen must definite position precisely to punch, but do not punch through the wall. Secondly, the holes must be symmetrical, and no tolerance is allowed.

The fourth step is to make staples. The making of the staples manifests the craftsmen's technical level, and the tenacity and making level of the staples determine the service life of the repaired ceramic ware. The staples could be divided into gold staple, copper staple and floral staple, and the size of the staple depends on the size of the ceramic ware and its damage degree. In this way, the repaired ceramic ware can't only be used to hold water without leaking, but also can add the ceramic wares with some special charms.

The last step is to well mix up the egg white with the ceramic powders to remedy the leakage to prevent the ceramic ware from leaking water. Then the integral ceramic repairing is achieved.

Meaning, Pass on the History and Culture

The traditional ceramic repairing technique in themes of inheritance and expression has only originally retained the ancient craftsmen's devout concentration and job oriented humble thought so as to be able to fully release and convey the implicit moral, customs and interest of the theme to the ceramic ware on hand, and also enable the viewers to clearly and adequately realize the great charm and peerlessness diffused out of the ceramic repairing technique.

Master Jiang took out a fragmentary ceramic vase and told the writer that this vase was a wedding souvenir for a customer's parents at that time. Except for the wintersweet and other auspicious patterns painted on the vase, the names of the customer's parents, sender's greeting and name were also on it. To the customer, the commemorative significance was far beyond the economic value. Master Jiang said he was ponding how to retain the fragmentary beauty and give it the second life.

The Innermost Words of the Craftsman

"When we are repairing the ceramic wares, we're also remedying the life. Meantime, we're actually disciplining ourselves. Calm down and concentrate on the job to work out a good result. If you can't calm down, you won't be able to do it well."

(Written and photographed by Huang Hui)

陶工金跃安：
在窑火中淬炼朴实人生

【老手艺项目】陶器烧制

中国是著名的陶瓷古国，陶器的出现距今有一万多年的历史。远在新石器晚期，我们的祖先就已经利用瓷土做原料，用高温烧成精美的硬陶。可以说，中华民族发展史中的一个重要组成部分，就是陶瓷发展史。中国人民在科学技术上的成果以及对美的追求与塑造，在许多方面都是通过陶瓷制作来体现的。浮梁县天宝水土宜陶，在相当长一段历史时期，陶器都是民间重要的生活日用品。随着时代的发展、物质的丰富，古老的陶器渐渐退离人们的生活，与此同时，烧制陶器这门技艺也在慢慢淡出人们的视野。

【匠人小传】

金跃安，原籍江苏镇江，18 岁开始学烧制陶器，那时村里几乎家家户户都烧制陶器，这是个很吃香的手艺。1974 年，他被聘请来到景德镇天宝烧制陶器。进入 20

世纪 80 年代，随着生活水平的提高，用陶器的人越来越少，做陶器的人也逐渐转行。然而，74 岁的金跃安老人却坚守这门古老的技艺 56 年，他成了方圆百里唯一干这行的人。2013 年，他被评为“景德镇传统柴窑烧成技艺”非物质遗产传承人。

【匠心之路】

受聘：远离家乡来天宝制烧陶器

天宝自然生态极佳，有着独特的制陶黏土，因此很早就有制作陶器的习惯。1974 年，原天宝乡政府为了开发当地资源，满足当时人们生产、生活所需的各种陶器制品，从江苏省南通聘请金跃安来天宝当把桩师傅。

金跃安以陶匠的独特眼光，对天宝周边进行了科学认真的考察后，就选址、规划、设计等重要环节做出了缜密的分析，决定在徐家窑的基础上对其迁修。新建的天宝龙窑位于高岭山脉的西南部，与瑶里、东埠、高岭所属同一区域。龙窑为东西朝向，窑体内部长 66 米、宽 2 米、高 1.8 米；外围长 66 米，宽 6 米，高 2.5 米，高 4 米；投柴口 73 个；烟囱口径 60 厘米，宽 1.5 米，高 4 米；坡度 30 度。在当地政府的配合下耗时 10 个月完成了龙窑的迁修工程，当年顺利投产，并在此基础上建立了天宝陶器厂，为当地的经济发展发挥了积极的作用。

坚持：传统的天宝龙窑制烧体系才得以完整保留

自 20 世纪 90 年代起，人们生活水平的不断改善，铝合金、塑料制品迅速取代了陶器制品，做陶器的人也逐渐转行。

“干这个不赚钱，都不愿干了。”金跃安说。他算了一笔账：一窑陶器全卖出去的话能收入 5 万元，扣除烧柴的花销以及挖泥、做坯、烧窑、搬运等费用，利润能剩下 30% 就不错了，这是近三个月的功夫钱，可东西没人要，卖不出去，就没的赚了。工人的工资都发不出来，天宝陶器厂面临倒闭。当时作为厂长的金跃安，不忍心自己亲自修建的龙窑就此荒废，在入不敷出的情况下，自掏腰包艰难地维系着龙窑的正常制烧。

因龙窑具备了一整套完整的传统制陶和柴烧技艺，并对陶瓷大学教育有着极大的教学和实践作用，天宝龙窑在陶瓷学术界的影响力与日俱增。在陶瓷学术界教授学者的呼吁下，在景德镇市委、市政府，浮梁县委、县政府的高度重视下，当地政府加大了对天宝龙窑的保护和开发。2013 年，浮梁县委、县政府安排专项资金用于天宝龙窑的修缮和建立相应的配套设施。今天所能见到的一整套传统的天宝龙窑制烧体系才得以完整地保留下来。这是目前全国仅存的完好的一座天宝龙窑。

复烧：真实地再现景德镇传统制烧陶的工艺

9 月 26 日，准备了一个多月的陶器开始装窑。制陶需要经过黏土成型、利坯、晾晒、上釉等工序。陶器有大陶缸、陶罐、陶瓷雕塑作品。金跃安找来帮工，把陶器从作坊往龙窑搬运，大的陶缸还需要两人抬运，金师傅则在龙窑里码放装窑。

他感慨万千，记得 20 世纪 80—90 年代，那时一年要烧上 10 窑、8 窑，窑窑都是满满的，有老百姓家家都要用的陶瓦片、水缸、陶罐。到了 90 年代中后期，随着人们生活水平的不断改善，各种生产、生活所用的陶器便不再具有广泛的市场需求，天宝龙窑也慢慢地完成了它的生产使命。出于对非物质文化遗产的传承和保护，在各级领导的重视下，天宝龙窑开始了它的新的艺术生命，以真实地再现景德镇的传统制烧陶器工艺，彰显出它耀眼的光芒。

28 日凌晨，金师傅带领他的传承人和学生在天宝龙窑进行了隆重而又简朴的祭拜仪式，对龙窑开始进行 6 个小时的暖窑，早上 6 点，龙窑点火燃烧……

83 个窑火口依序燃烧，窑火达到 1270 摄氏度，至晚上 8 点 30 分，历时 18 个多小时烧制，开始闭火闭窑。2 天后正式开窑。从泥料成型、制作到制烧成功，天宝龙窑整套工艺圆满完成，真实地展现了景德镇的陶器制烧技艺。

【匠人心语】

“我爱陶，一辈子都做陶，陶器已成为我生命中的一部分。”

（汪春荣撰文 / 摄影）

Jin Yue' an, a Potter: Tasting the Simple Life around the Burning Kiln

The Ancient Craft: Firing Pottery

China is a famous ancient country of ceramics. Pottery here has a history of more than 10, 000 years. In the late neolithic period, our ancestors could make fine hard pottery by using china clay as the raw material and firing it with high temperatures. It can be said that an important component of China' s national development history is the history of ceramics. The achievements of Chinese people in science and technology and the pursuit and shaping of beauty are reflected in many aspects through ceramic production. In a long period of our history, pottery was a folk important daily necessities. With the development of the times and the abundance of materials, ancient pottery gradually retreated from people' s life. Meanwhile, the art of firing pottery was slowly fading out of the field of view.

The Brief Biography of the Craftsman

Jin Yue' an, a native of Zhenjiang, Jiangsu Province, began learning firing pottery at the age of 18 years old, when almost every family in the village fired pottery. Firing pottery was a well-liked business at that time. In 1974, he was hired to make pottery in Tianbao, Jingdezhen. In the 1980s, with the improvement of living standards, fewer and fewer people used pottery, and people who made pottery gradually changed career. However, the 74-year-old Mr. Jin held on to this ancient art for 56 years and became the only person within a hundred miles making pottery. In 2013, he was honored as the bearer of the intangible inheritance of "The Traditional Firewood-kiln Firing Art of Jingdezhen" .

The Growth of the Craftsman

Being hired: Making Pottery in Tianbao Away from Home

With the unique pottery clay, the natural conditions in Tianbao is perfect for making pottery. So the practice of making pottery began at an early time here. In 1974, in order to develop the local resources, and meet the demands of the pottery required in production and life, the original Tianbao township government hired Jin Yue' an from Nantong in Jiangsu as the chief master worker in Tianbao.

With his unique thinking on making pottery, Jin Yue' an made a careful investigation around the area of Tianbao and gave a thorough analysis to the site selection, planning, and designing of a kiln. At last, he decided to relocate the Xujia Kiln and restore it to a new one. And then a newly built kiln—Tianbao Dragon Kiln was established, which was located in the southwestern part of the Kaolin mountains not far from the counties of Yao Li, Dong Bu and Gao Lin.

The Dragon Kiln was orientated in an east and west direction. The inside was 66 meters long, 2 meters wide and 1.8 meters high. The outside was 66 meters long, 6 meters wide, 2.5 meters high at the lowest part and 4 meters high at the highest part. There are 73 mouths in the kiln for firewood. The funnel with a caliber of 60 centimeters was 1.5 meters wide and 4 meters high. The slope of the kiln was at 30 degrees. With the help of the local government, it took 10 months to complete the relocation of the Xujia Kiln and building of the Dragon Kiln, which was successfully put into operation. Based on this, Tianbao Pottery Factory was established, and contributed a lot to the local economic development.

Persistence: The Traditional Pottery-firing System of Tianbao Dragon Kiln Has been Fully Preserved

Since the early 1990s, people' s living standards have been improving, aluminum and plastic products have rapidly replaced the pottery products, and people who made pottery have gradually switched into other careers.

"Firing pottery makes little money, so nobody likes to be in this line now." Jin Yue' an said. In the light of Jin' s caculation, if a kiln of pottery is sold out, the gross income is around 50000 yuan. With the cost of wood, dredging, making adobe, kiln firing etc. off, the net profit can only be left to 30% at most. In addition, this is earnings of three months. On the other hand, if the pottery is unsalable, no money could be profited, which would make the workers' wages be unavailable. This is why the Tianbao Pottery Factory is at the risk of bankruptcy. At that time, as the director of the factory, he couldn' t bear to let the Dragon Kiln he built in person fall into disuse, so under the condition of being unable to make ends meet, he paid his own way to maintain the normal firing of the Dragon Kiln.

Because the Dragon Kiln has integrated a set of complete traditional pottery-making and firing technique, and was especially helpful for the ceramic teaching in the Jingdezhen Ceramic Institute, its influence upon the ceramic research field grows day by day. Under the appeal of the professors and scholars in the ceramic academic circle, the local government increased the protection and development of Tianbao Dragon Kiln under the high attention of the county committee and county government of Fuliang and the municipal committee and municipal government of Jingdezhen. In 2013, the county government arranged special funds for the renovation of Tianbao Dragon Kiln and the establishment of its corresponding supporting facilities. That is how a complete set of traditional Tianbao Dragon Kiln system could be preserved intact today. This is the last and undamaged Tianbao Dragon Kiln in China at present.

Reburning: A Real Reproduction of the Traditional Pottery-firing Techniques of Jingdezhen

On September 26, 2017, the pottery that has been prepared for more than a month was loaded into the kiln. Pottery making includes many procedures: molding, trimming, drying, glazing and so forth. There were large pottery jars, pottery pots and ceramic sculptures. To get all the things into the kiln, Jin Yue' an found some assistants. For the large pottery jar, it needed two people to carry. And Jin' s duty is to adjust the place in the kiln.

He was filled with regrets. He remembered in the 1980s and 1990s, the kiln was full each time when it began working, though having to work 8 to 10 times a year. And there were many various potterywares, such as pottery tiles, pottery water tanks, pottery pots etc.. By the 1990s, with the people' s living standard improving, various pottery once used in production and necessary for daily life no longer had a broad market. And then, Tianbao Dragon Kiln has gradually completed its production mission.

For inheritance and protection of the intangible cultural heritage, which was greatly emphasized by the municipal leaders at all levels, Tianbao Drangon Kiln began its new life, with a purpose of truly reproducing the traditional techniques of pottery making of Jingdezhen to show off its dazzling light in the whole world.

In the early morning of the 28th day of this month, Jin, with his heirs and students, conducted a ceremonious and austere worship ceremony in front of the Dragaon Kiln, and then started the six-hour warm-up kiln for the Dragon Kiln. At 6 a.m., the fire in the Dragon Kiln was ignited...

83 mouths of the kiln was set on fire in sequence. The temperature reached 1270 celsius degree. Till 8 p.m., it had been burning for more than 18 hours. And then the kiln was sealed up and was not opened till two days later.

From the molding of the clay to the firing and success of making pottery, the Tianbao Dragon Kiln has finished a complete pottery making process, and showed truly well the ancient pottery-making techniques of Jingdezhen.

The Innermost Words of the Craftsman

"I love pottery and make pottery all my life, so pottery has become a part of my life."

(Written and photographed by Wang Chunrong)

铁匠周文彪：
心中的炉火永不熄

【老手艺项目】打铁

铁匠是一门古老的职业，他们以铁为原料，靠一把小小的铁锤打造出各式各样的生产工具和生活用品来养家糊口。铁匠一般都有一个自己的铁匠铺，有一座用来煅烧铁坯的火炉，早先的铁匠铺在火炉的连接处有一个大的用手拉的风箱，主要用来控制火的温度和力度，一般称为掌控火候。淬火和回火技术，全凭实践经验，一般很难掌握。

【匠人小传】

“周同兴”字号的铁匠招牌可谓瓷都名副其实的老字号，周文彪师傅家五代人都在中渡口以打铁、开铁匠铺谋生。

早先周师傅祖上的铁匠行有6座打铁的炉子，家里最多的时候有10多个人打铁。顾客要个什么锄头、剪刀之类的大小物件，凡是含铁的，都是要到这里来打。

【匠心之路】

祖上打铁的生意如火如荼

据周文彪师傅回忆，最早时，祖上的铁匠行是在坝上，后来因为河边要筑坝，就搬到了中渡口。当年中渡口最热闹的地方就是他家祖上的铁匠行。大家全都守在铺子门口，排着队等着，东西刚打好了，还没凉透就被急匆匆地拿走了。早先周师傅祖上的铁匠行打农用工具、瓷器行里利坯的道具和船钉。他很是自豪地说："早先镇上利坯用的工具，还有沿河船上的船钉基本上是我家'周同兴'铁匠行的。"

手工打的东西肯定比机械打的强

人生有三苦：打铁、撑船、卖豆腐。打铁是排在第一位的，这句老话说出了打铁这个行业的艰辛。夏日骄阳似火，大地像蒸笼一样热得让人喘不过气来，火苗被鼓风机吹得呼呼直蹿。"打制一件铁具，一般要经过多道工序：选料、加温、盯火候、锤打、挂生、淬火、磨口……"周师傅边说着边干手中的活。炉火烧得火红，他熟练地用火钳将要打的扒钉从煤堆中夹起，放在铁砧上，"叮当、叮当"一锤一锤地敲打着。扒钉的红色在煅打中暗淡了下来，又跟了几锤，然后将铁钉再次夹回炉中，煅烧、敲打、退火、再煅烧……如此反复，周师傅不厌其烦地进行了十几个来回。

终于，最后一次落锤，周师傅放下锤头，用手拿起那根扒钉凑在眼前仔细端详了一下，脸上的笑容舒展开来，将自己的"作品"摆在一旁的长凳上。

对于自己打的铁器，他很是自豪："古话说'百炼成钢'，煅得久，淬火久，铁器的密度就好。现在超市里卖的厨用刀，是机器压出来的，而经过煅打的刀，韧性好，不容易断，也容易磨。有人到超市买几百块钱的厨用刀，后来还是要到这里买手工的打刀，因为我打的刀就是好用呀。"

是的，不管岁月如何变迁，民间手艺人的智慧终将历久弥新。

打铁的手艺面临失传

据周师傅介绍，祖上的铁器行属于杂匠，什么铁器都打。但是现在管制刀具是不能打的。以前打一把菜刀是五块（元）六角，早先是一块（元）钱一天的工资。现在打一把菜刀一百块（元）钱左右，人工两个人也就是打两三把刀。所以现在做这一行，也只能是维持生存。

【匠人心语】

“现在打铁器的越来越少，利润薄呀，生存空间就少。也许过不了几多（多少）年，打铁这个传承千年的古老行当，也将会成为历史。我们这个属于濒危行业，应该要受到保护。社会给予一定的支持，生存的空间就大些。国家没有扶持，消失是必然的。”

（黄辉撰文 / 摄影）

Zhou Wenbiao, a Blacksmith: The Fire of Hope Will Never Die

The Ancient Craft: the Forge of Iron

A blacksmith is an ancient occupation in which they use the iron as the material and makes it into all kinds of production tools and household articles by a small iron hammer so as to support his family. A blacksmith generally has his own smithy where there is a stove to forge the iron, and there was also a big hand-pulled air bellow at the joint of the stove in the old smithy, which was used for controlling the temperature and intensity of the fire in general. The skills of quenching and tempering both depend on the practicing experience, so it' s generally hard to master.

The Brief Biography of the Craftsman

The signboard of the smithy printed with Zhoutongxing is an old and famous shop worthy of its name in the Porcelain Capital, and the five forefathers in Master Zhou Wenbiao' s family all lived on forging iron and running the smithy in Zhongdukou area. In the past, the smithies of Master Zhou' s ancestor had six stoves and more than ten blacksmiths worked at most. When the customers needed some hoes, scissors and other articles, so long as the articles concerned the iron material, they would all come here to buy.

The Growth of the Craftsman

The Business Boomed Like Raging Fire in the Ancient Smithy

Master Zhou recalled that the ancestral smithy was opened on the dam at the earliest time. Due to the construction of dam on the bank later, they moved the smithy to Zhongdukou. The most bustling area in Zhongdukou at that time was just situated near his ancestral smithy. The customers were all queuing outside the shop and waiting, and the articles were taken away in a hurry even if they were not completely cooled down as soon as they were forged from the stove. In early time, Master Zhou' s smithy produced the farm tools, the tools for trimming the ceramics and boat spikes. He said very proudly, "The tools for trimming the ceramics and the spikes on the boat along the river were basically made by Zhoutongxing smithy of my family."

The Ironware Made by Hand Must be Better Than Those by Machine

There were three types of hardship in life, and they were forging iron, punting and selling tofu. Forging iron was ranked first, and the old saying revealed the hardship in the industry of forging iron. In the summer, when the sun blazed like a fire ball, the land likes the steamer which made people breathless, while the flame was blown to flicker by the fan. "To forge a piece of ironware, generally goes through multiple steps such as material selection, warming, fire observation, hammering, hanging, quenching, blade sharpening and etc.." Master Zhou said while working on the ironware on hand. The fire burned fierily, and he proficiently tonged out the cramp iron to be hammered out of the coal pile, then put it onto the anvil and hammered it over and over again. The red color of the cramp iron turned dim in forging, and after hammered for times, the cramp iron was tonged back into the stove again. Calcining, hammering, annealing, re-calcining again and again, Master Zhou tirelessly repeated for more than ten rounds.

At length, after the last hammering, Master Zhou laid down the hammer, picked up that cramp iron and put it ahead of his eyes for scrutiny. Then the smile showed up on his face, and he placed his artwork on the bench aside.

Zhou was quite proud of his forged ironware, and he said, "There was an old saying that the steel was made after smelted for hundreds of times. The longer it is forged and quenched, the higher the density of the ironware is. The kitchen knives on sale in the supermarkets at present are all pressed by machine, but the knives is better in tenacity, hard to break and easy to sharpen if they are forged. Someone bought the kitchen knives at the price of several hundred yuan, but finally went to my shop for the handmade knives because my forged knives are better to use."

Yes, no matter how the times vary, the wisdom of the craftsman in the folk will be everlasting.

The Crafts to Forge Iron is in Danger of Being Lost

Master Zhou said that the ancestral smithy belonged to the miscellaneous craftsman, and all sorts of ironware were forged. But the controlled knives were not allowed to be forged nowadays. In the past, a kitchen knife costed 5.6 yuan, and the wage was one yuan per day previously. Now it costed around 100 yuan to forge a kitchen knife, and only two or three knives could be forged out by the manpower of two labors. So he could only subsist by working in this industry.

The Innermost Words of the Craftsman

"There are less and less people forging ironware nowadays due to the less profit and limited living space. Perhaps some years later, the ancient business of forging iron which passed down for millennium will be a chapter in the history. This endangered industry should be protected. The society imparts a certain degree of support, our living space will be larger. Without the support from the country, the disappearance will be inevitable."

(Written and photographed by Huang Hui)

白铁匠刘圣田：
敲打平凡而踏实的岁月

【老手艺项目】白铁匠

白铁匠手工切割铁皮，铁皮经过反反复复的敲打，被制作成水桶、漏斗、簸箕、烟囱和水舀子等生活用品。在 20 世纪八九十年代，白铁制品深受百姓欢迎。然而，随着时代的发展和新兴材料的取代，白铁匠的生存空间越来越小。茶山的刘圣田老师傅在羊角锤的敲敲打打声中，却坚守着这几十年的老手艺。

【匠人小传】

刘圣田，原籍都昌，65 岁。他 15 岁起就在景德镇市白铁社（后改名为景德镇市钣金钣铁厂）学徒。一把剪刀裁出轮廓，一把铁锤敲打形状，白铁匠刘师傅与白铁片打了 50 多年交道。不管顾客想要做出什么形状的白铁制品，他都能办到，而且成品既美观又实用，因此他也赢得了“白铁巧手”的赞誉。

刘师傅的白铁店在市里的茶山，店门外摆放着不少成品——大到白铁通风管、羊肉串烤炉，小到做“油墩子”的勺子、灌香肠用的漏斗、白铁喷壶和白铁盒子等，在他的店里更多的白铁制品是瓷厂作坊里用的瓷用烤炉、倒浆桶、过浆筛子、喷釉壶等瓷用工具。

【匠心之路】

在白铁社学徒的日子里

“刚开始学的时候很苦。”刘师傅说，“先从剪料开始，然后练习槌子敲。所有的东西都是凭自己的双手敲打出来的，有时候一敲就是整整一天。刚开始学剪白铁皮，手都剪起了血泡，但我还是坚持了下来。”据刘圣田回忆，那时学徒就学了 3 年，当时的工资每月 18 块（元）钱。做这一行难也不难，就是要认真。制作白铁器是从学做冲壶盖子开始的，那时候师傅都比较保守，特别是下料的时候，一般不让人看到。

刘师傅很喜欢自己钻研，不断地摸索，才有了今天的手艺。他意味深长地说：“这门手艺看着简单，但是没有十年八年的工夫，干不好哇。”

白铁匠的辛苦

据刘师傅介绍，白铁匠非常辛苦，笨重的工具和沉重的铁片全要靠人工搬动，大量的剪、切、敲、锤工艺也要靠手工来完成。而一般的白铁活计又都在门前空地上露天完成，长期的风吹日晒、弯腰低头使他们过早地衰老，在他们手上留下的是厚厚的老茧和开裂的血口。夏天还好，冬天里白铁冰手，手冻得像红萝卜也得干。有时碰到一件大活，成品出来就得敲几千大锤，即使是几十年的老工匠，晚上睡到床上也会腰酸背痛、动弹不得。

这手艺是项细致活儿

白铁匠的工具简单，一把钳子、一把剪子、一把锤子和一个笨重的铁砧，也

有用一截钢轨来代替铁砧的。加工制品时，先用圆规和尺子在白铁皮上画图，再用大铁剪剪裁、切割，切割要根据需要成型，或方、或圆、或直、或弯，这一切，都要靠手工来完成，借助于专用工具的地方很少。在白铁皮上画线、切割计算要非常精确，否则就对不上口，造成材料损失。

将把手艺坚持下去

虽然挣钱少，但是刘圣田师傅一直坚守着这门手艺，一是自己闲不住，二是不想把这门手艺丢了，在敲敲打打中过了大半辈子。

刘师傅顺手从桌上拿起一个小型吹釉筒向笔者介绍：这是吹釉用的筒子，他从 1988 年就开始做这个东西。现在他一天可以做好几十个。制作吹釉筒的关键在于吹的铁皮管子上，管子太粗了，上釉就会太浓、太厚；管子太细了，上釉就会太稀、太薄。“我制作的吹釉筒共有 4 种：3 两装的、半斤装的、1 斤装和 2 斤装的。”

“这也是白铁匠在景德镇的优势。”刘圣田说，“瓷厂作坊里的瓷用工具还是需要白铁制品的，就像这吹釉筒，前几天景德镇大学的学生就订了 30 个，我马上要送货过去。”

【匠人心语】

“要是店真的关了，以后再也不能敲敲打打了，我也没什么遗憾，只能说这是社会的进步吧。现在白铁通风管和瓷器作坊里的瓷用吹釉筒依然有它的市场，很多人还是需要我的。”

（昌南一芥 / 撰文　丰月 / 摄影）

Liu Shengtian, a White-iron-sheets Artisan: Striking out an Ordinary and Peaceful Life

The Ancient Craft: Galvanized Iron Sheet Craftsman

The galvanized iron sheet craftsmen cut the iron sheet manually and make it into various household commodities such as buckets, funnels, dustpans, chimneys, and bailers after hammering over and over again. In the 1980s and 1990s, the handcrafts from these craftsmen were very popular, while this group of people gradually lost their living space as the times progress and the new material takes the replacement. While the old master Liu Shengtian living in Chashan has been persisting in this ancient craft for dozens of years in the knocking sound of the claw hammer.

The Brief Biography of the Craftsman

Liu Shengtian, 65 years old, came from his birthplace in Duchang County. He apprenticed in Jingdezhen Galvanized Iron Sheet Association (renamed as Jingdezhen Galvanized Iron Sheet Factory later) at the age of 15. He has been dealing with the galvanized iron sheet for over 50 years to scissor the profile and hammer the shape. Whatever the galvanized iron sheet products the client needs in various shapes, Master Liu can make it, and his finished products are artistic and practical. So he is reputed as The Skilled Galvanized Iron Sheet Master.

Master Liu's store is located in Chashan of the city, where displays a great many finished products ranging from the vent pipe and the oven for grilling the shashlik to the spoon for frying carrot pies, the funnel for making sausages, sprayer, case and etc.. But the more we can see in his store are ovens for firing the porcelain, buckets and filters for ceramic slurry and glaze sprayers, all of which are widely used in the ceramic workshops.

The Growth of the Craftsman

In the Days When He Apprenticed in the Galvanized Iron Sheet Association

"It was very hard at the beginning," Master Liu said. "People started from the sheet scissoring, and then practiced hammering. All the works were hammered out by hand, and sometimes it would last for a whole day when you sat down hammering. When I started to learn to scissor the sheet, both hands were full of blood blisters. Nonetheless, I overcame and persevered successfully." Liu Shentian recalled his monthly salary at 18 yuan during his 3-year-long apprenticeship, and it was not so difficult to work but inevitable to be scrupulous in this industry. He learnt to make the lid for the kettle at first, but the masters at that time were a little bit conservative so they just hided this step and made it mystically.

Master Liu likes drilling and groping very much, and both help him to acquire the skill nowadays. "The handcraft of this industry looks simple, but it's impossible to be proficient without practice for several years." He said meaningfully.

The Hardship of the Galvanized Iron Sheet Craftsmen

Based on Master Liu's introduction, the galvanized iron sheet craftsmen's work is pretty laborious. The blunt tools and heavy galvanized iron sheet are carried by manpower, and lots of steps like scissoring, cutting, knocking and hammering are generally taken by hand in the open air. So the long hours' exposure to the wind blow and sun burning as well as the constant bow all drive the craftsmen to get aged earlier, and their hands are left with the thick callus and dehiscent wounds. It's even worse in winter than in summer. Their hands will be frozen as red as carrots by the chill iron, and they have no choice but to keep working. Sometimes they need to hammer for thousands of times before a finished product is made out and it is really suffering at night when lying on bed due to the fatigue, ache and rigor on the bodies even if they are proficient craftsmen working for dozens of years.

The Handcraft of This Industry is Exquisite

The tools of the craftsmen are as simple as a tong, scissors, a hammer and a heavy anvil which could be replaced by a length of steel rail sometimes. The craftsmen firstly use a ruler and compass to draft the size, and then cut the shape according to the demand by scissors. All these steps are completed by hand, and tools are not frequently used in the whole process. It must be precise to draw the border after calculating the size, otherwise, the parts can't be tightly connected and it finally results in a waste of material.

The Perseverance in the Crafts

Although the gains are less, Master Liu Shengtian perseveres in the handcraft of this industry because he is used to being busy on one hand, and he doesn't want to discard his skill after spending most of his lifetime on knocking and hammering the galvanized iron sheet.

Master Liu just took one glaze sprayer from the table and showed it to the writer, telling him that this was used for spraying the glaze on porcelains. He started to learn how to make this article from 1988, and he is able to make out dozens of such articles every day. The key of making such glaze sprayer lies in the iron sheet pipe, and it must be in the moderate size. Or else, the glaze on the porcelains is over thick and dense if the pipe is oversized and vice versa. The sprayers Master Liu makes can be divided into four types : the volumes of 150g, 250g, 500g and 1kg.

"The location in Jingdezhen is one of the galvanized iron sheet craftsmen's advantages," Liu Shengtian said, "and the demand for the tools like the sprayer is still great in the ceramic workshops. I am going to send 30pcs of such sprayers to Jingdezhen College right away for the students, they ordered days ago."

The Innermost Words of the Craftsman

"I won't have any regrets if I can't keep on hammering someday later when my store is closed down. Instead, it proves that the society is progressing. Right now the vent pipe and glaze sprayers made of the galvanized iron sheet are still demanded in the markets, so lots of people need my products."

(Written by Changnanyijie, photographed by Feng Yue)

篾匠章义：
把梦想编进平凡岁月

【老手艺项目】篾匠

篾匠是中国一门古老的职业，篾匠手艺是一门细致活，要经过多年磨炼才能达到精熟的程度。旧时，篾匠营生范围涉及人们的吃喝拉撒衣食住行，几乎哪里都有篾器的影子，可谓我国古代先民的一大创造。

【匠人小传】

章义师傅祖籍南昌，祖父是篾匠，父亲章复秀的手艺是跟爷爷学的。20世纪70年代，章复秀举家迁至景德镇谋生，靠祖传的手艺在当时人流量很大的中渡

口码头开了篾匠店，至今有30多年了。在章义师傅的老篾匠店里，大大小小、形状不一的竹制品放满了货架和店墙。一根根原本坚韧的竹子，在这里简直是脱胎换骨。

【匠心之路】

创业之艰

在章义师傅的记忆里，童年都是在清新的竹香中度过的。篾匠店开了30多年，墙上框架还有当年《景德镇日报》以《老篾匠的坚守》为题的头版头条的报道，店里还有父亲当年做的蒸笼、竹床、扁担、尿桶筐、篮子、鸡罩等民用篾器。后来父亲的身体不太行了，女儿也曾接手这店，但最终还是儿子章义接手了。

学艺之苦

谈起与篾器结缘的日子，章义也是非常感慨："家里从爷爷开始到我，三代都是以此为生。"章义师傅说，跟着父亲学艺是很苦的。东西做不好，就要受惩罚。最初学艺是学转眼，这是最基本的工序。眼要转的正，尺寸大小要对。有时一天转眼就要转几百个，他有时实在不想转了，就把工具丢一边，一丢就要被父亲打，罚跪、饿饭是经常的事。

学艺三年成，破篾要一年。刚开始破篾，手用多了，晚上吃饭端着碗都在抖。破篾的均匀度、韧性要把握好。篾薄了，做圆圈就会变形；篾厚了，弯度就不行，韧性就不够。篾的厚薄不均匀，产品的使用寿命就不会长。

生存之难

章义与笔者交流最多的，还是老篾匠店生存和发展的问题。干这一行利润很薄，学艺也很苦，所以现在做这一行的人越来越少了。章义师傅坦言说，随着机械化操作的流行，自己也很难做到父辈那样的技术和水平。有些客户需要订做的产品，也很难找到同行交流沟通。即便在同行中，有些艺人年龄大了，已经做不动了。

创新求存

谈及竹篾产品的创新求变，章义师傅如数家珍："我们做的产品，要随着社会潮流的变化进行创新。比如篾的抛光，在父亲手上就只是简单地打篮子，只要扎好就可以，注重的是实用性。现在还要锁边、修边、锁口，做竹篾扭的纹路要有美感，体现时尚感，在造型方面也有许多讲究。再比如一个竹篾装盘，以前就比较简单，平底装东西就可以。现在的顾客就要有盖子，这样就可以装干货，而且竹子的透气性很好，老鼠也不会偷吃。"

【匠人心语】

竹篾是我这一生最好的知己。在失意痛苦的时候，都有竹篾陪伴着我，让我耐住了寂寞，我将今生的希望和梦想都编进冰凉的摇篮和背篓之中，这一同编进去的，还有我平凡的岁月。

（黄辉 / 撰文　余琳超 / 摄影）

Zhang Yi,a Bamboo Artisan :
To Weave Dreams into the Time Line

The Ancient Craft: a Bamboo Strip Craftsman

A Craftsman making articles by the bamboo strips was an ancient occupation in China, and it is a very meticulous skill which must undergo years of practices before attaining to the proficient level. In ancient times, the business scope of the bamboo strip craftsmen concerned the every basic necessity of people' s lives, so the articles made of the bamboo strips could be nearly seen everywhere, and it could be regarded as a great invention for the ancestors in ancient China.

The Brief Biography of the Craftsman

Master Zhang Yi was born in Nanchang, and his grandfather was a bamboo strip craftsman before so his father Zhang Fuxiu apprenticed to his grandfather to learn the skill. In the 1970s, Zhang Fuxiu mitigated the whole family to Jingdezhen to make a living, and opened the shop for selling the articles made of bamboo strips in Zhongdukou which was very bustling at that time, so the shop has been there for more than 30 years by far. In Master Zhang' s old shop, the shelves and walls were full of bamboo wares in various sizes and shapes. The tenacious bamboos were thoroughly remolded in this place.

The Growth of the Craftsman

The Hardship of Starting up the Business

In Master Zhang' s memory, he spent his childhood in the smell of scented bamboo. The shop has been opened for more than 30 years, the newspaper with the report titled "the Insistence of an Old Bamboo Strip Craftsman" as the headline in the front page of Jingdezhen Daily in that year was still in a frame on the wall, and some bamboo strip articles made by his father such as the bamboo steamers, bamboo beds, shoulder poles, bamboo crates for closestool, baskets, bamboo cage for cocks and etc. were also in the shop. Later his father was in a poor state of health, and his elder sister once took over this shop, but the shop was finally passed down to him.

The Hardship of Learning the Skill

Referred to the day when he got the fancy with making bamboo articles, Zhang sighed with emotion, "Three generations from my grandfather to me all lived on this craft." Master said that it was very toilsome to apprentice to his father. If the bamboo strip articles he made were not good, he would be punished. At the beginning what he learnt was drilling on the bamboo, which was the most fundamental process. The position of the hole must be drilled upright, and the size must be appropriate. Sometimes he needed to drill hundreds of holes in one day, and sometimes he indeed didn't want to drill and dropped the tool aside, his father would beat him as soon as he did so. Punishing to kneel and not to eat was very frequent before.

It took three years to master the skill thoroughly, and one year to learn sharpening bamboo strip. If the strip was over thin, it would deform when it was wreathed, but camber would not be inadequate and the tenacity was poor if it was too thick. If the thickness of the bamboo strip was uneven, the lifetime of the products wouldn't be too long.

The Hardship of Survival

The most topics Zhang Yi communicated about with the writer were issues with the survival and development of the bamboo strip article shop. It was low in profit in this industry and toilsome to master the skill, so there were less and less people engaged in this industry now. Zhang frankly said that it was hard for him to attain to the skill and level of the elder generation as the mechanical operation popularized. Some customers needed to customize the products, but it was hard to find a peer to interchange the opinions and communicate with. Even if he found the peers, some were too old to make the bamboo strip articles.

Innovate to Seek Ways to Survive

Referred to the innovation of the products made of bamboo strips, Master Zhang was quite familiar with the subject and said, "Our products are innovated as the variation of the trend in the society. Take the polishing of the bamboo strip for instance, my father simply made the basket, and it was fine so long as it was firm, so he focused on the practicability. But now the basket must be overlocked, trimmed and fore shafted, and the twisted veins of the bamboo strips must be aesthetic to embody a sense of fashion, and there are more particular points in the field of the modelling. Take the bamboo strip container for another example, it was relatively simple in the past, so long as it was flat at the bottom and could hold stuff inside. But now the customers need a lid, in this way the container could hold dried food, and the container made by bamboo is good in air permeability, also the rats can't steal the food."

The Innermost Words of the Craftsman

"Bamboo strip craft is the biggest confidant in my life. When I was in frustration and misery, the bamboo strips were by my side, making me bear the loneliness, and I have weaved the hope and dream in my life into the cool cradle and pack basket, so have my ordinary years."

(Written by Huang Hui, photographed by Yu Linchao)

弹匠苏景春：
巧手温暖寒夜的梦

【老手艺项目】弹棉花

弹棉花，实际上指的是弹棉胎，也有弹棉褥（垫被）。棉花去籽以后，再用弦弓来弹，絮棉被、棉衣的棉，就加工到这一步。如过去女儿嫁妆的棉絮都是新棉所弹。一般人家也有用旧棉重新弹加工的。弹棉工具有大木弓，用牛筋为弦，还有木槌、铲头、磨盘等。弹时，用木槌频频击弦，使板上棉花渐趋疏松，然后由两人将棉絮的两面用纱纵横布成网状，以固定棉絮。纱布好后，用木制圆盘压磨，使之平贴、坚实、牢固。按民俗，所用的纱，一般都用白色。但用作嫁妆的棉絮必须以红绿两色纱，以示吉利。如旧棉重弹，须先除掉表面的旧纱，然后卷成捆，用双手捧住在满布钉头的铲头上撕松，再用弓弹。

【匠人小传】

苏景春，60岁，景德镇市浮梁县洪源镇人。他自幼跟随师傅弹棉花，走南闯北，走街串巷，技艺精湛，平易近人，颇受顾客欢迎。他从事弹棉花行业30多年，一路挥洒汗水，一路弹奏欢歌，一路播撒温暖，在平凡岁月中延续着一个弹匠执着的梦想。

【匠心之路】

退出历史的原始手工艺

一个骄阳似火的上午，我们在麻石弄找到了苏师傅的棉絮加工店。当时，苏师傅正在昏暗狭窄的工坊忙碌着。了解到我们的来意后，苏师傅一边汗流浃背地干活，一边与我们攀谈。

苏师傅说，机械化生产之前，弹棉花匠都是一弯弹弓、一张磨盘、一个弹花棰和一条牵纱篾走天下。这种原始的生产方式，工作效率很低，每人每日不过弹皮棉 8 斤。这种手艺的传承方式基本上是由师傅带徒弟或父传子。到了 20 世纪 80 年代，在中国大地上延续了千百年的弹棉花手艺发生了根本上的变化，弹花机的出现让弹棉花实现了规模化生产，弯弓、磨盘、弹花锤等弹棉花器械开始淡出了历史舞台。

弹棉花是个精细活

苏师傅说，在小孩的眼里，弹棉花是个很有趣的事情。小时候，每当听到“弹弹嘟嘟”的节奏声，孩子们就知道村里来了弹匠的，欢呼雀跃着，纷纷汇聚过来看热闹。

俗话说，没有金刚钻，别揽瓷器活。要想干好这一行，每个弹匠都离不开一把顺手的弹弓。这弹弓因人而异，可长可短。弹匠通过用榔头敲击弓上的弦，来沾取棉花，把棉花拼成方形，整理棉花都要靠这个“弓”。

“檀木榔头，杉木梢；金鸡叫，雪花飘”，这是过去弹匠对这门手艺的生动诠释。弹棉花不仅费力，也是个精细活，敲弓的时候要花大力气，才能把棉絮加工到位。而“拉线”则是细致的活儿，要有个帮手一起才能完成。纱线不盖好，棉絮就会脱落，最后前功尽弃。

拉完纱线，还需要用压盘经过多次的压磨。压磨也是个精细活，不仅要方寸俱到，还要用力匀称。否则，就会出现厚薄不匀，松紧不一。这套工序看似简单，做起来却挺费时间，因此，两个弹匠一天也就能弹上一两条棉絮。

弹匠是个苦差事

“一把弹弓走四方，心里苦来身上伤”，这是昔日弹匠辛酸命运的生动写照。因为日复一日弯腰劳作的职业特点，许多弹匠年纪轻轻就落下了腰肌劳损的职业病；更有甚者，长年累月在粉尘中呼吸，许多弹匠到晚年都患上了难以治疗的肺病——真是“辛苦赚钱半辈子，付之东流一夜间”。说到这，苏师傅情不自禁地长叹一声。

乡村弹匠的城市营生

后来随着市场经济的发展、改革开放的深入，弹棉花不再走乡串户了，而是固定在集镇上，弹棉花也从纯手工时代慢慢转换到机器加工时代。苏师傅的家在浮梁县农村，他就在景德镇麻石弄租了一间铺子弹棉花。随着家纺专卖店的兴起，在景德镇弹棉花的人越来越少。曾几何时，商贾云集的古镇到处都能够听到弹匠“弹弹嘟嘟”的弹奏声，现如今，全市不过十几家。

【匠人心语】

“我睡过蚕丝被、羽绒被，但总感觉没有棉被那么厚实温暖。真正让我感到厚实温暖的是自己亲手弹出来的棉被。我弹棉花已经弹了 40 年了，可以说算得上是很‘老’的老弹匠了，但是有了你们这样的先进机器，我还要弹很多年，争取弹到 100 岁！到时候我去申请吉尼斯世界纪录！”苏师傅如是说。

（陶阳客 / 撰文　余琳超 / 摄影）

Su Jingchun, a Cotton Fluffing Artisan: To Warm the Dreams in Chilly Nights

The Ancient Craft: Fluffing cotton

Fluffing cotton, in fact, refers to fluffing cotton tire, and fluffing the cotton pad (cushion). After the cotton seeds are taken out, then use string bow to fluff the cotton, the processing of making quilt and cotton-padded clothes is finished. For example, in the past, the daughter' s dowry cotton is the new cotton. In general, people can also reprocess old cotton. The fluffing tool has a large wooden bow, with ox tendon as the string. There are also wooden hammer, shovel head, grinding wheel and so on. During the spring, the cotton on the board becomes loose due to the frequent percussion of the wood, and the two sides of the cotton wadding will be arranged in a network of yarns in order to fix the cotton. After the gauze is finished, use wooden disc to press and grind, in order to make it flat stick, firm. According to the folk custom, the yarn used is usually white. But the cotton wool used for the dowry must be red and green yarn, as a sign of good luck. If the old cotton is reprocessed, the old yarn on the surface must be removed first, then rolled into bundles, the old yarns should be torn loose on the shovel head which is full of nails, and then processed with the bow.

The Brief Biography of the Craftsman

Su Jingchun, 60, from Hongyuan town of Fuliang County in Jingdezhen. Since childhood, he have been fluffing cotton with Master, travelling north and south, walking streets and alleys. Over 30 years in the cotton industry, he have been playing hard, singing happy songs and spreading warmth all the way. In the ordinary years, he have continued his dream of being a gunnery.

The Growth of the Craftsman

The Original Handicraft Which Withdrew from the History

a scorching morning, we found master Su's cotton processing shop in Mashi lane. At that time, master Su was busy in work in the dark and narrow workshop. After getting our purpose, master Su worked with sweat streaming down his back, while talking with us. Master Su said, before mechanized production, all the people who were flicking cotton went around with a bending bow, a millstone, a wooden hammer and a yarn pulling frame. The work efficiency of this primitive production way is very low—one person only flick 4kg cotton a day. This technology is basically passed down from master to apprentice or from father to son. In the 1980s, the technology of flicking cotton, which had lasted for thousands of years in China, changed fundamentally. The emergence of the machine made the large-scale production come true, and then the instruments such as bending bow, millstone, wooden hammer began to fade out of the historical stage.

Flicking Cotton is a Delicate Job

Master Su said, in the eyes of the children, flicking cotton is a very interesting thing. When I was young, every time the children heard the sound of flicking cotton, they knew that the people flicking cotton came to the village. Then they would gather round happily. As the saying goes, don't do porcelain work without diamond. To do this job well, every craftsman needs a good bending bow. The bending bow varies from person to person. It can be long or short. The craftsman taps the cotton through using the hammer to strike the string of the bow and squares the cotton, the craftsman finish the cotton also need the bow.

"Sandalwood hammer, fir tip; Golden cock crow, snow falls." this is the vivid interpretation of flicking cotton in the past. flicking cotton is not only a laborious job, but also a delicate job. The craftsman should take great pains to knock the bow, so that the cotton wad can be processed in place. "Wire-pulling" is delicate work that requires a helper to complete. If the yarn is not covered properly, the cotton will fall off and all previous efforts will be wasted. After the yarn is pulled, it needs to be crushed for many times with the press plate. Crushing is also a delicate job, the craftsman not only needs to make all of the yarns to be crushed, but also needs to crush evenly. Otherwise, there will be uneven thickness and different tightness. This process seems to be simple, but it always takes lots of time, so that two craftsmen can only make one or two cotton wads a day.

Flicking Cotton is a Tough Job

"Going everywhere with a bending bow, painful in the heart and wounded on the body ." This is a vivid portrayal of the bitter fate of the former craftsman. As a result of the day to day bending work, many craftsmen when they are young suffer from occupational disease such as lumbar muscle strain. At the same time, because of breathing in dust year after year, many craftsmen suffer from incurable lung disease in their old age—it is "earning money for half a lifetime, wasted overnight". "Although flicking cotton is a tough and low-income job, but I do not make money from adulteration "At this point, master Su couldn't help heaving a deep sigh.

The Country Cotton-Makers Live in the City

Later, with the development of the market economy, the deepening of the reform and opening up, the craftsmen no longer go around to work, they can be fixed on the town, fluffing cotton transforms slowly from pure manual age to the machine age, Su' s home is in a village of Fuliang County, he rented a shop in Mashi lane in Jingdezhen. With the rise of household textile stores, fewer and fewer people are fluffing cotton in Jingdezhen. Once upon a time, the old town was filled with the sounds of fluffing cotton, there are only more than ten stores nowadays.

The Innermost Words of the Craftsman

"I have slept in a silk quilt and a duvet, but they are not as thick and warm as a quilt. What really makes me feel thick and warm is the quilt that I made by myself. I have fluffed cotton for more than 40 years, I can say I' m almost an very old artisan, but because of the advanced machine, I also want to work for many years, and strive to work to the time when I am 100 years old! At that time, I will apply for a Guinness World Record!" Su said.

(Written by Tao Yangke,photographed by Yu Linchao)

藤匠李赛荣：
每一根藤条都带着人情味

【老手艺项目】手工藤器

藤器是世界上最古老的家具品种之一。早期，人们用水草、藤条、柳条、木材等材料手工编织成藤器品。我国藤器发展历史悠久，自汉代后人们就开始注重藤器的艺术设计，选用藤条来制造各种各样的家具，编织成各种图案、式样的藤编家用器具。

【匠人小传】

虽然李赛荣不像老艺人那样几代人或一辈子从事这手艺，但从 20 世纪 90 年代在竹藤厂“半路出家”学艺开始，到自己开藤器店，她手工编织藤器的时间，也有 20 多年了。

【匠心之路】

历史：消失的竹藤门市部

与其他手工行业一样，20 世纪 50 年代，市里的私人作坊式的藤器社并入了市手工业联社，地址在斗富弄的转弯角上，是几间老式的厂房，当时社里有 20 多个手工做藤器的老艺人。20 世纪 80 年代末，竹藤厂并入了市塑料一厂，成为其下属的竹藤门市部。

据李赛荣介绍，当时竹藤门市部有 40 多人。车间里的工种分为做架子和包藤条两种。做架子的师傅就几个人，均为男性。包藤条的有 20 多人，均为女性。以前厂里也曾在附近的农村招过一些女工学徒，这些女工在厂里住。刚开始学徒，先包藤器的脚和边，上手（出师）后才让其做较为繁杂的部位，比如藤椅的坐垫和靠背等部位。

2000 年，竹藤门市部正式解散。厂子解散后，李赛荣也成了市里唯一开过手工藤器店的手艺人。

开店：李赛荣曾开 3 家藤器店

“做这行表面看着轻松，可实际累得很，因为制作工艺复杂，人工成本高昂，所以手工藤器要比机制品贵出不少。但是，手工编制的成品，密度更高、更牢固，使用二三十年也不成问题。现在的手工编织藤器赚不了钱，但饿不死。”

市藤器厂解散后，李赛荣就接手了整个车间，并在斗富弄的拐角处租了店面，还聘请了几个手工师傅。后来，手工藤器的利润越来越薄，她索性一个人“单打独斗”，先后在斗富弄附近开了3家手工藤器店。现在，随着斗富弄的旧城改造，她的第3家店也关门了。

这门手艺传不下去

李赛荣告诉笔者，制作藤器的工具主要有藤刀、剪刀、架刀、小刀、码子等。藤刀也有多种，有用于破藤的，有用于编织的；制作藤架用架刀，藤匠师傅凭借高超的技艺，用架刀把采购的小杉树条砍削好，放入水中浸漂，若需要制作圆形用品，必须用码子校正，弯度可达到360度，不差丝毫。

做这行表面看着轻松，可实际累得很，一坐就是坐一整天。好比编织一张藤椅，就需要花费两三天的时间，编织藤席的时间更长。有时候为了赶货给人家，她从早上8点开始忙活到晚上12点多。

【匠人心语】

或许在这个时代，慢，是奢侈的。手工制作，可能赶不上工业品的速度，但是我们有理由相信，历经岁月变迁后，每根藤条中蕴含的心意，会随着时间沉淀下来。

（黄辉撰文 / 摄影）

Li Sairong, a Rattanwork Artisan: Every Cane is an Expression of Human Feeling

The Ancient Craft: Canework by Hand

The rattan articles are one of the oldest furniture varieties in the world. In the early days, people used water grass, rattan, wicker, wood and other materials to weave rattan articles. Canework has a long history in our country. Since Han Dynasty, people started to pay attention to the art design of the canework. They used all kinds of ratten to make various home appliances and furniture of different design and different patterns.

The Brief Biography of the Craftsman

Though unlike some old craftsmen, who had woven rattanwork for nearly a life time or whose ancestors had been in the same business, Li Sairong took it in the 1990s.Till now, she has been in this career for more than 20 years.

The Growth of the Craftsman

History: The Lost Bamboo & Rattan Department

In the 1950s, all the rattan workshops in the city, like other handicraft industries, were incorporated into the Handicraft Industry Association, which was located at the corner of Doufu Lane. The working place was just a few old buildings. At that moment, there were around 20 experienced craftsmen in the Association. In the late 1980s, the bamboo & rattan factory was absorbed into the First Plastic Factory, becoming a department of the latter.

According to Li Sairong, there were over 40 workers in the former Bamboo & Rattan Department. The work in the workshop was divided into two kinds: the frame making and the cane twining. There were a couple of male workers responsible for the frame making, and more than 20 female workers for the cane twining. Occasionally, the factory might hire the female workers from the nearby villages, who had to live in the factory. As apprentices, the new hired could only twine the foot and side parts of the rattanware. When they were experienced, they could make more complicated parts, such as the seat cushion and back of the canechair.

In 2000, the Bamboo & Rattan Department was officially disbanded. And after that, Li Sairong became the only artisan in the city who set up handmade rattanwork shop before.

Shop Running: Li Sairong Has Ever Had Three Caneware Shops

She told me that canework making is actually a tiring job, though it seems to be a easy task ostensibly. The process is complicated and highly labor costing. That is why the hand-made rattanware is much more expensive than that produced by machine. What' s more, the handmade ones are more tightly woven and much more durable. There would be no problem for you to use it for 20 or 30 years long. Now, making rattan chairs can' t give you much money, but can support your family.

After the city' s rattan factory was closed, Li took over the workshop and rented a store at the corner of Doufu Lane, and hired a number of artisanal craftsmen. Later, the profit of hand-made ratanware grew thinner and thinner, and then she simply fought alone in this business. Around Doufu Lane, she has ever set up three shops. Due to the old city rebuilding, her stores were all closed.

The Craft Can' t be Passed On

Li Sairong told me that the tools for making rattanware are mainly various knives, scissors. Every knife has its own task: some for cutting the cane, some for weaving, some for making the frame. For the frame, the experienced master worker may cut well the cedar wood first and then soak it in water. For making a round-shaped article, the frame must be corrected with a special tool and the curve of it should be able to reach 360 degrees.

This job is very laborious. Usually, once you sit down, it would be continued for a whole day. Take the rattan chair for instances, one such chair may take you several days. Weaving rattan mat may take longer. So she is often very busy from 8 a.m. to 12 p.m., especially when she got too many orders.

The Innermost Words of the Craftsman

Perhaps in this era, being slow means extravagance. Manual production may not catch up with industrial goods in speed, but there are still grounds for us to believe that the feeling contained in each rattan would be settled down in the end.

(Written and photographed by Huang Hui)

编斗笠的许献清：
风雨中的执着守望

【老手艺项目】编斗笠

斗笠虽小，但工序却挺复杂。从山上砍竹到破竹、剖篾，从捏蒂到套模，从箬皮或棕丝拼装到绕沿包边，从编笠顶到压实，细算起来不少于 15 道工序，且不能连贯做完。斗笠是早先农民生产生活中遮风挡雨的必配工具。随着时代的变迁，这门老手艺也随着时间的流逝而渐渐地快要消失了。

【匠人小传】

年满 72 岁的老人许献清，13 岁父亲就开始教他学编斗笠。据老人回忆，在乐平临港乡下，编斗笠早先似乎算不得技术活。这样的手艺，许多人都会。闲暇时，上山砍几根竹子，摘几把箬皮或棕丝，拿刀剖好篾，往往一早上的工夫，一顶斗笠就编好了。

之所以父亲这么早就教他学编斗笠的手艺，是想让他帮忙完成公社下达的任务。借此机会学会了编斗笠手艺的许献清，很快就成了远近闻名的编斗笠能手，手艺甚至超过了父亲，与篾匠师傅的手艺也不相上下，乡亲们都夸他编的斗笠结实、轻巧、美观、耐用。从事这门手艺59年，他算不清编了多少顶斗笠，现在临港镇只有他一个人在坚持了。

【匠心之路】

学艺：为帮父亲完成公社下达的任务

“说起我学编斗笠的事情，还和‘共库’挂得上边呢。”许献清老人回想起自己13岁开始学编斗笠的情景，记忆仍然那么清晰。

那是1958年，乐平县决定在涌山铜安埠村兴建江西18座大型水库之一的共产主义水库。坝址坐落在槎溪河（车溪河）上铜安埠村下游的蛤蟆塛，是东坑、董门、坦里3条支流的汇合点。槎溪河发源于婺源县西南的鸡公山（属大游山）和乐平的历居山，是乐安河北岸一条较大的支流。为此，乐平兴修水利指挥部调集民工32000余人，干部1000余人。指挥部给公社下达了编织30000顶斗笠的任务，许献清家也分到了800顶的任务。时间紧，任务重，村里的男女老少，都加入编斗笠的队伍，早起晚歇，从不间断。在灯火摇曳的静夜里，各家各户仍不时发出沙沙的声响。

有一天，许献清放学回家，父亲对他说：“来，我教你编斗笠。”当然，开

始教的不是编斗笠，只是给斗笠包边。包边学得很快，但需要手劲，而许献清年纪小，手劲不够，往往包得不紧，就用牙齿用力拽。包边的篾很薄很锋利，常常把他的嘴唇划破，弄出血来。就是靠着这股韧劲儿，他终于学会了编斗笠。由于他的帮忙，父亲也按时完成了公社交给的任务。

剖篾：编斗笠的基本功

“编斗笠手艺最重要的基本功就是剖篾。剖篾是个技术活，要剖得跟面条一样，宽窄厚薄均匀一致，编出的斗笠才美观大方。”许献清老人说完，才开始向我们介绍：把一根完整的竹子弄成各种各样的篾，首先要把竹子剖开，一根水竹对剖再对剖，剖成竹片，再将竹皮竹心剖析开，分成青竹片和黄竹片。然后再根据需要，竹皮部分剖成青篾片或青篾丝。剖出来的篾片，要粗细均匀，青白分明。竹的青篾丝柔韧且富有弹性，可以剖成细细的青篾丝，青篾丝一般包边用。黄篾丝柔韧性差，难以剖成很细的篾丝，故多用来编斗笠的底层。

剖篾的功夫好坏，体现在剖竹节巴上，因为竹节巴质脆、易断。在剖竹时两眼都盯着竹节，用左手的大拇指和食指捏着竹篾的一端，右手操刀，将竹篾剖开后，退一退刀，再用力将刀滑向竹节巴。新手一般很难将一大根竹干从上到下一剖到底，这是个技术活，稍不注意，不是竹节巴断裂就是篾丝割破手或篾刀切在手上。所以手艺人的手，总是布满一道道伤疤。

技艺：“巧”字源于艰辛的汗水

“这编斗笠，靠的就是个‘巧’字，熟能生巧，我闭着眼睛都能编。”许献清老人说完，开始演示给我们看，只见他一双生满老茧的手拿起细篾，一条一条又一条，来回飞舞，技术娴熟，十个手指宛如弹琴，不停地拨动着琴弦，细篾和细篾的碰撞，发出沙沙的声响。他先编织出斗笠的里子，然后在底层编织出面子，最后把里子和面子分开倒放，将箬皮铺满斗笠坯，进行拢合挤压，再用细篾稍微包一下边，缝合上下两顶斗笠坯。为了在缝合中达到上下两层固定和严实的效果，许献清老人还在上面放三块青石块。缝合好后，剪去伸出斗笠边沿多余的箬皮，

再用细篾细密地进行绕沿包边。我们细数了一下，一共经过了 15 道工序，一顶斗笠才算完成。看老人编斗笠，真是一种美的享受。

【匠人心语】

“斗笠虽小，但它能遮风挡雨，曾经是农民的一大宝呢。”
这是许献清老人选择最后坚持的原因吗？

（汪春荣撰文 / 摄影）

Xu Xianqing, a Rain Hat Artisan : The Persistent Watchman in the Wind and Rain

The Ancient Craft: Weaving the Rain Hat

Although the rain hat is small, the process of making it is complicated. It needs more than 15 working procedures, such as bamboo cutting, bamboo spliting and so forth. And all the procedures cannot be done successively. For the early farmers, the rain hat was an essential tool to get a shelter from the rain and wind. But as the time goes on, the old craft of knitting the rain hats has gradually disappeared with the passage of time.

The Brief Biography of the Craftsman

Xu Xianqing, aged 72 now, began to learn the craft when he was still 13 years old. In Xu' s memory, rain hats could not be counted as a craftwork before in the countryside of Leping city. Many people could do this. In the spare time, they might cut down a piece of bamboo from the mountains and then picked up a few indocalamus leaves and palm fibres, split off the bamboo skin, and one morning later, a rain hat may be finished.

The reason why his father taught him this so early was that he wanted Xu to help him with his task assigned by the commune. By this chance, Xu Xianqing grasped the skill of weaving rain hats, and became well known for his rain hats. His technique was more exquisite than that of his father, which could even compare with that of the craftsman who makes articles from bamboo strips. All the villagers thought his rain hats were stronger, lighter, more beautiful and durable. For 59 years, he couldn' t figure out how many rain hats he had made, and now he' s the only one who sticks to it in Lin' gang Town of Leping .

The Growth of the Craftsman

Learning the Craft: To Help His Father with the Tasks Assigned by the Commune

"As to the task of making rain hats that year, it had some relation with the Public Reservoir." Xu Xianqing revived the situation where he began his learning when he was 13 years old. It is still very clean in his mind.

In 1958, the government of Leping county decided to build a reservoir （The Communist Reservoir） in Tonganbu village of Yongshan town, which was one of the 18 largest reservoirs in Jiangxi province. The dam site was located in the meeting place of the three tributaries of Dongkeng, Dongmen and Tanli in Hamaguo, the lower reaches of Tonganbu village.

The Chaxi River originated from the Jigong Mountain in the southwest of Wuyuan County and the Liju Mountain of Leping city, which is a rather large tributary in the north of Le' an River. To build a reservoir, the Ministry of Water Resources of Leping city assembled more than 32, 000 villagers and 1000 cadres, and assigned a task of making 30, 000 rain hats. And Xu' s family took the task of knitting 800 rain hats.

The time was limited and the task was heavy. All the villagers, men or women, old or young, had to join in the task. Every day from dawn to night, they did their work without breaking. In the quiet night, there always came off the rustling sound from the houses with the soft candle light.

One day, when Xu Xianqing was going home after school, his father said to him, "Come on! I will teach you how to make rain hats." However, what his father taught him first was to wrap the edge. Edge wrapping was easy to learn but it needed strong hand power. Xu was too young then and had no such strengh, so in order to wrap it more tightly, he often had to use his teeth for dragging. The bamboo strip used for wrapping was thin and sharp, so Xu often got his mouth hurt and bleeding. Due to his persistence, Xu Xianqing finally acquired the skills of making the rain hat. As a result of his help, his father also completed the task assigned by the commune on time.

Cutting Bamboo Strips, the Basic Skill of Weaving the Rain Hat

"The most essential skill of weaving the rain hat is cutting the bamboo strips, which was a technical work. Only when the bamboo strips were thin and soft shaped like pieces of noodle, and uniform in the width and thickness, the hat you made might look more beautiful and elegant. " With these words, Xu continued his introduction, to get a complete piece of bamboo into all sorts of strips, and you have to split and sub-split again and again. The strips can be divided into the green strips （the skin part） and the yellow ones. According to the requirements, the green strips can be cut into the green slices and the green silks.The sliced strips should be evenly thick. And the green ones must be pliable and elastic and able to be cut into thin green silks for wrapping the edge. The yellow ones are not pliable and so hard to cut into thin silks, so they are often used to make up the bottom of the hat.

The skill of cutting bamboo strips could be well reflected in your dealing with the bamboo joints, because the joints are brittle and easy to break, and thus they are very difficult to handle. When coming to the joints, you must be very careful. With one end of the bamboo stick between the thumb and forefinger of your left hand and the knife in your right hand, first back off the knife a little, and them force it into the joint quickly. The abecedarin can't cut the bamboo smoothly from up to bottom, it is a skillful work. A little carelessness may get the joint broken or your hand hurt. So the hands of the artisan are always full of scars.

Techniques and Skills: Coming From Hard Work and Sweat

"Making hats relies highly on the techniques. But practice makes perfect. I can now handle with the bamboo strips proficiently, even with my eyes closed." Xu showed us how to make hats, he picked up the bamboo silk to weave, just like playing the piano with the hands plucking the strings continuously. The thin bamboo strips collide with each other in his hands and let out a rustling sound. He first weaved the lining, then he made the outer part on the base of the lining, next, he filled the indocalamus leaves between the two layers. After that, pressing the two layers and wrapping the edge, and wrapping the edge and then the two layers were stitched together. In order to make the hats stronger, Xu Xianqing always put three stone blocks on the top. After stitching, he cut out the extra indocalamus leaves and then wrapped it carefully around the edge of the hat. Till now, a rain hat was completed. I have made a counting and found there were 15 procedures for making one hat. Watching this old artisan weaving the rain hat was really a kind of enjoyment.

The Innermost Words of the Craftsman

"Though the rain hat is very small, it can protect us from the wind and rain. It used to be a great treasure for farmers."

Is that the reason why Xu Xianqing sticks to this craft?

(Written and photographed by Wang Chunrong)

木匠彭爱华：
弯腰做事挺胸走路

【老手艺项目】木匠

木匠是一种古老的行业。木匠以木头为材料，他们伸展绳墨，用笔画线，后拿刨子刨平，再用量具测量，制作成各种各样的家具和工艺品。传统木匠有过很长时间的辉煌。以前的习俗，除了平日里零散地添置家具外，盖新房特别是为儿子娶媳妇时，满堂的新家具是必不可少的。特别是传承有序的大户人家，留给子孙的则可能是经历了几世沧桑、边缘已经被岁月浸润得具有光泽的老家具。

【匠人小传】

84 岁的彭爱华师傅，17 岁便开始跟着父亲学木匠，曾经靠着这门手艺养家。他和那个时代的很多木匠一样，过上了“串百家门，吃百家饭”的生活。

【匠心之路】

随父学艺

他从小就看着父亲做木工活儿，对斧头、锯子习以为常，成为一名出色的木匠是理所当然的。更重要的是，木匠作为手艺人，人人尊重，“家财万贯，不可轻师慢匠”，是那个年代所有人的共识。

木匠世家出身，这让他能够做出复杂、精细的木制品，尤其是涉及机械原理的农具，比如犁车、水车，这是当时最重要的必需品。只要有人家中需要做木制品，主人家会亲自上门，请师傅到自家走一趟。待师傅把东西做好了，付了工钱，主人家还要好酒好菜招待师傅一顿，这是对师傅的感谢和尊重。彭爱华很幸运，不用拜师，跟着父亲学习便是。

学徒规矩

学木匠技术，关键是凿眼。俗话说“木匠好学，斜眼难凿”，所以师傅都要留一手，很少将凿眼的技术传于徒弟。民间有“祖传木匠本领高”的说法，就是说凿眼的功夫代代相传。后来，彭师傅也带了几个徒弟，也给徒弟开工钱，当时每天大概是七八毛（角）钱。“我的徒弟，现在没几个在世了。”彭师傅话语中不免感慨。

上户做事

“解放前，上户做事的工钱是每天一升半谷子。解放后就用现金了，大概是一元八角一天。比如打（做）一张八仙桌，就要做四到五天，打（做）一张床，要5个工，一个工2元钱左右。”

“有时候上户做事，早上要5点多出门，赶到东家那里吃早饭，来去有

30 多里路。中午吃饭，我坐在上方，徒弟可以坐在左右两边。下方一般是不坐人的，这是规矩。我对饭食从不挑剔，雇主给做什么吃什么。吃百家饭的人，什么样的雇主都能遇到，只要吃饱肚子，有力气干活就行。”

他以匠人的心智、灵巧的双手、辛勤的汗水，养家糊口。我们或许要重新拾起已被遗忘的匠心。

【匠人心语】

“有赃官赃吏，没有赃手艺人。手艺人坏了名声，连改正的机会都没得喽。”

是的，一个木匠只是为了生活而劳作，但是木匠有木匠的江湖规矩，那就是一辈子要规规矩矩地做事，规规矩矩地做人。

（黄辉 / 撰文　余琳超 / 摄影）

Peng Aihua, a Carpenter: Working with the Back Bent Down and Walking with the Head Held High

The Ancient Craft: Carpenter

The carpenter is an ancient career. They make wood into all sorts of furniture and artworks through stretching the line marker, marking, planing and measuring. The traditional carpenters have had a very longstanding glory. According to the previous customs, except for the furniture occasionally bought in ordinary days, the full set of new furniture was indispensable when building a new house, especially when the son got married. In particular in the orderly inherited big family, the ancestors might pass down the old furniture to descendants with the trims polished with gloss by years.

The Brief Biography of the Craftsman

Master Peng Aihua, 84 years old, followed his father to learn the woodwork at the age of 17 and once subsisted the family on this skill. Like most of the carpenters in that era, he led a life by working in the hundreds of families' houses and eating the meals cooked by hundreds of families.

The Growth of the Craftsman

Follow the Father to Learn the Skill

When he was still a kid, he saw his father did the woodwork, so he was familiar with the ax and saw and it was of course a dream for him to become an excellent carpenter. What's more important, as a craftsman, everyone respected the carpenters, and the proverb "Even a wealthy man shouldn't slight the teachers and craftsmen" was the common view for the people in that era.

Born in a carpenter's family, he was able to make out the complicated and delicate woodworks, especially the farm tools involving the mechanical principle, such as the plough and water wheel, which were the most important necessities at that time. So long as someone needs the woodworks, the host would pay a visit to the carpenter and invite the master to his home. After the master finished the woodworks and got paid, he would be served with good drinks and dishes by the host family to show their gratitude and respect to the master. Peng was quite lucky, as he didn' t need to apprentice to others but his father.

The Apprentice' s Rules

For learning the carpenters' skill, chisel is the key. As the saying goes, it' s easy to be a carpenter, but it' s hard to chisel an oblique hole. So all the masters would hold the trick and seldom pass on the chiseling skill to the apprentice. And in the folk, there is a saying that the skill of the ancestral carpenter is excellent, and that' s to say the chiseling skill is passed down from generation to generation. Afterwards, Master Peng taught a few apprentices and paid them for their woodwork at roughly 7 or 8 dimes each day at that time. "Few of my apprentices are still alive now." Peng said with emotion.

Go to Work at the Host' s

"Before the Liberation, the wage for the work at the employer' s was a litre and a half unhusked rice per day. After the Liberation, it was changed into the cash, and the daily wage was around one yuan and 8 dimes. For example, to make an old fashioned square table for eight people, it would take four to five days, and to make a wooden bed, five carpenters were needed with each charged two yuan around."

"Sometimes we had to go out at around 5:00 in the morning to work at the employer' s and had breakfast there, and the distance of a round trip was more than 30 miles. At lunch, I took the seat at the upside, and the apprentices could sit on both lateral sides, while no one would sit on the downside generally, and this was the rule. I was not picky with the food, and would eat what was catered by the host. The group eating at hundreds of families encountered employers of all sorts, so long as we were full up, we would have the force to work."

He supported his family through his intelligence, deft hands and arduous efforts. Perhaps, we need to pick up the forgotten spirits of the craftsman again.

The Innermost Words of the Craftsman

"There were corrupt officials but no corrupt craftsmen. Once the craftsman is notorious, he will have no opportunities to rectify."

As he said, a carpenter worked for making a living, but carpenters have their own rule in the social circles that is to say the carpenters should work in a proper manner and behave themselves well.

(Written by Huang Hui, photographedby Yu Linchao)

桶匠王杨柳：
内圆外方铸匠心

【老手艺项目】箍桶

桶匠这一行是从木匠中分出来的。人们把桶匠称作圆木匠，以与造房子打家具的方木匠相区别。桶匠做的木桶样式有洗脸盆、装米桶、饭甑、饭盆、饭桶、水桶、窝盖、大人取暖的火桶、小孩取暖的起桶、洗脚泡脚的脚盆、养土蜂的蜂桶、杀猪盆、装谷仓、马桶、尿桶、粪桶等，这些都是箍桶匠的手艺。有人在女儿出嫁之前，都要请桶匠师傅上门做几天手艺，做一对取暖的火桶、一只四脚盆、一只马桶给女儿。有些殷实的人家，竟做有数十种大小不等的木桶作为陪嫁的嫁妆。

【匠人小传】

王杨柳，原籍浮梁，现年65岁，15岁开始学徒，随师傅上户做手艺，学了三年，18岁出师。常言道："三百六十行，行行出状元。"他从事桶匠手艺40多年，选料、断料、推刨、拼接、打箍，再到加底板，每一道工序都做得很熟练，在景德镇乡村留下了无数各式实用的木桶。

【匠心之路】

王杨柳已是60多岁的人了，但可以看出他年轻的时候长得很清秀。他中年丧妻，没有再娶，一个人带大儿子并帮他成家。说起自己的手艺，他仍然兴致勃勃。

学徒：很苦很累，但手艺苦中学

当时对学徒的规矩、约束很多，除了三年没有工钱，端午节、中秋节和春节等三时三节还要向师傅送节外，收工回来后，还要帮师傅家担水、砍柴、劈柴、种菜和干其他农活。

那时候，师傅对他很严厉。有一次，他听说家乡晚上演戏，便谎称家里有事，请假回去看戏。虽然他过了戏瘾，但师傅知道后被罚在床前跪了一夜。正是因为师傅的严教，他才学到了一身过硬的手艺。

木工：看似容易，但做起来挺难

桶匠除了有木匠常用的锯子、刨子以外，还有圆刨和平刨。圆刨的刨口外凸呈弧形，用于刨木桶的内壁。平刨体形硕大，装两条腿，一头高来一头低，刨面朝天，像一条长凳。桶匠把木板放在朝天的刨面上推动，特别省力。

这些看似容易，但做起来挺难。有时不小心斧头砍到了手，他也从不上医院，随手把木板壁上的蜘蛛网刮下来，简单包扎一下止住血，然后继续干活。这时，他才真正领会“手不出血，不得手艺一绝”这句老古话的含义。

手艺：十里八村，村村留下好名声

“箍桶师傅本领高，刀一把来篾几条。弯板几块都失散，篾圈一个紧箍牢”，当地流传的这首顺口溜，夸赞的是桶匠师傅的精湛手艺。

可在家百日好，出门半日难。桶匠跟其他的手艺人一样，走家串户，这碗百家饭不是那么好吃的。先说吃肉，这也是很有讲究的：“一块先生，两块木匠、桶匠、锯匠，三块农户，四块轿夫。”当时家家都物资短缺，只有请师傅时才砍一斤肉，肉块也是算好了的。王杨柳也是农家子弟，自然懂得这些道理。虽然桶匠一餐可以吃两块，但他总是夹一块。他吃完饭喝口茶就做事，从不休息。完工后，东家有钱就付，没钱就先欠着，决不催讨。

日积月累，王杨柳一手绝活，加上做事不偷懒，人又通情达理好讲话，在十里八村赢得了很好的名气。知道的人没有一个不竖起大拇指，请他做事的人自然很多。

【匠人心语】

“做手艺，做惯了就成了传统艺术。”

“桶匠是从老辈人手上传下来的，虽然没有人学了，但也是一门手艺，我不想丢下它。只要做出的东西还有人要，我就会继续做下去。”

（汪春荣撰文 / 摄影）

Wang Yangliu, a Cooper: Square Outside and Round Inside

The Ancient Craft: The Art of Coopering

The cooper is actually a kind of carpenter. In order to distinguish it from the carpenters who make the furniture or build houses, people like to call the cooper as the wood-rounding carpenter. The woodware that should be made by the cooper was lavatory, ricer box, rice steamer, rice basin, rice bucket, water buckets, adult heating barrel, child heating barrel, the barrel for foot-bath, the bee barrels, basin used for killing pig, barn, a toilet, urine bucket, honey bucket, etc.. Which all demanded the arts of a cooper. Whenever there was a family wanted to marry their daughter, they would have a cooper work in their houses for a couple of days before the marriage. Usually, they would make a bucket for heating, a four-foot basin, and a toilet for her daughter as dowry. Some rich families would do dozens of wooden barrels of different sizes.

The Brief Biography of the Craftsman

Wang Yangliu, a native of Fuliang, now 65 years old, began his apprenticeship at the age of 15. He began to work with his master in the customers' houses. He studied it for three years and when he was 18, he could do the work alone. As the saying goes, "There are a wide range of professions in the world and each profession has its masters." He has been engaged in the hooper crafts for more than 40 years, and is very skilled in every working procedure like material selecting, cutting, planing, stitching, hooping, and floor fixing. Till now, he has left countless various practical buckets in the Jingdezhen's countryside.

The Growth of the Craftsman

Wang Yangliu is now in his 60s, but it can be seen that he was very handsome when he was young. Although he lost his wife when he was still middle-aged, he did not marry again. He brought up his son alone and helped him set up home. When speaking of his craft, he got very excited.

Being Apprentice: It's Hard and Tiring, But Skills Always Come From the Hardship

There were many rules for the apprentice. In the first three years, all the work he did would not be paid. In addition, he had to give his master presents at the Dragon Boat Festival, the Mid-Autumn Festival and the Spring Festival each year. What' s more, after he came back from work every day, he had to help his master carry water, cut firewood, split firewood, plant vegetables, and do some other farm work.

At that time, his master was very strict with him. At one time, he heard that a play would be put on in his hometown. He lied about his family and asked for leave to go back to see the play. Although he enjoyed the play, he was punished by his master—kneel in front of the bed for a whole night. It was because of the teacher' s strict teaching that he learned a hard trade.

Woodworking: It Seems Easy, But It Is Difficult to Do

In addition to carpenter' s common saws, planer, there are other tools, such as the rounding planer and flat planer. The rounding planer is outside-curved at the mouth, and is usually used for planning the inside of the barrel. The flat planer is very large and like a bench, with two legs and a high end and a low end. If the pail man works with the board on the planer, that would be quite effort-saving.

The work appears very easy, but actually very hard to do. Sometimes, your hand would be hurt by your axe. But he never went to the hospital. He just scraped the cobwebs off the boards and wrapped the wound with them for stopping bleeding and then went on with his work. At this time, he really grasped the meaning of the old saying "No bleeding, no top craftsmanship" .

Craft: Being Well-reputed in All the Villages

"The cooper is highly skilled; with a knife, several pieces of bamboo skin would be peeled out; the curved plates that are dispersively placed, would be fixed together tightly within the bamboo skin." These were the words widely spread at the time, praising the coopers' exquisite craftsmanship.

Being at home for thousands of day is better than being outside for half a day. The barrel-makers, like any other artisan, had to travel from house to house. Dining at others' home was not very comfortable. Take the meat-eating for instances. At that time, shortage of life materials was very common. So often, there would not be meat dishes unless a master was invited. But the amount of the meat was prepared previously according to the rules: one piece for the teacher; two pieces for the carpenter, cooper and the wood sawyer; three pieces for the hired farmer; four pieces for the sedan-chair bearer. Wang Yangliu is a farmer' s son, and naturally knows well these principles. Although the bucket maker could eat two pieces a meal, he always took one. He never rested when he finished his meal and the tea. After the completion, the owner would pay for the money. But sometimes payment would be delayed.

Over the years, Wang Yangliu has got top skills. Due to his diligence and good temper, he was well reputed in all the villages he had been to. Any person who knows him would have a thumbs-up for him. Therefore, he was very popular among the villagers in this business.

The Innermost Words of the Craftsman

"The traditional art is always formed from a long-term practice."

"The coopering skill was handed down from the old generations. Though nobody wants to take it up, it does be a craft. I don' t want to drop it. I will continue to do so as long as there is someone who needs it."

(Written and photographed by Wang Chunrong)

泥瓦匠黄明华：
愿得广厦千万间

【老手艺项目】泥瓦匠

泥瓦匠，其实简单来说就是从事砌砖、盖瓦等工作的建筑工人。泥瓦匠的工作是一种历史相当悠久的工作。泥瓦匠是一种技术性工作，不是经过简单的训练后，便任何人都可以做的工作。泥瓦匠所进行的作业如砌砖、抹墙等要求横平竖直。横平竖直，可以说是泥瓦匠的专业要求。

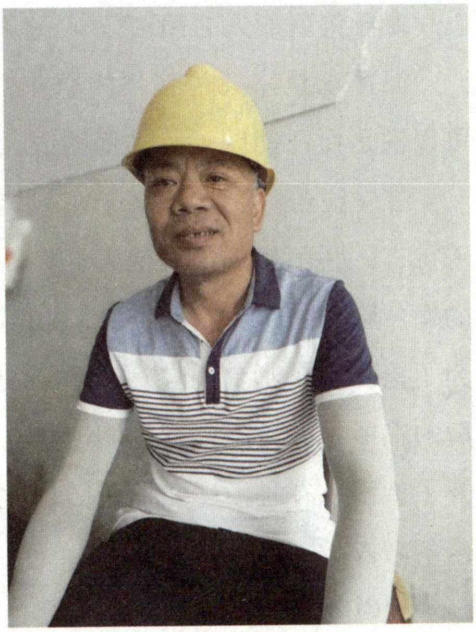

【匠人小传】

黄明华，62岁，15岁拜师学艺，从事泥瓦匠行业40多年。拌泥、切砖、盖瓦、砌墙、抹灰，样样精通。他做手艺一丝不苟，毫不马虎，业内口碑甚好。河西老汽车站、

十八桥基督教堂、莲花塘景德镇宾馆等等，景德镇一些像模像样的建筑都留下过他的汗水。2015 年，他从房管所退休，退休后，偶尔应邀去工地做些活计，赚些零用钱喝酒抽烟。

【匠心之路】

血汗铺就匠人之路

泥瓦匠是一门苦脏累的职业，非常辛苦。他从 15 岁入道，到退休回家，可以说是血汗铺就了黄师傅的匠人之路。

首先说苦。春去秋来，寒来暑往，泥瓦匠一年四季露天干活，风吹雨淋自不待言；骄阳似火的三伏天，在高温下干活，每年都要脱一层皮；在滴水成冰的寒冬腊月，双手抓着砖块，抹着水泥，几乎疼得失去了知觉。记不得多少回，为了抢工，黄师傅在 40 多度的高温下作业，结果闭了痧（中暑），晕倒在滚烫的工地上，被工友背到阴凉处，好半天不省人事。至于冬天，双手本来就冻开了口子，有时候还要抓着砖块往冷水里浸泡，刺骨的冰水渗入伤口，最让人苦不堪言。

再说脏。泥瓦匠和砖块与泥巴打交道，一天到晚蓬头垢面，一身工作服也

是堆满灰土，像个叫花子。所以过去泥瓦匠找老婆都很困难。

最后说累。泥瓦匠是个体力活，无论搬砖还是和泥，都需要过人的体力。所以泥瓦匠的饭量一般都比较大。每逢上门干活，雇主家里供饭时，尽管菜很一般，但米饭一定是要管饱的。否则，哪来力气为你卖力地干活？

做了这一行，苦脏累在所难免，工钱也不高。20 世纪 80 年代，黄师傅的月薪不过三十来元，仅够糊口。这些年，家装游击队颇受待见，其中泥瓦匠的工钱大幅提高，据说有的人一天下来能有两三百元。

【匠人心语】

万丈高楼平地起。泥瓦匠在俗人的眼里地位不高，我们不可把自己看低了。这就需要自身的本事过硬。本事不过硬，就做不成这一行。泥瓦匠虽然苦，但每当看着一幢幢崭新的房子从自己手下拔地而起，心里面还是有些成就感。不是吗？这个世界上如果没有泥瓦匠，也许人类至今还群居在阴暗潮湿的山洞里吧。

（芷林 / 撰文　余琳超 / 摄影）

Huang Minghua, a Mason: A Dream of Building Mansions

The Ancient Craft: The Mason

The mason, in a nutshell, is the construction worker who is working on the bricks, tiles, etc.. The work of a mason is a work with a long history. A mason is a technical job. It is not a simple job that anyone can do after simple exercise. The work of the mason such as bricklaying, wall painting requires to be horizontal and vertical. Horizontal and vertical, can be said to be a mason' s professional requirements.

The Brief Biography of the Craftsman

Huang minghua, 62 years old, learned art when he was 15 years old, he engaged in mason industry, for more than 40 years. Mixing mud, cutting brick, tiling, erecting wall, plaster, he is proficient in all of these. He is meticulous and not careless, so gets a very good reputation in the industry. The old bus station of Hexi, the Christ church of the 18th bridge, the hotel of Jingdezhen in lotus pond, etc., some decent buildings in Jingdezhen have left his sweat behind. Retired from the Housing Department in 2015, he was occasionally invited to work on the construction site to earn some money for drinking and smoking.

The Growth of the Craftsman

Sweat and Blood Pave the Way to Craftsmanship

A mason is a hard, tired and dirty job. From the age of 15 to his retirement, it can be said that blood and sweat paved the road to Master Huang' s career.

First, speaking of the hardness. The mason worked in the open air all the year round. In the hot days, working in a high temperature, he takes off a layer of skin every year. In the dripping-cold winter, he held on to the bricks with both hands and plastered the cement, the pain was almost unconscious. He cannot remember how many times he worked in more than 40 degrees high temperatures, in order to finish work on time, finally, he got sunstroke and fainted, at the construction site. The workers carried him to the shade place, he was unconscious for quite a while. In the winter, the hands were already frozen, and sometimes they had to hold on to the bricks to soak them in the cold water.

Besides, speaking of dirtiness. The mason worked with bricks and mud, unkempt from day to night, his overalls covered with dirt like a beggar. So it used to be hard for a mason to find a wife.

Speaking of tiredness finally. A mason is a manual worker, and it takes great physical strength to move bricks or mud. So masons should eat more. The employer will provide the workers with enough rice, even though the food is very ordinary. Otherwise, they have no energy to work hard .

In this kind of work, hardness, dirtiness and tiredness are inevitable, and wages are not high. In the 1980s, Huang' s salary was about 30 yuan a month, it was barely enough to make ends meet. In recent years, the home decoration guerrilla group is quite popular, among them the mason' s wages have increased substantially, it is said that some people can earn two or three hundred yuan a day.

The Innermost Words of the Craftsman

Tall buildings rise from the ground. The status of the mason is not high in the eyes of the vulgar, and they should not look down upon themselves, so they must be skillful. It takes a lot of skill. They cannot do this unless they are good at it. Though the mason was suffering, they felt a sense of achievement when they saw new houses rising from under their hands. Isn' t it? If there were no masons in the world, perhaps people would still be living in dark and damp caves.

(Written by Zhi Lin, photographed by Yu Linchao)

配锁匠杨文武：
以恒心打开人生之锁

【老手艺项目】配锁

锁匠是指具有无钥匙开锁和配钥匙技术的人，很多锁匠把这一行业当成终身职业。先前在景德镇的弄堂口、菜场等地随处可见锁匠的身影，一台配锁机、方桌上放几排钥匙片，再加上“修锁、配锁”的红字，就是这个行业的全部家当。自古以来，制锁与配钥匙的行业被视为秘密，全是家族世袭或师徒相传，而且完全是口传心授，并不形成文字记载流传后人。锁匠还必须值得人们信赖，而且最重要的是诚信。

【匠人小传】

年近七旬的杨文武师傅在河西农贸市场摆摊配锁已有30多年了。据杨师傅介绍说，以前配锁，没有配锁的材料，就自己找铁皮，然后用夹子夹好，全靠手工锉子一点点打磨出来，钥匙配得好不好，全靠眼睛看，自己也要琢磨。如今，各种新型的锁具层出不穷，钥匙也是五花八门。这些年来杨师傅配钥匙的机器就换了十几台，现在使用游标卡尺对钥匙进 v 行测量比较，应该说他对各种锁和钥匙了如指掌。

【匠心之路】

我只是个靠手艺吃饭的人

笔者见到杨师傅时，他正戴着一副老花镜，专注地打磨钥匙，偶尔与来往的顾客聊上一两句。在“嗤嗤”的金属声中，他一手轻扶着钥匙坯，一手控制着机器打磨的力度，按照顾客提供的样本在钥匙坯上打磨。十几分钟过去，一把新钥匙就基本打磨好了。他又取出一把锉刀，耐心地将钥匙的边缘一点点地磨得更光滑、平整。

打磨钥匙看起来简单，却需要手巧与心细，否则在钥匙坯上开的口大了或者小了，这把钥匙就用不了。有一次配一把四面开齿的十字钥匙，没有合适的钥匙坯。他端出几个沉重的老抽屉，里面是这几十年积累下来的零散钥匙坯。他徒手在里面一个一个翻动，铁屑刺着手，也没有找到完全一样的。有一个锁坯开齿部位长度差不多，但是太厚，他就用手锉来回打磨锁坯，再利用游标卡尺比对，用了很长时间配好了，顾客拿出了十块钱说不用找了，但杨师傅只收了一块五。

希望手艺有人传承下去

时光像流水，一晃 30 多年过去了。迈入老年的他，仍然活跃在修理各种各样的锁事上。儿女们都很争气，有了更好的工作。于是杨师傅面临技术失传的老大难问题。

【匠人心语】

“做了一辈子的手艺，扔不掉了。修锁这一行，想 100% 地搞好，就要拿出 100% 的精力。”杨师傅说话时带着坚定的手势。

（黄辉 / 撰文　余琳超 / 摄影）

Yang Wenwu, a Locksmith :
To Unlock the Door of Life with Perseverance

The Ancient Craft: Making Keys

A locksmith refers to a person with the skill to unlock without keys and make keys, and lots of locksmiths treat this job as their career for the whole life. In the past, the locksmiths could be seen everywhere, such as the mouth of the lane, the food market and etc., and a key machine, rows of keys on a table with the post printed with "lock repairing" and "key making" are all the facilities for this industry. Since the ancient times, lock production and key duplication were regarded as a confidential industry in which the skill was lineal in a family or inherited from master to apprentice, and it was passed down to descendants orally but not in the form of words. If the locksmiths want to gain people's trust, then the integrity is the most important virtue.

The Brief Biography of the Craftsman

Master Yang, who is nearly 70 years old, has been running his booth in Hexi Farm Product Fair for more than 30 years. Master Yang said there was no material for duplicating the keys in the past, so he had to find some iron sheets, then fasten it by clamp and use the file to polish out the keys by hand. And a key's quality was utterly dependent on the master's eyes and thought. However, all sorts of new locksets emerge endlessly nowadays, and the keys are also various. In recent years, Master Yang has changed more than ten machines for making keys, and started to use the vernier caliper to measure and compare the keys, so he should have been quite familiar with all sorts of locks and keys.

The Growth of the Craftsman

I am Making a Living on My Skills Only

When the writer met Master Yang, he was focusing on polishing the key wearing a pair of glasses, and chatting with the customers occasionally. In the metal sound made by the polishing machine, Yang took the key billet by one hand, and controlled the strength of machine by the other hand to polish the crude key according to the sample provided by the customer. More than ten minutes passed, a new key was basically polished out. And then he took out a file to patiently polish the trim of the key smoothly and neatly.

Polishing keys seems to be very simple, but it requires the deftness and meticulousness, otherwise, the open mouth on the crude key would be over big or small, and the key would be useless. Once he duplicated a cross-shape key with teeth on four sides, while there was no suitable key pillet. He took out some heavy iron drawers in which they were scattered crude keys accumulated in the past decades. He sought one by one with the hand barely exposed to the sharp and stabbing scrap iron but failed to find out an identical one. But he got one crude key with the almost same length of the open mouth, while it was too thick, so he just polished it with the file repeatedly and made comparison by the vernier caliper, he took a long time to accomplish the key. Then the customer paid 10 yuan and asked him not to give back the changes, but Master Yang only charged 1.5 yuan.

The Wish to Pass Down the Craft to Someone

How time flies! And 30 years passes in a flash. The aged man is still active in repairing locks of all sorts. All his children are living well and having better jobs. So Master Yang is confronted with the great trouble of failing to pass his craft down to successors.

The Innermost Words of the Craftsman

"Having been working with the skill for my whole life, and I can't cast it away. In the lock repairing industry, you must devote the full vigor so as to do it well." Master Yang said with a firm gesture.

(Written by Huang Hui, photographed by Yu Linchao)

油漆匠陈来水：以虔诚擦亮生命底色

【老手艺项目】油漆匠

民间老漆始于秦汉，盛于明清，据记载已有几千年的历史。我国出土文物中最早的漆器，距今有两千多年的历史，色泽艳丽如新，远非现代合成漆所能媲美。

漆匠的工艺流程先后有10多道工序，调料、刮底、打磨、上底漆、油漆灰补洞、打水磨，再上底漆，打磨光滑后上面漆，最后抛光。

【匠人小传】

年近六旬的陈来水师傅从事油漆行业34年了。从1984年开始，陈师傅就在景德镇从事漆匠行当。他说，旧时，涂刷器物用的是天然漆，俗称老漆。操作时，一般可用天然丝蘸漆反复去搓，油漆层数越多，光洁度越高；也可用棕刷子去刷。木器漆好后，四周支起蘸有水的席子，使之阴干。如今，人们使用的大多是人造合成漆，以毛刷或机械化喷漆的方法取代了传统的做法。

【匠心之路】

传承：从学徒到授业

学徒一般是学做两年才能出师。徒弟跟着师傅上户做事，是没有工钱的。学徒先要学会熬光油。将桐油放入铁锅，先大火后小火熬制，不像熬灰油那样添加“驮生”和“籽土”（含氧化铅和二氧化锰的添加剂，主要作用是催干），等油熬到能拉丝迅速降温，免得油熬老火了，不利于涂刷和流平。

学会熬油后，再学刷油漆。先将坯油和纯生漆按一定比例勾兑并充分搅匀，再用牛尾刷刷涂到物体表面，操作中多粘重刷，开油、理油、顺油工序不能少，要用足够的力道操作，免得漆膜堆积。

陈师傅说，从入这一行开始，他先后也带了 10 多个徒弟，到了 1997 年就没人再学了。现在，陈师傅一直从事手工油漆行当，景德镇的手工油漆有一定的市场，有一些陶瓷店或装修仿古店面时，就要用到手工油漆。

老漆：豆腐猪血作底色

陈师傅说，当年的木料都是漆老漆，老漆是用植物或矿物质提炼的。老漆相当耐用，具有耐腐蚀性。有些寿料（棺材）用老漆，葬在地下几百年都不会腐烂。出土文物中的漆器在地下埋了几千年，它的漆面还是光亮如新。所以它还有一个更好听的名称——国漆。

在上漆之前，要用豆腐、猪血打底，也就是在木料上刷上豆腐猪血，这主要是起到承上启下的作用，因为豆腐猪血既可以和木料相结合，又可以和油漆相结合，使得油漆的黏性效果更好。

早先的漆匠所用的油漆多是老漆，这是天然漆的一种，不进行任何加工的叫生漆，或叫毛漆。色乳白或灰白，与空气接触会变色，先后变成粉红、红、深红，最后变成黑色。

生漆干燥快、牢度好、硬度高。经过日光翻晒后过滤的叫熟漆，加进熟桐油的叫广漆，或叫黄漆。生漆做出的器具漆面光泽差，色彩单调（只有黑色）。广漆、

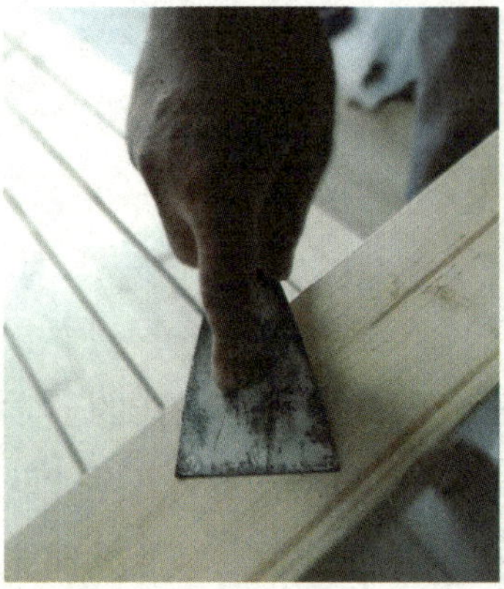
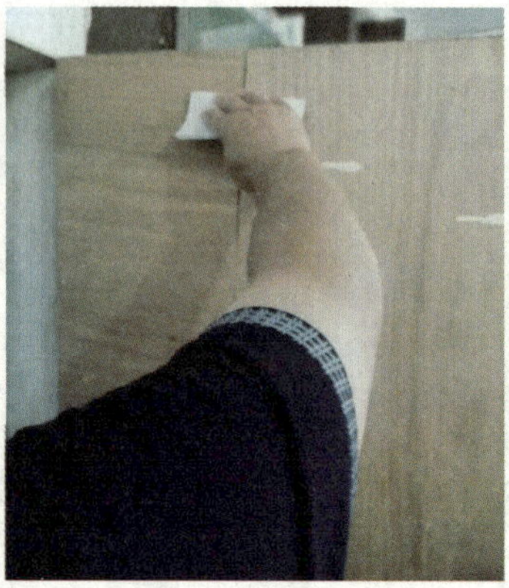

黄漆做出来的色调多样，漆面光亮如镜，而且能显现木纹，色调有淡金黄、黄棕、红棕、深棕。色调与桐油的加入量相关，桐油加入量越多色越淡。

手艺：漆好老人“万年空”

陈师傅说，漆好老人“万年空”熬漆最关键。那时，漆寿材多用生漆，生漆漆出来的东西透亮耐久，据说是从山里漆树上割下来的。有人天生不能接触生漆，一沾上全身就害漆疮流脓，做不成漆匠还落一身痛苦，能吃这行饭的人就是不简单了。人家主人自然领会漆匠师傅的话，嘱咐主妇宰了老母鸡炖汤。

除中间歇两天，漆匠师傅共要跑五六趟，每次都是半天，俗话说，漆匠活那叫“漆半天”，中间还要等干哩，半天就抵一天工，看似轻巧，其实做好也不容易，不能怠慢人家手艺人。漆匠师傅手艺不凡，最后一遍生漆罩上，效果就出来了，那死木头竟黑亮照人，仿佛成了一尊艺术品。完活那天，主人要给漆匠师傅敬酒，结了工钱还送他一些礼物。

【匠人心语】

传统老漆好在哪里呢？陈师傅说：“因为苦脏累，跟我一起做油漆匠的同行，许多人都改行了，只要人们有需要，我依然会坚持做下去。我对传统老漆有着特殊的情结。老漆是从漆树上割下来的，属于纯生物产品，对人体没有毒害。我更希望有人能把油漆这门技艺传承下去。”

（黄辉撰文 / 摄影）

Chen Laishui, a Lacquer Plasterer: Polishing the True Color of Life with Piety

The Ancient Craft: Lacquering

The lacquer began in Qin and Han dynasty, and was popularized in Ming and Qing dynasty. It has a history for thousands of years according records. The earliest lacquer ware unearthed in our country has a history of more than two thousand years. It is so bright and beautiful that the modern synthetic one cannot be compared with it.

The technological process of lacquering has more than 10 procedures: seasoning, bottom scraping, polishing, priming paint daubing, paint-ash filling, water grinding, priming paint daubing again, top paintcoat daubing, and burnishing at last.

The Brief Biography of the Craftsman

Cheng Laishui, aged nearly 60 now, has been engaged in this business for more than 34 years. His work as a lacquerer began in 1984. He told us that the lacquer used in the early times was the natural one, which was commonly called old lacquer. When lacquering, there were two methods for you: one was to rub with the natural silk soaked with the lacquer; the other was brushing with the palm-fiber brusher. After the lacquering was finished, cover it with a wet mat, keep it away from the sunlight and wait for it to be dried. Today, most people use the synthetic lacquer and mechanical spraying method, instead of the traditional one.

The Growth of the Craftsman

Inheritance: From Apprenticing to Lecturing

Usually, to finish the apprenticeship required two years time. During this period, there was no wage for the apprentice. The first thing the apprentice must learn was to decoct oil. Firstly put the tung oil into the wok, and boil it with big fire first and small fire later. Different from decocting the ash paint, decocting the tung oil needed no "Tuosheng" and "Zaitu", additives for drying. When the oil was boiled to a proper condition, cool it down quickly, in case it was over boiled and became too dry for brushing.

And the next learning content was lacquering. First, mix the base oil and the pure raw lacquer together in a certain proportion and stir it fully, and then coat it to the surface evenly with the ox-tail brusher. In the operation, there needed enough strength. Otherwise, the lacquer might be piled up on the surface.

Mr. Chen said he had taken more than 10 apprentices from his beginning of the business. But since the year of 1997, there has been no one who would like to pick it up. Now, Mr. Chen is still engaged in the manual lacquering job. In Jingdezhen, there is still a certain market for the manual lacquering, which may be needed in some ceramic shops , and decorating the antique stores will use it too.

Old Lacquer: Tofu and Pig Blood are Used as the Background Color

According to Mr. Chen, the lacquer used in the early times was the old lacquer, which was processed from the plant and minerals and so was very durable and corrosion resisting. Some coffins lacquered in the old lacquer would not decay though buried for hundreds of years. Lots of unearthed lacquer ware has been buried underground for thousands of years and shines brightly still just like the new ones. Therefore, the old lacquer has a loftier name—the national lacquer.

Before lacquering, get some Tofu and pig blood as the base, that is, brush them on the wood surface. This is mainly for the effect of sticking. Because the tofu and pig blood could permeate into the wood and also they could well integrated well with the lacquer, which may improve the stickiness of the lacquer to the wood.

Generally, the lacquer the earlier lacquerers used is the old lacquer, which is a natural one that needs no processing and is also called unripe lacquer or raw lacquer. It is milky white or gray, and will change color when exposed in the air, from pink to red, to crimson, and finally to black.

The raw lacquer can be dried fast, with strong firmness and hardness. The sun-dried and filtered raw lacquer is called ripe lacquer, and the ripe lacquer which boiled tung oil is added is called light lacquer or yellow lacquer. The lacquer ware brushed in raw lacquer has a poor gloss and monotonous color (only black), while the yellow lacquer can present a wide range of colors, like light gold, yellow brown, red brown, dark brown etc. Besides, the surface lacquered in the yellow lacquer is always as bright as mirror. Also the wood grain can be shown through it. Actually, the color it presents depends on the amount of the tung oil added to the lacquer. The more the tung oil the lacquer contains, the lighter the color is.

The Craft: Highly-skilled Lacquerers are Quite Rare in the Past Years

Chen said highly-skilled lacquerers are quite rare in the past years. For lacquering, the most important part is lacquer decocting. In the old days, the coffin was often lacquered in the raw lacquer, because the raw lacquer may be glossier and more durable. It was said that it was cut off from the lacquer trees. But some people are born allergic to it and get sick once touching it. So sometimes the lacquerer might tell his customer that to earn a living by this business was not that easy. The customers of course could understand his words and would serve him a delicious chicken soup while having the meal.

For each business, the lacquerer has to go to his customer' s home five or six times. And each time, he could only do his work half a day. Because he has to wait till it is dried. So there was an old saying for the lacquering work: half-day lacquering. But though it seems to be an easy job, lacquering is actually very tiresome. So the lacquerer could not be ignored. Due to the lacquerer' s extraordinary craft, the dull wood after being lacquered may shine brilliantly just like the artistic creation. When all the lacquering work is finished, the customer would give a toast to the lacquerer and pay him the money for his work.

The Innermost Words of the Craftsman

What is the advantage of the traditional old lacquer? "Since the lacquering work is hard and tiring, many lacquerers that once co-worked with me have switched to other business. But I will go on with it, as long as it is still needed. I have a special feeling for the traditional old lacquer. The old lacquer is cut off from the lacquer trees and is a pure bioproduct. So I think it would not be harmful to our health. I hope more that someone may pick it up and pass it down."

(Written and photographed by Huang Hui)

制笔匠于冬梅：
一丝一毫见精神

【老手艺项目】毛笔制作

瓷用毛笔是手工制瓷过程中必不可少的一种工具。在景德镇，就有一个因毛笔而命名的里弄，叫“笔家弄”，后谐音为“毕家弄”。据史料记载：元时应青花绘制之需，景德镇开始了制作瓷用毛笔的历史，随后逐渐出现了专门用于写画青花的写画笔、挞笔、水笔、釉笔，明代五彩的盛行开始出现勾笔、填笔。到清康熙年间，青花出现混水工艺，料分五色，出现了专门的混水笔。随着康熙五彩、雍正粉彩和珐琅彩的出现，钩笔、填笔、单双料画笔、洗染水笔、金笔等等也补充进来。清末新彩的引进，又开始出现各种用于釉上彩瓷的油笔、条幅、楷笔、钩笔、扫相笔、开相笔、修相笔、扁笔、鸡毫等等。至此，景德镇瓷用毛笔的制作技艺已自成体系，成为景德镇民间手工技艺中不可或缺的一个部分。

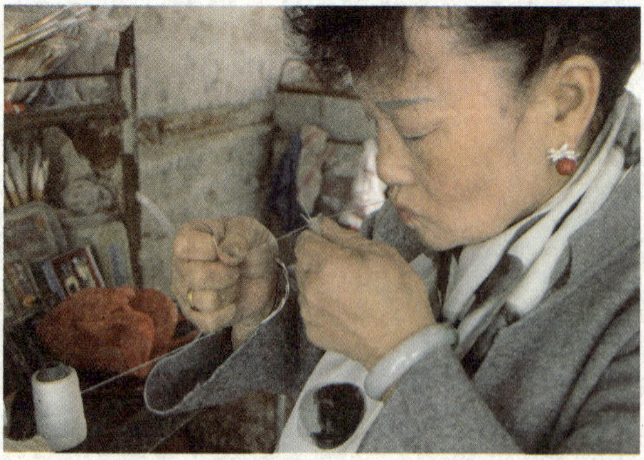

【匠人小传】

66 岁的制笔艺人于冬梅，在景德镇瓷用毛笔厂工作了 40 多年，直到退休。1976 年，20 多岁的她就进厂跟师傅学制笔的手艺。据于冬梅老人介绍，制作每支瓷用毛笔都要经过几十道工序才能完成。她把一辈子的时间和精力都倾注在一支支手工制作的生花妙笔之中。

【匠心之路】

据于冬梅老人回忆，当年因为国家政策，她的大姐下放到农村，她则留城，进了景德镇市瓷用毛笔厂工作，当时是每个月 18 元的工资。当年在厂里上班，每个工人每月要做 10000 多支毛笔，有时赶货每月要做到 12000 多支毛笔。谈及毛笔厂的历史，于冬梅老人又沉浸在回忆之中。

工艺：毛笔制作全凭手上“功夫”

据于冬梅老人介绍，制作毛笔之前先要把毛放在石灰水里熬，再用清水洗。然后才正式进入制笔流程。

首先是选毛，根据绘画要求选择不同的毛。

第二是梳毛，这是一项细致的活，要把毛梳理整齐，毛要用刷子一根一根梳理好。一支毛笔需要多少毛，全靠手上的功夫，如果毛多了，手就会感觉到发胀，就要把毛拔下来。当然，毛少了也不行，就需要补上去。

第三就是吊藤，俗称吊石头，目的是让细绳把笔头绑得更紧，在吊藤的过程中还要复绑，也是为了把笔头绑得更紧。

第四是制作笔筒。选取当地山林的野生苦竹，经过打磨、剪切、打孔和抛边后备用，打孔的大小根据笔头大小而定。

第五是装毛。将制作好的毛笔头装进竹制的笔筒内。于冬梅介绍，瓷用毛笔装毛时可不用上胶，毛笔经过水浸后自然膨胀，会牢牢固定在笔筒内，不易掉落。

装毛完成后，还要进行完工前的验收——试锋，用毛笔在制瓷泥胎上绘画，如果笔锋过尖就要进行修剪，直到适合绘画为止。

于冬梅老人说，做瓷用毛笔全是凭经验和手感，瓷用毛笔中主要是画笔较难做，画笔在制作过程中要起毛、礅尖、剪尖，礅尖是要把毛礅得笔直笔直的。

辉煌：瓷用毛笔与瓷业发展密不可分

据于冬梅老人介绍，在20世纪80年代，景德镇瓷用毛笔厂内职工达到80人。厂里分新花组（羊毛加狼毛）、画笔组、拔毛组、补水笔组（粗货）、贴花组、打箍笔组等6组。当年的毛笔厂除了和景德镇各大陶瓷厂有固定商业往来外，每年厂里还面向全国开产品定销会，来自邯郸、淄博、澄陵、福建、广西等各地的客户都纷纷前来购买毛笔，盛况空前。可以说，20世纪80年代至90年代是景德镇瓷用毛笔厂最鼎盛的时期，这和当时的政策、经济及整个景德镇瓷业发展状况应该是密不可分的。

遗憾：瓷用毛笔厂宣告解散

进入20世纪90年代后，随着景德镇十大国营瓷厂的相继倒闭，毛笔厂开始走下坡路，渐渐地，毛笔厂的发展开始呈衰败之势。厂里开始将毛笔分发给工人，让工人分组到各瓷厂进行上门销售。慢慢地，工人们自己掌握了销售，就开始自己在家里做笔再自己拿去卖，这样毛笔厂就再也无以为继了。1997年，厂里开始全面停产。2001年，企

业改制，瓷用毛笔厂彻底宣告解散。

应该说，这也是市场经济体制形成过程中景德镇小手工业行业所要经历的一个必然的阶段。

于冬梅说："厂子解散后，有的职工便在家中制作毛笔，我也在原先的厂门口摆起了这个摊子。我们制作瓷用毛笔的人，被大家称为三百六十行之外的人，但我们一直在幕后默默地注视着景德镇制瓷业的发展。"

【匠人心语】

一丝一毫，力求精工细作，一笔一画，绘就瓷业豪情。瓷用毛笔制作技艺代表了景德镇陶瓷艺术赖以存在的重要根基。

（黄辉撰文 / 摄影）

Yu Dongmei, a Writing and Painting Brush Maker: Every Single Line Bears a Deep Love

The Ancient Craft: Brush Making

Porcelain brush is a necessary tool in the process of hand-made porcelain. In Jingdezhen, there is a lane named after the brush, called "the pen lane" , and the later homophone is "Bijia lane" . According to historical records, Yuan Dynasty had the demands of drawing the blue and white porcelain, Jingdezhen began the history of making porcelain brush, then the writing brush, pen, tart pen painted blue and white porcelain emerged gradually, until Ming Dynasty, other pens appeared. To the Kangxi period of the Qing Dynasty, porcelain appeared mixing process, materials divided into five colors, the special mixing pen emerged. With the emergence of Kangxi porcelain, Yong Zheng pink porcelain and enamel porcelain, many sorts of pens were also added. The introduction of new porcelain in the late Qing Dynasty led to the emergence for a variety of color glazed porcelain of the pens. At this point, the production techniques of Jingdezhen porcelain brushes have become an integral part of the folk handicraft in Jingdezhen.

The Brief Biography of the Craftsman

Yu Dongmei, an 66 years old artist, worked at the Jingdezhen Porcelain Brush Factory for more than 40 years until she retired. In 1976, she was more than 20 years old and entered the factory to learn the skills with her master. According to the introduction of Yu Dongmei, the production of each porcelain brush is accomplished by several dozens of processes. She spent her whole life and energy on the hand-made brushes.

The Growth of the Craftsman

According to Yu Dongmei's recollection, because of her national policy, her elder sister went down to the countryside. She left the city and went to work in Jingdezhen Porcelain Brush Factory. It was 18 yuan a month at that time. When they worked in the factory, each worker should make more than 10000 brushes each month, and sometimes had to make more than 12000 brushes to catch up with the goods. Talking about the history of the brush factory, Yu Dongmei was immersed in the memory .

Craft: the Brush is Made All by Hand "Kung Fu"

According to the introduction of Yu Dongmei, before making the brush, we should put the hair in the lime water and then wash it with clean water. Then it was formally entered into the pen making process.

First of all, selecting feathers. According to the painting requirements to choose different feathers.

Second, combing feathers, this is a meticulous work. The hair should be combed neatly with a good comb brush. How many feathers a brush needs depends on hand "kung fu", if the feathers are more, the hand will feel bloated, it is necessary to pull down the feathers. Of course, less hair is not good, it needs to be added.

The third is hanging vine, commonly known as hanging stone, the purpose is to bind the pen more tightly with strings, and bind it again in the process of hanging vine, the purpose is to string the pen more tightly.

The fourth is to make a pen container. Choose the local wild bitter bamboo, after sanding, shearing, punching and polishing edge, it could be used in the future. Meanwhile, the size of the depends on the size of the head of the pen.

The fifth is to install feathers, that is put the made brush head into the bamboo pen container.. Yu Dongmei introduced that the porcelain brush cannot be used with glue when the brush is hairy, and the brush is soaked naturally after water. It will be firmly fixed in the pen, and it is not easy to fall.

After the completion of feather installing, the acceptance test is necessary: painting with a brush on the porcelain clay billet to test its tip, if the tip is too sharp then trim the pen tip to make it be suitable for painting.

Yu Dongmei said the brush making depended on experience and hand feeling, the painting brush is difficult to make.

Splendor: Porcelain Brushes are Inseparable From the Development of Porcelain Industry

According to the introduction of Yu Dongmei, in the 1980s, the staff of the Jingdezhen Porcelain Brush Factory reached about 80. The factory is divided into 6 groups such as new flower groups (wool and wolf hair), painting brush group, hair pulling group, pen group of water supplement (coarse goods), applique group, hoop pen group and so on. Apart from the business with major ceramics factories in Jingdezhen, the factory also opened for the annual product sales, the customers from Handan, Zibo, Fujian, Guangxi, Chengling and other cities have come to buy brushes, it was unprecedented. It can be said that, from 1980s to 1990s, it is the most prosperous period of Jingdezhen Porcelain Brush Factory. It is also closely related to the policies, the development of the economy and porcelain industry of Jingdezhen.

Regrets: the Porcelain Brush Factory Declares the Disbandage

Since 1990s, with the liquidation of Jingdezhen ten big state-owned porcelain factories, brush factory began to decline, gradually, the development of brush factory began to decline. The factory began to dispense brushes to workers, let the workers sell the porcelain brushes to the porcelain factories. Slowly, the workers have mastered the sales and began making pens at home to sell, so the brush factory were hard to survive. In 1997, the factory began to stop production in an all-round way. In 2001, the enterprise was reformed, and the porcelain brush factory was completely disbanded.

It should be said that this is also an inevitable stage of the small handicraft industry of Jingdezhen in the formation of the market economic system.

Yu Dongmei said: "after the dissolution of factory, some workers stayed at home to make the brushes, I also set up a booth in front of the gate of the original factory. People who make porcelain brushes are called 'the people out of three hundred and sixty industries'. But we have been watching the development of Jingdezhen porcelain industry silently behind the scenes."

The Innermost Words of the Craftsman

Each tiny bit strives to be crafted carefully, each stroke path paints porcelain pride. The art of making porcelain brushes represents the important foundation for the existence of Jingdezhen ceramic art.

(Written and photographed by Huang Hui)

皮鞋匠汪普乐：
手工鞋让你走进慢时光

【老手艺项目】手工皮鞋

世界上最早用皮革做鞋子的是中国人，据历史记载，3000多年前的商朝宰相伊尹就“用革做履”。现代皮鞋制作技术是从国外传过来的，历史也只有100多年时间。皮鞋的造型、款式、结构以及穿着功能都胜于其他鞋类，因此皮鞋成为人们服饰类中“举足轻重”的产品。景德镇在20世纪60年代有了第一家皮革厂，当时的皮革厂制鞋工艺大部分还是以手工为主，一双鞋要经过几十道工序。手工制鞋因为融入更多的人性化工艺，穿起来脚感舒适；而定制一双手工皮鞋也成为

古镇许多新人婚前婚后的美好愿望。

【匠人小传】

汪普乐，今年45岁，初中毕业后就进入景德镇皮革厂做工，勤奋好学的他在厂子里待了近10年，把制鞋的整个工艺流程全部掌握了。20世纪90年代末期，皮革厂倒闭后，他自谋职业，开了一家小店从事手工制鞋。从1998年开始做皮鞋，至今已经有20年的手工制鞋经历，当年的小伙如今已年过不惑之年，成了一名老鞋匠。

【匠心之路】

勤奋刻苦技艺精

1989年，汪普乐初中毕业后进入当时景德镇唯一一家制作皮鞋的厂子——"景德镇皮革厂"。做学徒时，他每天从磨刀、削皮开始刻苦练习，一次削皮时不小心把手上的一块皮削到了，到医院连缝了9针，疤痕到现在还清晰可见。

由于他勤奋刻苦，善于学习，不到两年时间，除了掌握自己本岗位的技术，他还在其他师傅身边偷学了很多技艺。在皮革厂工作了10年，他一直是厂里的技术能手。1998年，皮革厂效益不景气，大部分职工都下岗了，下岗回家的汪普乐并没有感到迷茫无出路，凭着娴熟高超的制鞋技艺，他找到了属于自己的发展之路，开了一家手工制鞋店。

技高仁善生意火

汪普乐的手工制鞋店选在市九中旁边的斜坡上，鞋店虽小，可曾经生意很红火。当时还不满30岁的他，有的是干劲与梦想，又天生能吃苦，所以生意做得挺火的。20年前，还没有车直达温州、杭州，每次去进鞋料，他都得熬夜坐一天一夜的硬座，辛苦自不必说。在进料的同时，他抽空考察市场，把浙江的新款鞋带回来，作为自己工艺改造的参考样板。

他做的鞋不仅款式新，而且真材实料，穿着舒服不硌脚，经久耐穿，一双鞋可以穿四五年。有时制作一双几百块的高质量的鞋用到的皮革，需要消耗将近大半头牛的原革料。定做的鞋子用的皮料是厚实紧密的背部皮革，雨天都可当雨鞋穿。那些比较薄的皮革他就拿来练手试作新产品。而且汪普乐做鞋从不偷工减料，一双鞋按正常工序需要钉上100枚以上的鞋钉，一些制造商家为节约人工成本，一般只钉50枚左右。鞋子做好后用鞋楦定型很重要，至少要两天才能保证鞋型的深度固定，有些商家直接上烤炉烘烤，既省时又省力，而他几乎是坚持用老办法自然晾干，这样不会伤及鞋面皮质，鞋子更耐穿。

市场冲击渐低迷

生意场上没有永久的春天，伴随着机械化制鞋成本的降低，以及网络购物的热度，手工制鞋行业日渐走入低谷，汪普乐的鞋店生意也越来越清淡，行业中的人大多转行做机械制鞋，可汪普乐仍坚守着老本行。他说：“与流水线生产出的产品相比，手工制作的每双鞋是独一无二的，每道工序经过了一丝不苟的打磨，经得起岁月考验。”

【匠人心语】

作为一个手艺人，重要的是用心去做事，通过自己的手打造出最好产品，做手艺，就是做到老，学到老。现在，能从头到尾做出一双手工皮鞋的人寥寥无几，我最大的希望，就是能让这门老手艺传承下去，可这种吃苦卖力的事已没有年轻人愿意做。

（蓝田玉 / 撰文　黄辉 / 摄影）

Wang Pule, a Shoemaker : Handmade Shoes Help You Approach the Time Leisurely

The Ancient Craft: Handmade Leather Shoes

The earliest shoes made of leather was produced by Chinese, according to the historical record, Yi Yin, the chancellor in Shang Dynasty, made his shoes out of the leather 3000 years ago. The modern technique of making leather shoes was brought from abroad, and the history was as short as more than 100 years. The leather shoes are superior to other types of shoes in shape, style, structure and wearing functions, that's why the leather shoes are a decisive product in people's costumes. As early as the 1960, the first leather shoes factory was established in Jingdezhen City, and majority of the techniques for leather shoes production in that factory was handwork, so a pair of finished shoes would go through tens of processes. The handmade leather shoes felt more comfortable as more humanized techniques were taken into the production. So it is a nice wish for many of newly married couples to own a pair of customized handmade leather shoes at that time.

The Brief Biography of the Craftsman

Wang Pule, who is 45 years old this year, started to work in Jingdezhen Leather Factory after graduation from middle school, and this diligent man stayed in the factory for nearly 10 years, completely mastering the whole technical process of making the leather shoes. In the late 1990s, he started with his own business by running a small shop embarking on handmade shoes production after the factory closed down. Since 1998 when he started to make leather shoes, he has been working on handmade leather shoes for 20 years, and the youngster in that year has been in his 40s, becoming an old shoemaker.

The Growth of the Craftsman

Diligence Makes the Excellent Skill

In 1989, Wang Pule entered into the sole factory producing the leather shoes in Jingdezhen after graduation from the middle school, and it's Jingdezhen Leather Factory. Being an apprentice, he practiced hard starting from sharpening knives and peeling the leather, and once he carelessly peeled the hand and was sent to hospital for 9 stitches with the scar still clearly visible right now. As he was working hard and good at studying, he secretly learnt lots of skills from other masters except for the basic skill for his post less than 2 years. He was always the technical expert during the ten years when he stayed at the factory. In 1998, the majority of workers were redundant for the economic depression in the leather factory. However Wang Pule didn't feel puzzled over his prospect after layoff, instead, he found a development way for himself through his proficient and excellent shoemaking skill and opened a shop for handmade shoes.

Being Merciful with Excellent Skill Makes Good Business

Wang Pule's handmade shoe shop is located in the upslope beside No. 9 Middle School in the city, although the area of the shop is small, but the business was very good before. At that time he was less than 30 years old, and he was stuffed with vigor and dreams, also he could bear the hardship innately, so the business was quite good. 20 years ago, there were nonstop trains to Wenzhou and Hangzhou, so he had to take the hard seat for a whole day whenever he went to buy the material for the shoes, which is for sure painstaking. Meantime, when he bought the material, he would spare some time to investigate the market by purchasing some new–style leather shoes in Zhejiang and brought them back as the reference samples for improving his own skills.

As his shoes were not only possessing new style, but also made of real stuff, the customers felt comfortable when wearing them. And his shoes are durable, which could be worn for four or five years. Sometimes making a pair of high–quality shoes valued a few hundred yuan would nearly use up more than half of the original leather from an ox. The leather material for the customized shoes was the thick and compacted cowhide from its back, and such shoes could be worn in rainy days. The comparatively thin leather would be used for exercising the skill to make new products. Meantime, Wang Pule never cheated on workmanship and materials when making shoes, and a pair of shoes must go through the regular process by hammering more than 100 spikes. While some merchants usually hammered less than 50 spikes into the shoes for saving labor cost. When the shoes were made out, it was important to fix the shape by using the shoe last, and at least two days were required to ensure the shape of the shoes deeply fixed. Some merchants would directly put the shoes onto the oven to dry them, which was both timesaving and laborsaving. Nevertheless, he almost persisted in the old method to dry the shoes naturally, and in this way the surface of the shoes wouldn't be damaged, so the shoes were more durable.

Being in Depression Gradually Due to the Market Impact

The prosperity in business won't last permanently, as the shoemaking cost is lowered for the mechanization, and online shopping is popularized, the industry of handmade shoes is gradually falling into its low point, and business in Wang's shoes shop is no longer booming gradually. Most of the craftsmen in this industry all shift to make shoes by machine, but Wang Pule still perseveres in his old profession. He said, "Compared with the products manufactured out of the production line, each pair of shoes made by hand are unique, and they could withstand the test of the time because each of the processes goes through the meticulous handling."

The Innermost Words of the Craftsman

"As a craftsman, it is important to put your soul into the work to make out the best products by your hands, and it's never too old to learn. Nowadays, there are scarcely craftsmen who can make out a pair of handmade shoes through the integral process from stem to stern, and my greatest wish is to pass down the ancient crafts. However, there are no such youngsters who are willing to sacrifice the comfort and energy to this industry."

(Written by Lan Tianyu, photographed by Huang Hui)

修鞋匠黄树芳：
坚守40年的老行当

【老手艺项目】补鞋

黄师傅的木箱里有补鞋用的皮子、胶水，钉鞋用的钉子，绱鞋用的木楦子等，其他工具还有钳子、启子、尼龙线等。右边一台补鞋机，左边一只工具箱，前面是叠得高高的半圈鞋子，黄师傅系着围裙，坐在一把矮矮的旧竹椅上，忙着手上的活儿。这巴掌大的一隅已然成为黄树芳一辈子的谋生之地和半个“家”。

【匠人小传】

70多岁的修鞋匠黄树芳师傅，从1971年开始就在斗富弄摆修鞋摊。在40多年的摆摊

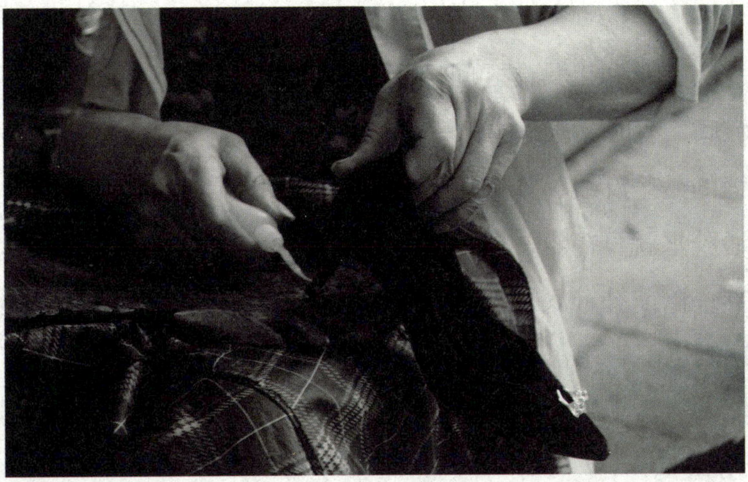

修鞋生涯中，黄师傅一直未离开过斗富弄，从 20 世纪 70 年代的牛皮毡顶棚的菜市场到现在的古街，他在弄口边的四个角落都摆过摊。

【匠心之路】

一门手艺谋生计

据黄师傅回忆，他原籍湖北，父母当年毕业于九江师范，分配到湖口教书。之后，父母都被打成“右派”下放到湖口县的农村。再后来，政府落实政策，黄师傅随着妻子来到景德镇。黄师傅的妻子顶替了自己父亲的工作，进入大集体单位，黄师傅则跟一位老皮匠学补鞋。或许他也没想到，这一干就是大半辈子。

黄师傅告诉笔者，40 多年了，修鞋的工价从 1 毛钱左右到现在的 10 元左右，说明大家的生活有了大改善。这期间，黄师傅也曾与买帽子的、做裁缝的 3 人抱团租门市，每月 30 元一间的店面，但他还是觉得摆地摊自在。

做最接地气的活

补鞋看似简单，其实是一门手艺活，全靠手工进行。黄师傅说，有些皮鞋很难弄，“意大利”的皮鞋皮质坚硬，上线很难，还有以前烧窑师傅用的工作鞋很难修理。

黄师傅修补鞋子时，头在鞋和工具盒之间来回转动，右手拿起不同的工具，有时挑断线，有时插入鞋底，有时又敲敲打打……

他告诉笔者，以前缝的是苎麻线，如今用的是涤纶线；以前补的大多是元宝套鞋、解放鞋，一瓶普通胶水就可搞定，如今上手的是各种款式的皮鞋，必须学会翻新、补色，上光滋养；以前补鞋底用的是臭皮钉和铁锤，如今女士的高跟鞋里有“腰铁”，修理时钢锯也不管用，非得用砂轮切割机不可。

40 年补鞋摊汇聚街坊情

在摊子的长凳上，坐着两位耄耋之年的老太。她们是这里的老街坊，只要天气好，黄师傅的摊子就成了街坊老人的闲聊之处。附近扫街的清洁工也在此逗留，大家一起歇息闲聊。渐渐地，这小摊成了人气指数挺高的聊天吧。

“都是街坊邻居，手艺人讲的是诚信。”黄师傅是这样说的，也是这样做的。很多时候，顾客送来的鞋不能随补随取，要过一段时间再来拿。可是，由于各种原因，不少顾客不能如约来取鞋，他就一直候着，如果当天没等着，就暂时带回家，第二天即使下雨落雪，他也一定把摊摆出来，以备顾客随时前来取鞋。可是，有的会过几个月甚至一年后再来拿，还有的几年、十几年也没再回过鞋摊，但黄师傅还是把这些早已补好的鞋保管着。他常说：“鞋匠，修补的是鞋子，讲的就是街坊的感情。”

【匠人心语】

“修鞋是相当苦的，我是吃了很多苦的。如果没吃那么多苦，或许我就没有这样的耐心了。我一辈子没有进单位，但我靠自己的手艺活得很安心。”

是的！黄树芳师傅坚守的，就是匠人的本心。

（黄辉 / 撰文　余琳超 / 摄影）

Huang Shufang, a Cobbler : Sticking to the Old Profession for 40 Years Long

The Ancient Craft: Repairing Shoes

Master Huang' s wooden case is full of the material for repairing shoes like the alternative leather, the glue, the nail, the wooden shoe last for stitching the soles, etc., and tools like tongs, screw driver, nylon threads and so on. With a shoe repairing machine on his right, and a tool case on his left, Master Huang is aproned and seated on a short bamboo chair behind a pile of shoes stacked highly, focusing on his work on hand. And such a small area has been the place for Huang Shufang to make his life and equals to his home to some extent.

The Brief Biography of the Craftsman

The 70-year-old cobbler Huang Shufang has set up his booth in Doufu Lane for repairing shoes since the year of 1971. In the past 40 years, he never left this lane but changed his position in four corners at the mouth of the lane, from the old fair here which was full of sheds covered by felts in 1970s to the retro street.

The Growth of the Craftsman

A Skill to Subsist

According to Master Huang' s recall, he was born in Hubei, and dwelled in Hukou County after his parents graduated from Jiujiang Normal University and were assigned to teach there. However, his parents were both classified as the Right Deviationists and banished to the village in Hukou County soon. And after that Master Huang followed his wife and came to Jingdezhen City according to the governmental policy at that time. His wife took over her father' s job and entered into a collective unit and Master Huang apprenticed to learn the shoe repairing from an old cobbler. Maybe he never perceived at that time that his choice might last for his whole life.

Master Huang told the writer that the cost for repairing shoes had been increased from one dime around to 10 yuan around today in the past 40 years, in another word, people' s lives have been improved greatly.

Also Master Huang once shared the rental of a shop with a hat seller and a tailor at the cost of 30 yuan per month, but he still preferred to run his business in a booth freely.

The Most Grounded Industry

"It looks simple to repair shoes, nevertheless, it's virtually a skill relying on the handwork." Master Huang said, "Some shoes are not so easy to repair, for example, the texture of the leather shoes made in Italy is pretty hard, and it's difficult to thread the shoes, so are the boots worn by the masters working in the kiln firing the porcelains."

When repairing the shoes, Master Huang's head turns back and forth between the shoes and the tool case with his right hand taking different tools to pick and cut the thread, to pierce into the soles or to knock on the shoes sometimes...

He told the writer that the stitching thread was made of ramie before but it's dacron now. And what he repaired before were mainly the overshoes and rubber-soled shoes, so a bottle of common glue could work. But they are the leather shoes of all types now, so he must learn to refurbish, to complement the color, to polish and nourish the shoes. In the past, the nails and hammer were enough to repair soles, but he has to use the abrasive wheel cutting machine now as even the saw doesn't work because of the iron bone inside the high-heeled shoes.

The Gathering of Neighbors' Sentiment at the 40-year-old Booth

On the long bench at the booth were two very aged women, and they were the old neighbors living on this street. Whenever the weather was good, Master Huang's booth would turn into the place for the old in neighborhood to gather for chatting. Also the dustmen sweeping this street would stay here for a rest and chat at leisure. Gradually, this small booth has become a very popular chat bar.

"The craftsman attaches importance to the integrity, and most customers are in neighborhood." Master Huang said so and did as what he said. Sometimes, the shoes could be repaired as soon as they were taken to Huang's booth, and the customer needed to fetch after some time. However, many customers might not come as appointed to take their shoes back for various reasons, and Master Huang would stay late there. If the shoes were not taken away that day, he would take them home temporarily but came out to run his booth on the following day regardless of the weather conditions so as to facilitate the customers to fetch their shoes anytime. Nonetheless, some shoes might be kept at Huang's booth for months or even a year before they were taken away, and some might not leave after years or longer. Master Huang always keeps these repaired shoes in good condition, and he often says, "The cobblers do not only repair the shoes but also value the neighbors' relationships."

The Innermost Words of the Craftsman

"As a craftsman working on shoes repairing, I suffered a lot. But I may not be so patient without these bitter experiences. I've never entered into any units, but it makes me feel relieved by living on my crafts."

That's right! What Master Huang does persist in is just the craftsmen's instinct.

(Written by Huang Hui, photographed by Yu Linchao)

修伞匠石贵爱：
妙手呵护风雨人生

【老手艺项目】修伞匠

过去的雨伞大都是油布或油纸伞，都是竹木做骨架，只有伞面是油纸或油布，虽然有些笨重，但是使用起来还是得心应手。雨伞与其他人们使用的物件一样总得有个坏，雨伞坏了就得修，于是就有了修伞匠。修伞匠没有特定的“行头”，有人肩背一副“褡裢”，也有挑挑儿的，还有推独轮车的，虽然“行头”各异，但修伞的家伙、材料都一样，如手摇钻、刀铲、桐油、刷子、竹管、竹签、铅丝、麻绳、高丽纸等。

【匠人小传】

石贵爱，58岁，走街串巷从事修伞行业30多年，修伞无数。她曾经在跃进瓷厂做过工，企业改制后重操旧业，摆摊设点以修伞为生。因为她技艺精湛，为人和善，收费公平，颇受顾客称道。

【匠心之路】

修伞匠，已不多见了。究其原因，有主观上的原因——随随便便在便利店买把雨伞，便宜的不过八九块钱，也就吃碗炒粉的钱。真要脱了线或破了个洞，随手一扔，弃若敝屣，少有人会敝帚自珍地浪费几块钱去修理，用镇上人的话说，那是“豆腐花了肉价钱”；也有客观上的原因，那就是物质生活质量提高了，人们已经抛弃了朴素的底色，一件件穿了几回的衣、一碗碗白花花的米饭、一盘盘未动筷子的佳肴都可以毫不顾惜地扔掉，更遑论一把破雨伞。

善心温暖风雨岁月

一个骄阳似火的夏日午后，在景德镇中渡口老街区的偏僻一角，石贵爱正在埋头忙碌：粗糙的手捏着细细的针，一下一下地将伞布与伞骨缝在一起，针脚细密精致……

在这片偏僻的老街区，石贵爱与伞已打了多年的交道。环视小摊一隅，架子上摆满了修伞工具：尖嘴钳、剪刀、钢锉、螺丝刀、成卷的铁丝……角落里还静静站立着修好和未修的雨伞。

早些年，为了寻一碗饭吃，石贵爱经常推一辆自行车走街串巷四处吆喝，一把钳子、一个锥子、几根铁丝，就是她营生的家伙。换一个伞柄两三元，换一根钢骨子一块钱。如果仅仅是缝根线，她就分文不收。时间长了，镇上大街小巷许多人都认识她，一些老太太妇人家即便没事找她，也会客气地请她坐下来歇口气，喝口水。

后来她在跃进瓷厂做过工，企业陷入困境后，

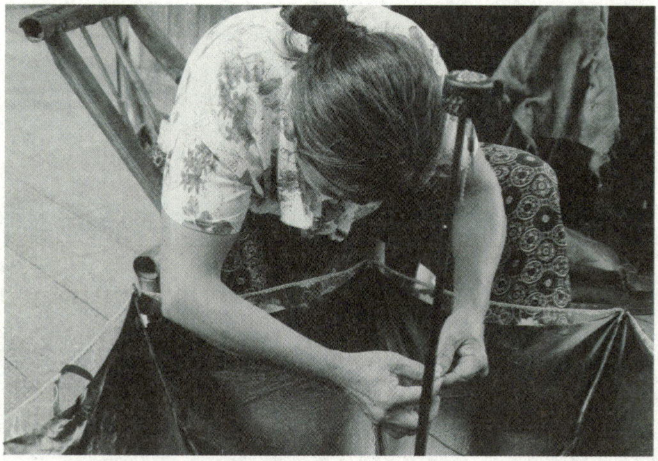

为了生计，她重操旧业，摆摊设点，成了专门的修伞匠。从那时起，石贵爱每天早晨7点出摊，傍晚收摊。修伞铺周边的建筑拆了建，建了拆，唯独这个摊子一成不变。

生命不息　风雨兼程

“修伞最大的难处是无处购买老款雨伞的配件，我手头的这些零配件，很多都是在已经无法修理的破伞上拆卸下来的，还算是比较齐全。”说话间，她拿出一把半新的自动伞。

这把伞的主人是东门头的一位老先生，他将伞放在家中十几年，一直舍不得用，前段时间找出这把伞，却发现伞骨已坏。老先生四处打听，最终听说中渡口有个修伞的女师傅，他当即从东门头赶了过来。两人相见时，老先生说的第一句话让石贵爱印象深刻：“这把伞是老朋友送我的，很有纪念意义，请师傅务必帮忙修好。”

石大姐常年修伞，锋利的伞骨断口常会将她的手弄伤，但她干起活来依旧灵巧，无论是穿针引线，还是接骨换架，都干净利落。而前来找石贵爱修伞的，大多是回头客。

【匠人心语】

“有人很好奇，说现在怎么还有修伞的人呀！”她笑着说，“可别小看了修伞这手艺，要修好，还真得下一番功夫。客人找我修伞，说明市场还有需求，我会继续干下去。”石大姐憨厚地笑了笑，继续忙她手中的活。

（陶阳客 / 撰文　余琳超 / 摄影）

Shi Gui' ai, an Umbrella Renovator: Caring the Bumpy Life with the Deft Hands

The Ancient Craft: The umbrella-repairman

In the past, umbrellas were mostly oil-cloth or oil-paper umbrellas, whose skeleton were made of bamboo and wood, only the umbrellas were made of oil-paper or oil-cloth, although they are heavy but can be used conveniently. An umbrella, like any other object used by people, is broken down. When it breaks down, it has to be repaired. So there was an umbrella repairer. umbrella repairer has no specific "outfit", someone shoulders a "the wallet", someone pushes the unicycle though "outfit" is different, materials and tools are all the same, hand drill, knives, sickles, tong oil, brushes, bamboo tubes, bamboo sticks, lead wire, hemp rope.

The Brief Biography of the Craftsman

Shi Gui' ai, 58 years old, has been engaged in the art of umbrella repair for more than 30 years. Once worked in the Yuejin Porcelain Factory, Shi went back to the old business after the factory reformed, and set up a booth to repair the umbrella for a living. Because of the exquisite skill, her kindness, the reasonable charge, Shi receives the customer' quite commendation.

The Growth of the Craftsman

The umbrella-repairman is rare. The reason for this is subjective—buy an umbrella at a convenience store for as little as eight or nine yuan, which equals to the cost of eating a bowl of fried noodles. If the umbrella takes off the thread or breaks a hole, just throw it away . Also there are objective reasons, that is material quality of life improved, people have abandoned the impression of plain, the clothes just worn for several times will be thrown away, uneaten food can be thrown away, not to mention a broken umbrella.

Kindness Warms the Stormy Years

A scorching summer afternoon, at a remote corner of Zhongdukou block in Jingdezhen, Shi is busy in working, her rough hands held thin needle, which will stitch the umbrella cloth and bone together with fine and dense delicate stitches...

In this remote old neighborhood, Shi has been dealing with umbrellas for years. Around the corner, the shelves are filled with umbrella repair tools: needle-nosed pliers, scissors, steel files, screwdrivers, rolled wire. The repaired and unrepaired umbrellas stood in the corner.

In the early years, in order to find a bowl of rice to eat, Shi often pushed a bicycle around the streets with yo-heave-ho, a plier, an awl, a few iron wire are her tool of work. Two or three yuan for an umbrella handle and one yuan for a steel bone. If it's just sewing a thread, she will di it for free. For a long time, many people in the streets of the town knew her, and some old women would politely asked her to sit down and have a drink.

She later worked in Yuejin Porcelain Factory. When the business was in trouble, she went back to her old business and set up a booth to make a living. She became a professional umbrella repairer. From that time on, Shi Gui'ai went out at 7 o'clock in the morning and closed the booth in the evening. The buildings around the umbrella booth were demolished and built, only this one remained unchanged.

Life Goes On and On

"The greatest difficulty is nowhere to buy accessories of old umbrella, I have some spare parts, many of them are removed from the broken umbrella, the accessories are relatively complete." As she speaking, she took out a semi-new automatic umbrella.

The owner of this umbrella is an old gentleman at the east gate. He has kept it at home for more than ten years and has been reluctant to use it. The old gentleman inquired about it everywhere, and at last he heard that there was a woman who repaired an umbrella at Zhongdukou. When they met, the first words of the old man impressed Shi Gui'ai deeply: "this umbrella was given to me by an old friend of mine. It is very memorable."

Shi has been repairing the umbrella all year round, and the sharp break of the umbrella bone will often hurt her hands, but she ais still dexterous in her work, whether thread needles or drag thread, or replace bone, is all clean and neat. Most of the people who come to find Shi to repair their umbrellas are old customers.

The Innermost Words of the Craftsman

"Somebody is very curious, saying that why the person still repairs an umbrella now." she said with smile. "don not underestimate the skill of building an umbrella. The customer asked me to repair the umbrella, indicating that the market still needs it, and I will continue to work." Shi smiled innocently and kept busy with her work.

(Written by Tao Yangke, photographed by Yu Linchao)

磨刀匠梁家福：
宝刀锋从磨砺出

【老手艺项目】磨刀匠

“磨剪子嘞，戗菜刀……”这是样板戏《红灯记》中的经典台词，每当听到这种熟悉的吆喝声，人们就会不由自主地想起当年那些走街串巷的磨刀匠。

一条旧板凳，两头绑块磨刀石，板凳底下再放个电喇叭：“磨剪子嘞，戗菜刀……”不一会儿，就围上来了几个顾客。这是老一辈镇巴佬记忆犹新的旧时光景。

时代变了，磨刀匠正逐渐从城市消失，想见到他们还真不容易。偶然遇到一个磨刀匠，听到一声吆喝声，让人真有恍如隔世的感觉。

【匠人小传】

梁家福，1968年生人，安徽省安庆人。自幼跟随叔叔学习磨刀技艺，几十年来走南闯北，从事磨刀手艺养家糊口。近年来长驻景德镇走街串巷专门从事磨刀营生，对于景德镇的街道里弄了如指掌。因为磨刀技艺过硬，收费合理，颇受镇上老太太和家庭主妇的欢迎。

【匠心之路】

20世纪七八十年代，磨刀这个行业的生意相当红火。庭院里、小巷中、街道上，到处充斥着“磨刀哇……”的吆喝声。记忆中，那叫唤声响亮而清脆；记忆中，磨刀匠总是肩扛一条长板凳走街串巷。

梁师傅自幼生活在安庆农村，家里兄弟姐妹5个，家境贫寒。梁师傅读了两年小学就辍学回家务农了。面朝黄土背朝天的农村生活，不仅辛苦，而且枯燥无味。梁师傅有个叔叔是老磨刀匠，一年四季走南闯北，梁师傅甚是羡慕。经他多次软磨硬缠，叔叔终于收他为徒。东奔西走学了大半年磨刀技艺，叔叔让他另立门户开始单干。就这样，梁师傅开始了30多年的磨刀匠生涯。这些年来，每逢农闲时间，他就扛着一条板凳四海为家，从事磨刀营生。浙江、湖南、江西大地，都留下了他的脚印。每到一个城市，他都是找到最便宜的小旅馆住下，一直做到寒冬腊月才回家过年。

“磨刀这活儿看起来简单，其中也是有技巧的，用力要均匀，做事要细心，这样磨出来的刀才会耐用。磨刀、磨剪子中，最难的是磨剪子，磨的时候不光要掌握角度，力度也要合适，不然磨出来的剪子不好用。价格方面磨刀是5元，如果还要戗菜刀就再另加3元。”梁师傅说。

以腿毛试刀

别看磨一把刀才收三五元钱，梁师傅干活从来都是精益求精，从不敷衍顾客：先在砂轮上狠狠打磨几分钟，再在磨刀石上进行精加工。每磨一遍，都要看一下刀刃的厚薄和锋利程度。10 分钟后，一把刀磨好了，还拿起刀在自己的小腿上削了两下。“真正的快刀是能削断腿毛的，我验收了以后才放心交货。”他如此费力地用心干活，每次都是大汗淋漓。

【匠人心语】

只要功夫深，铁杵磨成针。磨刀讲究的不光是一股牛劲马力，更要掌握适可而止的手上功夫。这好比烧柴做饭一样，差一口气饭不得熟，过了火候饭就烧焦了。世界上万事万物都同此理。

（芷琳撰文 / 摄影）

Liang Jiafu, a Knife Grinder: Good Honing Gives a Sharp Edge to a Sword

The Ancient Craft: Sharpening Craftsman

"Grinding scissors, peak-cutting knives…" this is the classic line of the model play "the red light". When people hear this familiar cry, they cannot help but think of the grinders who walked on the streets.

An old bench, two ends tied pieces of grindstone, the bottom of the bench put an electric horn: "grinding scissors, peak-cutting knife." A few customers soon gathered round him. This is the old days that the old townspeople remember vividly.

Times have changed and knife grinders are disappearing from the city. It is hard to see them. Meeting a knife grinder by chance, hearing a call, let a person have the feeling of geniality.

The Brief Biography of the Craftsman

Liang Jiafu, born in 1968, is from Anqing in Anhui. Since childhood, he has been learning knife grinding skills from his uncle. For decades, he have traveled all over the country to earn a living as a knife grinder. In recent years, he have been living in Jingdezhen engaged in sharpening knives. He knows the streets of Jingdezhen very well. He is popular with old ladies and housewives in the town because of his excellent skill and reasonable charge.

The Growth of the Craftsman

In the 1970s and 1980s, the business of sharpening knives was booming. In the courtyard, in the alley, on the street, everywhere is full of "grinding knives wow…" In memory, the call was loud and clear; In memory, the grinder always walked around with a long bench on his shoulder.

Mr. Liang lived in the rural area of Anqing since he was a child. After two years of primary school, Mr.

Liang dropped out of school and went back to be farmer. Life in the countryside facing the loess is not only hard but also dull. Master Liang had an uncle who was an old knife grinder. His uncle finally took him in as a apprentice after he pleaded for several times. After learning the art of sharpening knives for more than half a year, his uncle asked him to start his own work. In this way, Mr. Liang began his career as a knife grinder for more than 30 years. All these years, in his spare time, he carried a bench on his back and worked as a grinder. Zhejiang, Hunan, Jiangxi, all left his footprints. Every time he went to a city, he found the cheapest small hotel to stay in. He did not go home until the winter came.

"The job of grinding a knife looks simple, but it is also skilled, and the force should be even and careful, so that the knife will be durable. In the process of grinding knives and scissors, the most difficult thing is to grind the scissors. When grinding, you should not only master the angle, but also have to hold appropriate strength. The price of peak–cutting knife is 5 yuan." Mr. Liang said.

Using Leg Hairs to Test Knife

Although grinding a knife just costs 35 yuan, the work of Mr. Liang is always seeking for perfection, he never palters with the customers. Firstly, grinding wheel hard for a few minutes, and then processing carefully on the grindstone. Every time you grind it, you need to see the thickness and sharpness of the blade. 10 minutes later, a knife was sharpened, and the knife was cut twice on the lower leg. "The real sharp knife can cut the hair off the legs, and I won't be able to deliver the goods until I have accepted it." Working is so hard that I sweat every time.

The Innermost Words of the Craftsman

As long as you work hard, the iron pestle becomes a needle. Sharpening the knife needs not only strong power, but also needs to master the appropriate skills. It is like burning wood to cook a meal. The rice will be adust if the fire is to big, not ripe if the fire is not enough. Everything in the world is the same.

(Written and photographed by Zhi Lin)

剃头匠黄银根：
毫末技艺顶上功夫

【老手艺项目】剃头匠

“剃头”是自清代开始的老式叫法。辛亥革命以后，人们的头上没了辫子，称之为“剪头”或“推头”。直到新中国成立，“理发”一词才时兴起来。而今时代发生了变化，剃头的称谓改叫“美发”了，剃头匠也便称为美发师。

【匠人小传】

黄银根，79岁，景德镇人，13岁起拜师学艺，从事剃头行业将近70年了。几十年来，他在老板店里打过工，在华电瓷厂国有理发店做过师傅，至今还在自家摆摊设点为人剃头，发挥余热。有的顾客从出生到离世，一辈子的头发都是他打理的。凭良心做事，凭本事吃饭，是他的口头禅。

【匠心之路】

含辛茹苦的小徒弟

黄师傅早年丧父，童年时代非常辛酸。13岁那一年，因为生活所迫，继

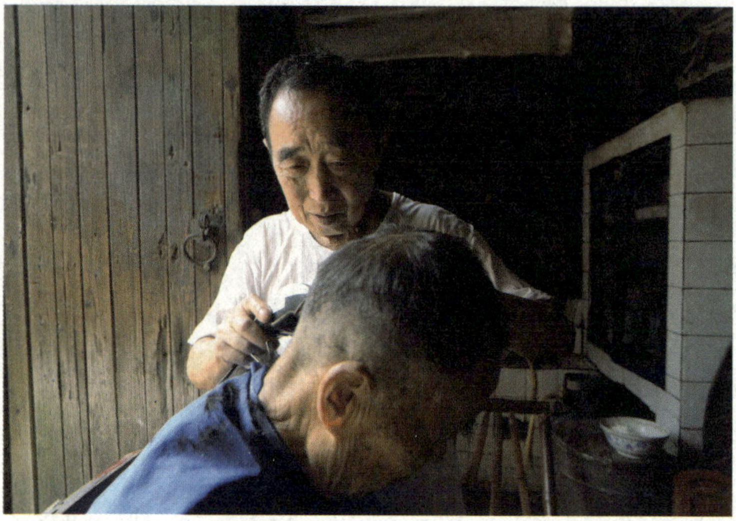

父把在私塾里读书的他委托给一个剃头匠的熟人学徒，为的是他能够混口饭吃。在继父看来，既然无钱读书，也没有本钱做生意，如果能够做个剃头匠，养家糊口是没有问题的。因为，无论什么朝代，也不管男女老少或富贵贫贱，每个人都需要剃头，而且一辈子都需要剃头。

学徒数年，黄师傅不但没有工资，很长一段时间都只是帮助师傅打下手——烧水、扫地、搓毛巾、磨刀，还有一件事让他记忆犹新：那时候没有电风扇，每当骄阳似火的夏日，理发店就在屋梁上悬挂一块厚厚的帆布，吊着一根长长的绳子，安排专人在下面拉扯摇摆，使之产生一阵阵凉风。他就是那个汗流浃背摇摆“人工风扇”的少年。

头破血流的“处女作”

熟练掌握剃头的刀法是每一个剃头匠应有的基本功。恰当地拿捏锋利的剃刀，需要有几分恰到好处的手上功夫，如果用力过头就会伤及顾客。

打杂半年，师傅开始给他授艺。为了让他掌握刀法，师傅想了一个刀刮膝盖的绝招让他训练——每天用锋利的剃刀刮自己的膝盖。这个动作既枯燥无味，又需要聚精会神；稍不留神，膝盖就有可能被刀子刮破。练了将近半年时间，师傅想让他试试水，就安排他给一个挑瓷坯的张师傅剃头。咔嚓咔嚓给顾客剪完头发后，他开始给张师傅刮脸。不知是因为第一次剃头过于紧张，还是因为技术不过硬，一不小心削掉了张师傅脑门上一个不起眼的癞痢包。张师傅顿时血流满面，抱头痛哭。这一幕可把小银根给吓坏了，拿着一把剃刀僵硬地站在原地，双手哆嗦着，脑子里一片空白。师傅见状，赶紧放下手中的活计，跑过来一边给张师傅赔不是一边拿毛巾为他止血。这头再也无法剃了，张师傅用手捂着伤口，呻吟着，悻悻离去。小银根的“处女作”就这样失败了。最后的代价是停发一个月的工钱。提及此事，黄师傅依然心有余悸：“还好，张师傅是个非常马虎的人，没有胡搅蛮缠找我麻烦。否则，我后面就做不成剃头匠了。”

慢工方能出细活

剃头匠收入不高，但也饿不死人。20 世纪 50 年代，剃一个头也就一毛多钱，60 年代上涨到两毛。随着物价的上涨，剃头的价钱也跟着上涨。一些美发店的价格更是有些离谱，一两百元洗个头染个发是家常便饭。但是，直到今天，黄师傅剃个头依然不过 10 块钱。为什么不涨价？因为来摊子剃头的大多数是老人家或农民工，经济都比较拮据。自己有退休工资，生活不成问题。之所以舍不得放下拿了近70年的剃头刀，并非仅仅为了赚钱，而是为了老有所为，老有所乐。只要还有人进不起美发店，还需要他这个剃头挑子，只要自己还能动弹，就一直会干下去。

【匠人心语】

“我一辈子没做什么大事，就是与人头打了几十年交道。人与动物不同之处，就在于人懂得剃头，否则就觉得面目可憎。所以，一个人即使再穷，也会把剃头看成是头等大事。为了人们能够体面地走出去，我愿意做一个老老实实做事的剃头匠，直到自己拿不起剃刀。”

（陶阳客 / 撰文　丰月 / 摄影）

Huang Yin' gen, an Old Barber : The Finest Art for Every Single Hair

The Ancient Craft: The Barber

The expression "clipping hair" began in the late Qing Dynasty. Since the revolution of 1911, the long pigtails disappeared and then it was called "shave hair" or "razor hair". The word "haircut" don't come into use until new China founded. Now as the time changed, the appellation for cutting hair has become "hairdressing", and the old barber is also called hairstylist.

The Brief Biography of the Craftsman

Huang Yin'gen, 79 years old and a native of Jingdezhen, started to be a apprentice since he was 13 years old. And now he has been engaged in barber business for nearly 70 years.For decades, he ever worked in others' stores and also worked as a master in a state-owned barber shop of the Huadian Porcelain Factory. Until now he is still having a stall to shave hair for people and making contributions to society.Some customers had their hair shaved by him from birth to death.His mantra is that work with conscience and keep alive with ability.

The Growth of the Craftsman

A Little Hardworking Apprentice

Mr.Huang lost his father when he was very young and his childhood was bitter.When he was 13 years old, Mr.Huang who was studying in an old-style private school was entrusted to a shaving craftsman by his stepfather with the purpose of ensuring his living. In his stepfather's opinion, though he had no money to study or do business, being a shaving craftsman was not bad for supporting a family, because in any dynasty, everybody, whether they were poor or rich, has to get their hair shaved during their whole lifetime.

When being an apprentice for several years, Mr.Huang didnot get any payment, even if he helped his master do many easy things each time, such as heating water, sweeping the floor, rubbing towels and sharpening knives.There is another thing that remains still fresh in his memory. At that time, there was no fan. In the hot summer, in the barber shop there would hang a thick canvas and a long rope on the beam. Each time there came a customer, there should be a person under the beam pulling the rope to make cool breeze. And generally, he was just the sweating boy who swang the "artificial fan".

A Very Badly-beaten Debut

The first condition for being a barber is his proficiency in using the knife. Properly pinching a sharp razor, needs a most proper and right force on it.An excessive force may hurt the customer.

Having been the assistant for half a year, he could finally began his learning.In order to let him master the skill of using the knife, the master thought out a way for him: shave his own knees with a sharp razor every day. That was very boring but required close attention. Any carelessness would get the knees hurt. After he practiced this for nearly six months, his master wanted to give him a try and arranged for him to serve a porcelain heaver named Zhang. With the sound of cuting hair, he finished his hair cutting, then he began to shave face for his customer. Maybe it was because of his excessive nervousness or lack of skill, he cut off a small flesh scab on Zhang' s head accidentally. Immediately, Zhang' s face was covered with blood. Seeing Zhang crying with his face in his hands, he was frightened, holding the shaver in his trembling hand, his mind went blank. Quickly, his master put aside his work and ran over to Zhang and appologized to him while stopping bleeding for him with a towel. With groaning and his hand pressing on the wound, Zhang left away. Huang Yin'gen' s debut thus failed this way. The price for it was deduction of one month' s salary. Even now when speaking of this, Huang' s heart still flutteres with fear. "Fortunately, Master Zhang was a very careless person and didnot pester me later. Otherwise, I could not be a barber."

Soft Fire Makes Sweet Malt

The barber could not earn much, but their income was enough for supporting a family. In the 1950s, the price was just more than one dime. And in the 1960s, it went up to 2 dimes . As prices rose, so did the price of cutting hair. The price offered in some hairdressing rooms is even more outrageous: that one or two hundred yuan for washing hair or dying hair is very common now. But until now, Huang' s price is still only 10 yuan. Why not increase the price? Because most of the people who come to his stall are elderly or migrant workers, they are not that wealthy. With his retirement pay, there is no problem for him to keep alive. The reason why he does not want to put down the razor which he has hold for nearly 70 years is not just for the sake of making money, but for the sake of the accomplishment in the old age and the joy gained from it. As long as there is someone who can' t afford a hairdressing and needs him, if he is still strong enough, he' ll keep going with it.

The Innermost Words of the Craftsman

"There were no major events in my life. I have dealt with man' s head for tens of years.People are different from animals in that man know how to shave hair. Otherwise, they will be quite repulsive. Therefore, any one, no matter how poor he is, will regard shaving hair as the most important thing. In order to let people go outside decently, I' d like to be a honest barber until I can' t pick up the razor."

(Written by Tao Yangke, photographed by Feng Yue)

食艺
Food Processing Art
一夫／摄影
Yifu \ photo

榨油匠祝自发：
木榨声里的“流香岁月”

【老手艺项目】传统手工榨油

传统手工榨油（压榨法）是一种历史悠久的榨油方法，约始于汉代，早在北魏贾思勰的《齐民要术》中，就有压榨取油的记载。在元代的《王祯农书》、明代的《天工开物》中，都有木榨机和榨油方法的记载。北宋时期就已经出现大型的木榨机，后来慢慢形成了具有规模性的专业榨油作坊。木榨，是一种古老的榨油技艺，现如今木榨已成为一种文物，机器早已替代了古老的木榨，但它是中国劳动人民智慧的象征，在机器时代，我们必须保护传承这种古老技艺。

【匠人小传】

祝自发，现年 51 岁，在安徽宣城一个偏僻农村长大，家族世代以榨油为业。其父辈为远近闻名的榨油匠，一年四季走南闯北以榨油为生。因此，祝自发从十几岁跟随父亲在油坊做学徒，走村串户在木榨坊里谋生。20 世纪 80 年代后，榨油作坊的木榨机逐渐被机器榨油取代，农村也迎来传统工艺的萧条，祝自发只得去景区办的木榨油坊打工，才得以重拾起这个几乎要失传的手艺。

【匠心之路】

接过父亲手中的撞锤

祝师傅家族世代以榨油为业，父亲祝长江是当时村里远近闻名的老油匠，周边村庄常请他去建榨油作坊，然后留下传授榨油技艺。祝长江一生走南闯北，在许多村庄建过油榨坊，每走一个地方，都留下他精湛的技艺。20 世纪 70 年代末，他曾带着独子祝自发从安徽来到景德镇浮梁县，给偏僻的乡村建木榨油坊，在浮梁待了几年。

直到 2016 年，一个偶然的机遇，他走进了婺源篁岭景区，在景区内的古法榨油坊落脚。祝师傅说，他很感谢景区领导给了他施展一技之长的平台。他的想法就是在展示传统木榨油工艺的同时，可以保护和传承千年传统技艺。

木榨里流溢出醇香

榨油的工艺很复杂，从选籽、炒籽、磨粉、蒸粉、踩饼、上榨、插楔、撞榨到接油有十多道工序，全部靠手工完成。问起出油量的高低有什么诀窍，祝师傅说，年成好时收获的菜籽、芝麻出油会更高；炒籽要根据不同的原料掌握火候，火候不能过了也不能嫩了，比如山茶要炒嫩一点出油就多，花生稍老一点榨出的油更香；磨粉也很重要，磨得越细越好，出油率就越高；蒸粉也是一道很关键的程序，主要是为了让油菜籽粉充分吸收水分，增加黏度；蒸好的粉倒进垫了无纺布的圈中包起来，然后穿上草鞋将粉饼踩平，踩结实了才能拿起来，才能把它放进木榨的槽里。

接下来是最辛苦的环节——上榨。把踩好的粉饼装进木榨的凹槽，然后往榨荷里装进尖头的楔子。通过用榨锤用力击打，就可以不断挤进楔子压迫粉饼，榨出油了。

从稻草到布料：匠心之外见仁心

在祝师傅谈榨油操作过程时，笔者注意到他说包粉饼用的是无纺布，问起他为什么不像别人一样用稻草时，他道出了其中原委。他说："现在的稻草大多在生长期间用农药喷洒，稻草充分吸收了农药成分，我从来不用稻草包粉饼，而是改用无纺布，既避免了稻草中残留农药渗入到粉饼中，又节省了资源，稻草不能重复使用，而无纺布洗干净后下一次还可继续使用。"

【匠人心语】

在谈到古法榨油技艺的传承时，祝师傅颇为担忧。如今，很多地方的木榨都被效率更高更省力的电力榨油机取代，像这样的老榨坊几乎已绝迹。因为古法榨油费时费力，几乎没有年轻人会愿意吃这份苦，来学习这古老手艺，这门传统手工榨油技艺恐怕不久也将失传。目前他在这里所做的工作，就是在尽力保护与传承这门古老手艺，希望收一两个愿意干这一行的年轻人。

（蓝田玉撰文 / 摄影）

Zhu Zifa, an Oil Artisan: The Pleasant Time Flowed away with the Rhythem of Wood Striking

The Ancient Craft: Manufacturing Oil by Hand

Traditional manual oil extraction （pressing method） is a time-honored method of oil manufacturing, dating back to the Han Dynasty, which was recorded in "The Techniques Essental to Qi Nation" by Jia Sixie in Northern Wei Dynasty. The "Wang Zhen's Manuals for Farmers" in Yuan Dynasty and the "Heavenly Works" in Ming Dynasty also listed the method of pressing oil by wood. In the Northern Song Dynasty, there appeared large-sized wooden oil-pressing machines, which gradually developed into professional oil mills with certain scales. Pressing oil by wood is a kind of ancient techniques. Nowadays, the wooden oil-squeezing machine, which was replaced by the modern ones long before, has become a cultural relic. But it is the symbol of Chinese working people's wisdom. In the machine age, we must protect and inherit the ancient skills.

The Brief Biography of the Craftsman

Zhu Zifa, now 51 years old, grew up in a remote village in Xuancheng, Anhui province. All generations in his family regarded oil-pressing as the means of livelihood. His father was a well-known oil-pressing artisan. To earn a living, his family had to travel frequently. Zhu Zifa began learning the skill as he was still a teenager. Since the 1980s, the wooden oil-pressing machine was gradually replaced by the modern machine, which ushered the depression of traditional crafts in the rural areas. At last, Zhu Zifa had to work in the scenic spot, which enabled him to pick up the craft which was almost lost.

The Growth of the Craftsman

Taking over the Hammer from His Father

Zhu's ancestors all lived by pressing oil. His father Zhu Changjiang was a famous oil-pressing artisan in the village. The surrounding villagers often asked him to build the oil mill, and teach them the skill of squeezing oil. Zhu Changjiang travelled extensively in his life and built a large number of oil mills. Wherever he went, he would leave his exquisite skills there. In the late 1970s, he, together with his only son Zhu Zifa, came to Fuliang County of Jingdezhen, helped the local people to build a wooden oil mill, and didn't leave until several years later.

In 2016, Zhu, by accident, walked into the scenic spot of Huang Mountain in Wuyuan and settled down in the workshop of pressing oil by ancient methods. He said he was very grateful to the leaders of the scenic spot for giving him a platform to show his skills. His main idea was to preserve and pass on the traditional techniques of squeezing oil.

The Fragrance Flowing out of the Wooden Oil-squeezer

The process of extracting oil is very complicated. It needs ten or more procedures: selecting seeds, stir-frying seeds, grinding seeds, steaming seed-powder, pressing the oilcake, loading, inserting the wedges, hammering etc. All of them were done by hand. When asked for the tips to get more oil, Zhu said that it depends largely on the quality of the seed and sesame. However, there is one thing should be mentioned: when stir-frying seeds, the fire should be commanded according to the raw materials. If the raw material is camellia, the fire is not too strong, while if it is the peanut, the fire should be strong. Grinding seeds is also important, the finer the powder is, the higher the oilyield is. The powder-steaming is also a key procedure, the purpose of which is to allow rapeseed powder to absorb enough water so as to increase its viscosity. First, let the steamed powder be poured into a round vessel and wrap it; then put on a pair of straw shoes to stamp the powder until it is flat; and then when it gets hard enough, put it into the groove of the wooden squeezer.

And then there comes the hardest part—wedge-fixing and striking. Put the pressed-powder into the grooves of the wooden squeezer, and then insert the wedges into the squeezer. By punching hard with a hammer, you can squeeze the wedge and press the pancake, and the oil will be squeezed out.

From Straw to Cloth: Benevolence Can be Seen Beyond the Craftsmanship

While talking, we noticed that Zhu used non-wovens as the wrapper for the powdercake. When asked why not use the straws like others, Zhu let out to us his secret. He told us, "Most straw now will be sprayed on some pesticide during its growing period. Inevitably, the straw has absorbed fully the pesticide. So I use the non-wovens instead of the straws to pack the powdercake. Because the non-wovens can be used for many times and thus is resource-saving."

The Innermost Words of the Craftsman

When it comes to the inheritance of the ancient techniques of squeezing oil, Zhu is worried. Today, most wooden oil-squeezers have been replaced by the high efficient power-driven machine and the old mills of squeezing oil are practically extinct from today's society. As the old method wastes time and energy, there are no young people willing to take this hard work. And this traditional manual oil skill will be lost soon. His purpose of working here is just want to preserve and pass down the ancient craft, hoping to find some youngsters who want to pick it up.

(Written and photographed by Lan Tianyu)

制茶师江贵宝：
天祥茶号的传世绝艺

【老手艺项目】手工制茶

说起浮梁茶叶，不能不提天祥茶号及其辉耀百年的“浮梁祁红”。19 世纪中叶，谙熟祁红工艺的严台乡贤江流芳在这片钟灵毓秀的家园厚土，率领族人开发出 500 多亩高山茶园，并创立了自己的“天祥茶号”。由于天祥茶号出品的浮梁祁红（简称浮红）品质上乘，色香味俱佳，有口皆碑，很快闻名遐迩，供不应求。

【匠人小传】

天祥茶号及其以智慧和汗水铸造出来的浮梁祁红“1915”金字品牌，不仅是浮梁茶业的宝贵遗产，也是中国茶人的骄傲。有人听闻天祥茶号当年获得的“1915”金牌依然珍藏在第三代传人江贵宝手里，并且是迄今我

国保存完好的茶业界唯一一块1915巴拿马金牌实物，便悄悄找到他，愿以10多万元的高价购买，被深明大义的江贵宝先生严词拒绝。1989年8月，江贵宝先生在家人的支持下，将金牌交给了复县不久的浮梁县人民政府。为了表彰这一义薄云天的善举，浮梁县人民政府向江贵宝先生颁发了荣誉证书及4万元奖金，成为浮梁茶业和当地群众津津乐道的佳话。

【匠心之路】

钟灵毓秀的一方水土

在浮梁县群芳争艳的种种茶叶中，天祥茶号及其辉耀百年的"浮梁祁红"即是其中出类拔萃的金字品牌。严台的祁峰山为浮梁县与安徽祁门县闪里镇的交界，这里富含钾、钠、铁、镁、铜、锌等矿物质的土壤，特别适合种茶，因此种茶制茶盛行，自古以来，百姓以此为业，延续千年而不衰，严台由此成为世界三大高香茶之一"祁门香"珍品的核心产区。

独具特色的制茶工艺

中国制茶历史悠久，自发现野生茶树开始，从生煮羹饮到饼茶、散茶，从绿茶到各种茶类，从手工制茶到机械化制茶，其间经历了复杂的变革。茶类的品质特征的形成，除了受到茶树品种和鲜叶原料的影响外，加工条件和技艺是重要的决定因素。在手工制茶的过程中，以下一些步骤的细微变化与革新，都可能导致生产出色、香、味、形品质特征不同的浮梁祁红。

摘叶："浮梁祁红"的手工制作从摘叶开始就精益求精，要求茶叶采摘要选择良种茶园，按照统一的标准进行，通常在1芽1叶或1芽2叶初展时采。采摘时注意"四不采"，即不采雨水叶，不采病虫叶，不采紫色叶，不采瘦弱芽叶。采用提手采摘方法。采后挑拣大小均匀的鲜叶，及时薄摊在阴凉通风的地方晾6~8小时，当日制作。

杀青：在铁锅内进行。制前把锅壁磨光洗净。杀青时锅温先高后低，手掌心

距锅底 30 厘米左右有烫感时，投下叶片，每锅投鲜叶 400~500 克。刚下锅时，双手均匀翻炒，以焖为主。当感到叶子烫手并蒸发大量水分时，翻炒加快，以抛为主。要抛得高，撒得开，捞得净，使茶叶均匀受热，水分快速蒸发，避免焦边红叶。当叶质柔软，叶色变暗，清香扑鼻时，迅速将杀青叶取出，放入圆篾盘内抖散摊晾。

干燥：江贵宝不像一些茶叶公司那样利用干燥机以热风烘，而是采用自然风干，使其含水量低于百分之四，既利于贮藏运销，又保持了茶叶的原生态口味。

从传统手艺来看，江贵宝制茶更像是在制造一件艺术品，具有深厚的文化底蕴。传承见证的是几千年来的茶文化之馨香！

【匠人心语】

无论机器化生产技术多么发达，永远都无法掩盖手工制茶工艺的智慧之光；因为机器化生产提升的是茶叶生产的效率，而手工制茶倾注的是制茶人的匠心精神。

（惠风 / 撰文　江建鸿 / 摄影）

Jiang Guibao, a Tea Maker: Tea-making Stunts Unique to Tianxiang Tea Shop

The Ancient Craft: Hand Made Tea

The Ancient Craft: Hand Made Tea

Speaking of Fuliang tea, we must mention Tianxiang tea shop and Fuliang Qi which is famous for hundreds of years . The middle of the 19th century, Jiang Liufang from Yantai who is familiar with the skill of Qi led his clansmen developed more than 500 acres of mountain tea, and created their own brand called "Tianxiang tea" . Because of its excellent quality, color, scent and taste, the tea called "Fuliang Qi(Fu Red) " which was produced by Tianxiang tea shop was famous and in short supply.

The Brief Biography of the Craftsman

Tianxiang tea shop and its 1915 gold brand of Fuliang Qi, is not only the precious heritage of Fuliang tea industry, is also Chinese pride. Someone heard that 1915 gold medal was still enshrined in the third generation Jiang Guibao' s hand, it is the only physical good of 1915 gold medal in tea industry of China, then that man quietly found him and wanted to pay a high price of about 100000 yuan, Mr. Jiang Guibao strictly refused. In August in 1989, Mr. Jiang Guibao, under the support of his family, handed over the gold medal to the Fuliang County People' s Government. In order to commend the righteous spirit of charity, the Fuliang County People' s Government issued a certificate and a bonus about 40 thousand yuan to Mr. Jiang Guibao, it became a good story which is always talked about by the Fuliang tea industry and the local people.

The Growth of the Craftsman

A Region Endowed With Natural Resources

In all kinds of tea in Fuliang County, Tianxiang tea and "Fuliang Qi" is one of the outstanding landmark and gold brand. Qifeng Mountain of Yantai is the junction between Shanli town of Fuliang county and Anhui Qimen County, here is rich in potassium, sodium, iron, magnesium, copper, zinc and other minerals in the soil, especially suitable for tea planting, so planting tea and making tea is popular here. Since the ancient times, people make a living by tea and the industry continued for thousands of years without failure. Yantai became one of the core areas Qimen tea which is one of the three high-fragrance tea in the world.

Special Tea Making Process

Chinese tea has a long history. Since its discovery, from the methods of making to the external patterns, from green tea to various kinds of tea, from hand-made tea to mechanized tea making, all changed greatly. The quality, feature and form are affected by the type of tea trees, material, processing condition and skill. In the making process of hand-made tea, the subtle change and innovation of the following steps may led the production of different Fuliang Qi whose color, fragrance, taste and shape are diverse.

Leaf picking: the making of "Fuliang Qi" has a very high requirement from the beginning of leaf picking. The tea picking should be conducted in the great tea garden for picking tea to choose varieties of tea, according to the unified standard, usually the tea leaves are picked off when its 2 or 3 tender leaves come out. When picking, we should pay attention to "four non harvest", that is, not to pick up the rainy leaves, not to pick up the leaves of the diseases and insects, and not to pick up the purple leaves, and not to pick up the thin and weak buds. Use the hand picking method. Picking out the uniform fresh leaves, then timely spread the leaves in a cool and ventilated place to dry for 6 to 8 hours, the production should be finished on the same day.

Stir-frying: it is finished in the iron pot. Wash the wall of the pot before making it. The temperature of the pot is high first and low later. The palms feel the hot feeling at the place which are 30 centimeters away from the bottom of the pot. The leaves are thrown into the pot, there are 400 to 500 grams of fresh leaves in each pot. Stir-frying your hands evenly and stewing is the main method. When the leaf is hot and a lot of water evaporates, Stir-frying quickly and throwing is the main method. It should be thrown high, spread out, and get clean, so that the tea is evenly heated, the water evaporates quickly to avoid the leaves to be adust. When the leaves get soft, darken and fragrant, quickly carry them out, and put them into the round bamboo plate and shake them around to let them get cool.

Drying: Some tea companies use the dryer to dry the leaves with hot air, but Jiang uses natural air drying to make its water content less than four percent, which is good for storage and marketing, and is also good for keeping the original taste of tea.

Jiang makes tea just like making a piece of art and it has a profound cultural background, inherit and witness the sweet smell of tea culture for thousands of years!

The Innermost Words of the Craftsman

No matter how advanced machine production technology, light of wisdom in the handmade tea process can never be covered, because the machine production enhances the efficiency of tea production, while the workers of hand-made tea devote themselves to the tea with the great spirit.

(Written by Hui Feng, photographed by Jiang Jianhong)

水酒酿造师廖金水：
百年水酒香再飘

【老手艺项目】百年水酒

水酒就是用糯米蒸熟后拌上酒曲发酵酿制的糯米酒，江西老表们习惯管它叫“水酒”。在物资匮乏的年代，每年入冬后，家里的老人们就开始做米酒了，准备年节喜庆时喝，而平时爱喝几口水酒的汉子们，只有去街头巷尾寻个水酒店一解酒瘾。20世纪七八十年代，水酒店这门营生在景德镇进入鼎盛时期，光是十八桥、戴家弄两地就汇集了十多家水酒店，古老的水酒酿造技艺随之又发展下去。

【匠人小传】

廖金水，65岁，一个几代靠酿酒开水酒店生存的手艺人，自解放初随做水酒为生的父亲来到景德镇，之后一直在景德

镇经营家族水酒店，当年在水酒行业被同行尊为行业老大，廖家的水酒店在戴家弄是妇孺皆知，酒客盈门。

【匠心之路】

底层百姓的“休闲会所”

廖金水自 70 年代末就接过父亲的水酒铺独撑门面，水酒铺在当时的戴家弄街口。说起几十年前的水酒营生，廖金水如数家珍，一一道来。

当时百姓家都不富裕，家里要是有个好喝几口的就得奔离家近点的水酒店解解酒馋，当时一斤水酒一毛两分钱，水酒馆只供应凉菜，通常是兰花豆、豆腐干、炸花生米、油麻花等，一小碟才 5 分钱。上店里来的多是最底层的劳动人民，窑巴佬、拉板车的、杀猪卖肉的。有些熟客到月底给不出酒钱了，通常先赊账，等发工资了再补上。廖金水说，令他记忆尤深的是一个经常来店里拉板车的汉子，每天 7 点钟店门一开，他必定第一个闯进店，仰脖喝上一碗酒再出工，有时连小碟下酒菜都免了。

酿好酒全凭经验

谈到酿酒的技术，廖金水随口说出 8 个字来：发面做酒，不充老手。再好的酿酒师傅，也会偶尔有失手的时候，追问原因，廖师傅道出了酿酒的关键所在——

水酒的酿造程序其实很简单，做水酒要想酒水出得多，就选陈糯米，新糯米做酒糟好。糯米在水中浸 2~3 小时，用清水冲净滤干盛入饭甑用大火蒸。蒸饭的火候很重要，俗语说得好，做酒的是徒弟，蒸饭的是师傅。糯米蒸得太透了，做出的水酒会混沌不清；没蒸熟的米饭又不会发酵。

饭甑端下后，用凉开水冷却，当饭甑底部漏出来的水不烫手后，然后将略有余温的米饭和酒药充分搅拌（酒药要根据米的多少配料），倒入大缸中发酵。廖金水说，整个过程对温度的把握也是酿好酒的关键，一般 38℃至 39℃酿出来的

米酒口感最好，温度过高会发酸，夏天正常温度下，一般放3~4天米酒就发酵完成，冬天可以生火加热。廖师傅还说起旧时酿酒作坊的诸多规矩，闲杂人等不准进入，尤其是女人更不得入内，“酒娘子”是随便得罪不起的，否则一缸酒就坏了。

好的米酒，开坛即有香味，一坛米酒做成功了，还需“滤酒”，就是将酒糟滤出。要用干净凉开水过滤酒糟，过滤后的酒就是“水酒”，最后将其装入酒缸中出售给顾客。有的人喜欢喝原酒浆，我们这叫“玉兰酒”，即从开坛之时，从坛里取出没有加水、由原酒浆酿成的酒。玉兰酒味道极好，是水酒中的上品，价格也卖得高。

【匠人心语】

无论社会如何发展，底层的消费者都存在。水酒铺不仅满足了普通工薪底层消费者的低消费要求，也为他们提供了更为健康的饮酒方式。这是纯正的糯米酿造的粮食酒，不含伤害身体的酒精，适量喝点水酒有益健康，希望自己的百年水酒铺成为瓷都人民最乐意光顾的小酒店。

（蓝田玉 / 撰文　余琳超 / 摄影）

Liao Jinshui,a Rice Wine Brewmaster: The Rice Wine Aroma Lingers on for Hundreds of Years

The Ancient Craft: Hundred-Year-Long Watery Wine

Watery wine is made out of the steamed glutinous rice blended with distiller' s yeast after fermentation, and people in Jiangxi all conventionally call it watery wine. In the years when the substance was in shortage, the old people would make watery wine in each winter to prepare it for drinking at the celebrations for the Spring Festival, while the men who liked drinking the watery wine would look for a watery wine restaurant to satisfy their craving for the wine. Between the 1970s and 1980s, the business of the watery wine was in its prime period in Jingdezhen, and there were more than ten watery wine restaurants just in the area of Eighteen Bridges and Daijia Lane, so the ancient technology of brewing watery wine was moving forward.

The Brief Biography of the Craftsman

Liao Jinshui, 65 years old, is a craftsman living on running watery wine restaurant for past several generations. In the early years after the Liberation, he came to Jingdezhen with his father who also lived on brewing watery wine and ran his restaurant here all the time, and he was honored by peers as the head of this industry. Liao' s watery wine restaurant in Daijia Lane is well-known even to the women and children, so it' s often full of the drinkers.

The Growth of the Craftsman

The Recreation Club for the Underprivileged People

Liao Jinshui took over the watery wine restaurant alone from his father since the end of the 1970s, and the restaurant was located in the street corner of Daijia Lane. Referred to the operation of the watery wine in the past tens of years, Liao was very familiar with the subject and elaborated on it.

At that time, the common people were not affluent, and the people with the habit of drinking wine in the family would run to the watery wine restaurants in neighborhood to satisfy their craving. The watery wine per 0.5kg was priced at 0.12 yuan then, and the restaurant only offered the cold dishes such as diced bean, dried bean curd, fried peanuts, fried dough twist and etc. which were all at the price of 5 cents.

Most of the customers coming to the restaurants were the labors living at the bottom of the society, such as the workers in the kilns, handcart carriers, butchers and etc. Some of the frequent customers couldn't pay for the wine, so they would buy on credit and pay off when getting wages at the end of the month. He said what was the most impressive in the memory was a handcart carrier who must be the first to burst into his shop for a big bowl of watery wine before going to work once his shop was opened at 7:00am every day, and sometimes he didn't even need the dishes for the wine.

Brewing out the Good Wine Utterly by Virtue of Rich Experience

Referred to the skill for making watery wine, Liao spoke out without thinking that it's better not to pretend to be a sophisticated master when leavening dough. No matter how skilled the master was, he would have the chance to fail, and when chased for the reason, Liao revealed the key to brew the watery wine lied.

The procedure to brewing the watery wine was quite simple, if more wine was expected, then the stocked glutinous rice should be used, and the new rice was more suitable for making vinasse. After the glutinous rice was immersed in water for 2 to 3 hours, it should be rinsed, drained and then put into the steamer to be steamed with high heat. The duration and degree of heating is crucial to steaming rice, as the old saying went that it was the apprentice to make wine but the master to steam rice. If the glutinous rice was over steamed, the watery wine would be turbid, but rice wouldn't ferment if it was less steamed.

After the steamer was taken off, it should be cooled down by the cold water, when the water dripped from the steamer bottom was not so hot, the rice remaining kind of warm would be adequately stirred with yeast whose content was determined by the quantity of the rice, then the rice would be poured into a big vat for fermentation. Liao said the control of the temperature in the whole process was also a key to brewing the good wine, and the watery wine was the most tasteful if it was brewed at the temperature of 38℃ to 39℃, otherwise, the wine would be sour if the temperature was too high. At the normal temperature in summer, it would take 3 to 4 days to ferment the watery wine, and in winter, it could be heated by fire. Master Liao said there were lots of rules in the wine workshop in the old times, miscellaneous people without duty and women in particular were prohibited to enter, as the "Wine Lady" couldn't be offended at random, or else the whole vat of wine would go bad.

The good wine could be smelt once the vat was opened, and filtration was also essential for making a vat of good watery wine, which was filtrating out the vinasse. The vinasse was filtrated by the clean cold water, and the liquid after the filtration was the watery wine, which was eventually poured into the wine jar for sales to the customers. Someone liked the original wine syrup, and we called it "Magnolia Wine" here which was the pure wine syrup taken out from the vat without adding any water. Such wine tasted pretty good, and it was the top grade of the watery wine which was sold at high prices.

The Innermost Words of the Craftsman

No matter how the society develops, there will be the consumers at the bottom of the society. The watery wine restaurant doesn't only satisfy the common salariat and bottom consumers' low consuming demand, but also offers them a healthier drinking way. This is the pure grain wine brewed out of the glutinous rice, so it doesn't contain any harmful alcohol, and it is good for health to drink moderate watery wine. He hoped that his hundred-year-long watery wine shop could be the restaurant for people in Jingdezhen to patronize willingly.

(Written by Lan Tianyu, photographed by Yu Linchao)

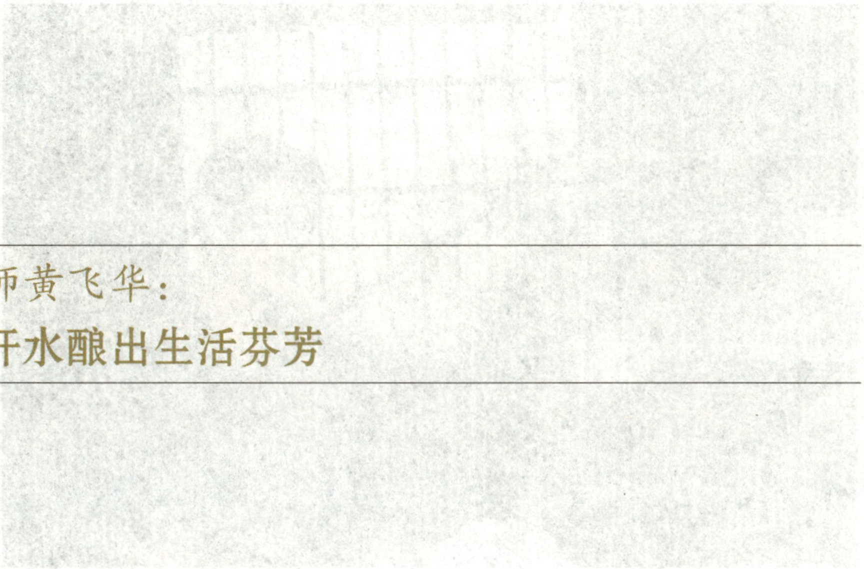

吊酒师黄飞华：
苦涩汗水酿出生活芬芳

【老手艺项目】民间酿酒

酒在中国已有五六千年的历史，与中华文明的发展同步。酿酒，是农村人家年年都要做的重要事情。小灶酿酒是一种酿酒方法，也是前人智慧的结晶，酿酒要提前发酵好酒酿，然后拿到酒甑子上利用蒸馏的方法得到白酒。

景德镇农村不少地方还在传承着小灶酿酒的技术。小灶酿制的酒俗称小灶酒，多用五谷杂粮酿造，它口感更好，更纯正，一般为酿酒者自己饮用或者待客。

【匠人小传】

黄飞华师傅从20多岁就开始酿酒，这祖传的手艺是从他爷爷那辈传下来的。走近三龙乡这处位于山里的酿酒作坊，闻到的不是老屋常有的霉味，而是佳酿特有的醇香。今年46岁的黄师傅祖上就靠酿酒谋生。

在景德镇的老酿酒艺人之间流传着一首《烧酒歌》：“火烤胸前热，风吹背后寒。只知饮酒乐，哪知酿酒难。”它便真实地道出了酿酒师傅们的艰辛。传统的酿造工艺，让黄师傅格外珍视酿出的每一滴纯酿。

【匠心之路】

坚守：只为酿一灶好酒

说起祖传的酿酒工艺，黄师傅头头是道，俨然是一位经验丰富的“酿酒师”。黄师傅说，刚开始他用谷子酿酒，但谷酒喝多了会“打脑”，也就是喝多了会头痛。后来他就用麦子酿酒。麦酒不“打脑”，喝了也不会口干。

黄师傅告诉笔者，自己的小灶酿酒靠的主要是气候和祖传的工艺。“俗话说‘气候是做酒的师傅’，气温高、气温低都不适宜调酒，还有就是气候变温的时候也不能调酒。酿造白酒的最好时间是秋冬和早春季节，其他时间都不适合制酒。100 斤麦子可以酿出 20~30 斤的酒。酒渣用来养猪，我养了好几十头香猪。”黄师傅开心地笑了起来。

“现在我一年可以酿造 10000 斤左右的白酒。酒酿好后，一般要等到半年以后才可以喝，酒还是陈的香嘛。”黄师傅高兴地说。

工序：传统酿酒保生态酒质

在黄师傅的酿酒作坊里，一口土灶显得很注目，上面倒扣着一只大木桶，里面被倒进了约 30 斤麦糟。在烧火之前先将木桶的四周用细纱布密封好，这样就可以点灶火。

随着灶火渐渐旺起来，木桶里装满的麦糟逐渐往下沉。然后在麦糟上放用细绳绑好的长方形木片，让其漂浮在麦糟上，这主要是起引导器的作用，下端与一根铁管相连，通向木桶之外。

当木桶里的水达到一定温度，就在木桶的上面盖一个铁皮锅，木桶上面有很大空间，用于注入冷水冷却用的。水是起循环作用，底下是蒸汽。当上面注入的冷水温度过高了，就必须放掉，再注入冷水，有助于酒蒸气的冷却。

蒸馏，是制酒的最后一道工序。黄师傅说，这种方法自古以来就在用，酒精的沸点是 80 度左右，水的沸点在 100 度，当下面加热，蒸汽在锅盖穹顶徘徊，遇到上面的冷水冷却，形成液体，就是酒。

【匠人心语】

“现在的人对酒的理解不是‘勾兑’就是‘小烧’，早没有传统酒的记忆了。”黄师傅不无感慨地说，“酿酒很磨人，酿酒时要时时刻刻看着，看火候、看蒸汽、看出酒，也就是一定要专心。”

（黄辉撰文 / 摄影）

Huang Feihua, a Brewmaster of Chinese Liquor: A Fragrance of Life Brewed out from the Bitter and Sweat

The Ancient Craft: Wine Brewing in the Folk

The wine has a history as long as more than 5000 years in China, and it synchronously develops along with the Chinese civilization. Wine brewing is an important thing for each family in the countryside every year. Making wine on the small hearth is a brewing way, and is also the valuable outcome of ancestors' wisdoms. The fermented glutinous rice needs to be prepared in advance, and then it is placed onto the bamboo steamers to get the white spirit by distillation.

The skill to brew wine on the small hearth is still inherited in many places in the countryside of Jingdezhen. The wine made on the small hearth is named after its technology, and mainly made out of miscellaneous grains, so it tastes better and purer, and the maker usually retains it for drinking himself or entertains the guests.

The Brief Biography of the Craftsman

Master Huang Feihua started to make wines from the age of 20, and the ancestral skill was inherited from his grandfather. When approaching the winemaking workshop located in the hill scent of Sanlong Village, the writer didn't smell the musty odor of the old house as usual, but the mellow scent of the vintage wine. The ancestors of Master Huang at the age of 46 this year lived on making wines.

There was a song named "white spirit song" prevailed among the ancient winemakers in Jingdezhen, and the lyrics were "The fire burned the chest hot, and the wind blew the back coldly. People only enjoyed drinking wine, but they never knew the difficulty of making wine", which truly revealed the hardship of the winemakers. So Master Huang cherished every single drop of the pure spirit made through the traditional winemaking technology in particular.

The Growth of the Craftsman

Persist Just for Brewing a Steamer of Vintage Wine

Referred to the ancestral skill to brewing wine, Master Huang was clear and logical, who deserved his career as a veteran winemaker. Master Huang said that he used the unhusked rice to brew wine at the beginning, while people would get headache if they drank too much cereal wine. Later he switched to make wine out of the wheat. The wheat wine won't make people feel headache and thirsty after drinking.

Master Huang told the writer that his wine made on the small hearth depended mainly on the climate and the ancestral technology. "It's inappropriate to brew wine if the temperature is either high or low, so is it when the climate gets warm. As the old saying goes, the climate is the master of making wine. The best time to make white spirit is fall, winter and early spring, and it's not suitable in other time. 50 kilos of wheats could brew out 10 to 15 kilos of wine. Then the wine residue could breed the pigs, and I bred tens of pigs in this way." Master Huang laughed delightfully and said.

"Now the annual output from my wine workshop is around 5000 kilos. After the wine is brewed out, it will be stored for half a year before drinking, because the longer the wine is in cellar, the more aromatic it will be." Master Huang said happily.

Assure the Ecological Wine Quality by Following the Traditional Winemaking Process

In Master Huang's wine workshop, a mud hearth was very attractive, and it was covered by a wooden bucket inversely in which around 15 kilos of wheat was poured. Before firing, the surrounding of the bucket would be sealed by the gauze, and then the hearth could be ignited.

As the fire inside burned up gradually, the wheat inside the bucket slowly went down. Then he placed a rectangle hub bound with a thread and let it float on the wheat, the main function of the hub was like a trigger. The other end of the thread was connected to an iron pipe which led to the outside of the bucket.

When the temperature of the water inside the wooden bucket reached up to a certain degree, an iron wok would be put onto the top of the bucket and cover it, and it was spacious above the bucket, which was used to pour the cold water for cooling down. The water was in circulation and the vapor was underneath. When the temperature of the poured-in water above was over high, it must be drained, and pour the cold water again, which was helpful for cooling down the vapor of the wine.

It was the last process to use the bamboo steamer for distilling. Master Huang said such a method has been used since the ancient times. The boiling point is 80℃ for alcohol while it is 100℃ for water. The vapor wandered along the dome of the pot cover when it was heated underneath, the vapor cooled down after contacting the cold water above and turned into liquid, which was the wine.

The Innermost Words of the Craftsman

"In modern people's mind, the wine stands for either the blending wine or the regular wine with 56% alcoholic density, and the memory of the traditional wine has vanished for long." Master Huang said with emotion, "Winemaking is very torturing, as you need to keep a close eye on it every second to watch the fire, the steam, the wine flown out, and you must be concentrating on it."

(Written and photographed by Huang Hui)

“豆腐西施”章茶凤：踏实做事清白做人

【老手艺项目】做豆腐

景德镇的豆腐坊，有着悠久的历史。据史料记载：解放前有70多家，大多开在街头弄尾，如河西老街上、三间庙，河东上自四图里，下到小港嘴等地，开豆腐坊都是夫妻一起做。这是一个辛苦行业，半夜叫天光，十分劳累。

【匠人小传】

“世上三般苦，撑船、打铁、磨豆腐。”这是流传在景德镇的一句老话。家住罗家茶叶四队的章茶凤就是一名磨豆腐的手艺人。在她的作坊里，有一台年纪和她相仿的石磨。这台有50多年历史的石磨，竟然是她出嫁时娘家陪的嫁妆。据了解，章茶凤祖上包括爷爷奶奶和父母都曾开过豆腐

坊。章茶凤嫁到茶叶四队后，就在家里开起了豆腐坊，跟丈夫一起干起了祖辈的老行当，这一干就是 20 多年。

【匠心之路】

传承：章茶凤家三代开豆腐坊

今年 50 多岁的章茶凤是峙滩人，祖传三代都开豆腐作坊，她 20 岁不到就学了一手磨豆腐的好手艺，嫁到茶叶四队后就与丈夫一起在家里开起了豆腐作坊。

章茶凤与街坊四邻的关系特别好。作坊里的豆腐渣，一直免费供街坊中喜欢吃的人带回去摆弄着吃，多余的就用它喂牛或猪。豆腐浆给大家用来洗脏衣服，去灰去油效果好，比肥皂、洗衣粉还好用。尤其冬天临近年关的时候，村里家家为过年焕然一新，都要集中洗衣，滴水成冰的冷天里，豆腐浆还是热的——章茶凤的豆腐作坊，就成了妇女们的热闹处，自然也成了孩子们的乐园。

开豆腐作坊要起早贪黑，十分辛苦，下午 5 点多就要泡豆子，做豆腐一直要干到第二天凌晨，一般上午到集市卖豆腐，下午在家中睡个回笼觉。一年下来，虽然发不了财，但温饱是不成问题的。她也担心，总会有一天磨不动，想把自己的这门老手艺传承给更多的人，特别是年轻人。原本指望儿子能接他们的班，但是又不太愿意儿子干这种苦活累活。

手磨豆腐比机器做的口感更好

章茶凤表示，手工豆浆做出来的豆腐口感较粗，吃起来更有质感，只是现在都是高科技，手工太费事，没有机器快捷。磨豆腐又是非常辛苦的活。“就是要能吃苦，以前做豆腐凌晨两三点就要起来，做好了豆腐去卖。现在是下午 5 点多泡黄豆，要忙到凌晨。”

她向笔者简要介绍了传统做豆腐的技艺：将干黄豆分批倒进一台土砻中碾压脱壳，再让脱干净壳的黄豆片在清水中浸泡四五个小时；然后用人力转动一台石磨，伴和着清水将黄豆片磨成豆浆，通常由 2 人操作，即一人用一支砻臂不停地转动石磨，一人负责加黄豆和水；之后用一个密实的面粉袋装上豆浆，然后用力将浆液挤出；再将纯豆浆倒进一个大鼎，经煮沸后装进一个按比例配以石膏水的木桶里，并用一支木桨搅匀，然后让其冷却凝结；最后是加压成形：取几块长约 60×60×4 厘米的槽形木板，板面呈方格状，并各垫上一块白布，然后用葫芦瓢将已凝结的豆腐花舀到几块木板槽里，用槽里的白布盖住，再压上一块木板和石头，以减少含水量并成形。一个多小时后，搬开石头和木板并将其反转过来，除去白布，一板乳白色呈方格状的豆腐便新鲜出炉了。

【匠人心语】

“做豆腐跟做人一样，要实在，最关键的是用心！”谈起自己的卖豆腐经，章茶凤正色说道，“人在做，天在看，我一直觉得，无论做什么都要对得起自己的良心，在做豆腐上，我也一直这么要求我自己。”

几十年来，章茶凤跟丈夫每天起早磨豆腐。诚然，豆腐在清寡中暗含了某种精神层面的气质，古人称赞豆腐有“和德”，吃豆腐的人能安于清贫，而做豆腐的人当然也懂得“顺其自然”。

（黄辉 / 撰文　丰月 / 摄影）

Zhang Chafeng, a Beautiful Tofu Maker: Honest in Work and Clean in Life

The Ancient Craft: Making Tofu

Jingdezhen' s tofu (bean curd) shop has a long history. According to historical records: there are more than 70 such shops before liberation. Most of them were located at the ends of the lanes. Generally, it was run by a couple. Tofu making is a hard work and it is very tiring.

The Brief Biography of the Craftsman

"There are three tough businesses in the world: boating, ironing and tofu making." this is an old saying circulating in the past Jingdezhen. Zhang Chafeng is such a craftman of making tofu. In her workshop, there is a millstone about her age, which was actually her dowry. The stone mill has a history of over 50 years. According to Zhang, her ancestors including her parents and grandparents had ever had a tofu shop. So when she was married, she inherited from her ancestors the technology and set up a tofu shop in her home. Till now she has been in this career with her husband for more than 20 years.

The Growth of the Craftsman

Inheriting: Three Generations in Zhang' s Family have ever Opened Tofu Workshops

Zhang Chafeng is now over 50 years old. Her hometown is Zhitan. Three generations above her run the tofu business. She grasped the skills when she was still younger than 20. Therefore, since she was married, she opened a tofu workshop in her home with her husband.

Zhang Chafeng got along very well with her neighbors. The tofukasu in her workshop was always free for her neighbors who liked eating, and the rest was used to feed her cows or pigs. Tofu slurry was also offered free for those needing to wash dirty clothes. As it' s known, it works even better than the soap and washing powder. When the new year was impending, wifes would get together for washing. At this moment, it was always so cold, and the water in the river is chilly. The tofu slurry in Zhang' s workshop, however, was warm and hot, so her workshop often became the wives' meeting place, and then the paradise of the children.

Tofu business was very tiring, which needed getting up very early and working very late. At about 5 p.m. every day, she had to begin soaking beans. The process of making tofu was usually continued to the next ealy morning. In the next morning, she still had to be in the market selling y tofu, so she could only have time for a rest in the afternoon. The profit a year couldn't get her quite rich, but it was sufficient to support a family. She was worried that one day she would get too old and have no strength to grind the beans. She wants to pass on her skills and techniques to more people, especially the young. She had wanted her son to pick it up, but disappointedly, her son can't endure the hard work.

Hand-made Tofu Tastes Better Than the Machine-made

According to zhang, hand-made tofu is more rough and so gives more textured feel. The manual work is laborous and time-consuming than the high-tech equipments. Grinding beans and making tofu is quite toilsome work. "To make tofu," Zhang said, "you have to endure the hardship, getting up at 2 to 3 in the early morning; after your tofu is finished, you have to sell it in the market; in the afternoon, you have to soak your beans at 5p.m. and then work continuously into the deep night."

She gave a brief introduction to the art of making tofu: first pour dried beans into a huller for removing the shell, and then soak the unshelled beanslices for four to five hours in water, and next turn the millstone to grind the beanslices into soyabean milk. During this procedure, two persons are needed: one turns the millstone and the other adds water.

After that, get the soyabean milk into a flour bag and squeeze the bag for seriflux; pour the seriflux in a large tripod and boil it; when the seriflux is boiling, put it in a wooden bucket proportioned with gypsum water and mix it with a wooden paddle, then let it cool and coagulate.

The final step of tofu making is shaping. In this step, you need a groove-shaped container, which should has a flat and square bottom. First, line the bottom with a piece of white cloth. Second, scoop up the coagulated beancurd jelly into the container and cover it with the white cloth. Third, place over the jelly a plank to reduce the water content, or sometimes add a stone over the plank. About one hour later, remove the stone and plank and turn over the container and take off the cloth, a sheet of ivory-white square-shaped tofu is finished.

The Innermost Words of the Craftsman

"Making tofu is the same as being a human. The most important thing is to be careful!" Zhang Chafeng said seriousy when speaking of her experience of selling tofu, "While we are doing, the god above is watching. So I always hold whaterver we do should be done out of conscience. That is the principle I always sick to in making and selling my tofu."

For decades, Zhang and her husband have been making tofu every day. Obviously, Tofu now, though not so profitable, has got something spiritual. The ancients said tofu indicated "harmony and virtue", and those who liked eating tofu could stand deprivation and poverty. So those who make tofu should know how to go with the flow and let the nature take its course.

(Written by Huang Hui, photographed by Feng Yue)

养蜂人汪长成：为谁辛苦为谁甜

【老手艺项目】养蜂

养蜂即蜜蜂养殖，是人工饲养蜜蜂而取其产品（如蜂蜜、蜂王浆、蜂胶、花粉、蜂蜡、蜂蛹及蜂毒等）的事业，包括在广义的畜产内，所以广义地说蜜蜂也是家畜。蜜蜂养殖的历史有数千年之久，蜂蜜的利用是从渔猎时代开始的。

【匠人小传】

61 岁的养蜂人汪长成，小时候最喜欢吃蜜糖，自然对蜜蜂很喜欢。放学后，经常跑到哥哥汪长水家，近距离地观看蜜蜂从蜂桶里进进出出，这时候是他最开心的时候。当地有一种说法，蜜蜂养得多的人家，运气好。他家养蜜蜂，纯属偶然。2000 年，那时他哥哥年纪已大，见他特别喜欢蜜蜂，就把自己家的 10 桶蜜蜂全都转让给了他。现今，他家蜜蜂已经发展到30多桶，成了当地有名的土蜜蜂养殖户。

【匠心之路】

摸索：积累了丰富的养蜂经验

接手哥哥的10桶蜜蜂后，汪长成如获至宝，自然欢喜得不得了。除了吃饭睡觉，他一门心思琢磨着如何养蜂。天长日久，汪长成积累了丰富的养蜂经验。观察蜜蜂傍晚收工的早迟，他能推断次日的天气。如果太阳落山后，蜜蜂收工了，说明第二天天气晴好；如果天黑了，蜜蜂还飞进飞出，忙个不停，说明第二天要下雨。

时间长了，他对乱哄哄的蜂群渐渐熟悉了。一个蜜蜂群体有几千到几万只蜜蜂，由一只蜂王、少量的雄蜂和众多的工蜂组成。蜂群中，蜂王虽然被称为“王”，但它实际上并不领导蜂群，它在蜂群中的作用就是繁衍后代，蜂群中大部分的蜜蜂都是它的后代。在春季繁殖高峰时，一只蜂王每天会产卵2000多个——总的重量甚至超过了它的体重。工蜂会时刻围绕在蜂王的周围，像“侍者”一样照应它的需求，比如提供食物、清理垃圾等。蜂王是生殖器官发育完全的雌蜜蜂，由受精卵发育而成。通常每个蜂群蜂王只有1只，体较工蜂长1/3，腹部较长，末端有螯针，翅仅覆盖腹部的一半。蜂王在不同的生理状态，其释放的蜂王信息成分及含量明显不同。足不如工蜂粗壮，后足无花粉框，有吸引蜜蜂的作用。蜂王的寿命有4~6年，而普通蜜蜂的寿命一般才60天。

蜜蜂是很勤劳的小生灵，只要花开，天气晴好，每天天不亮就外出采花粉蜜。在高峰期，经常人还没有起床，蜜蜂就已经在花丛中“嘤嘤嗡嗡”地忙开了。蜜蜂每次在花上吸饱一肚子花粉蜜后，就飞回蜂巢，把花粉蜜吐在蜂脾正六角的孔里。晚上，蜜蜂用翅膀扇风，使蜂蜜里的水分蒸发，慢慢变稠。当蜂房中的蜂蜜贮满后，蜜蜂就用蜂蜡封住，叫封盖糖，以备过冬。这时，有经验的养蜂人没等蜜蜂把蜂蜜封住，就开始取蜜。

为了加快新陈代谢，汪长成要培养新蜂王，代替老蜂王。在天气晴好的日子，他将培养好的新王——处女王快速放飞高空，大量的雄蜂尾随而去，只有飞得最

快的雄蜂追上处女王，在离地三十米的高空交配，可谓“浪漫的婚礼”。交配结束，雄蜂完成使命，数分钟后自行死亡。交配后的处女王就会产卵，叫新王，以替代产卵量不大的老王。蜂王一辈子专门产卵，繁殖后代。在高峰期，蜂王一夜之间所产卵的重量，甚至超过自身体重。

每当三、四月份，正是蜂群分桶的季节。这时蜂群经常从蜂桶里飞出来，顿时漫天飞舞，这是他最开心的事。只见他不慌不忙地拿来早准备好的竹曾皮，走在蜂群的前面，这时黑褐色的蜂群很听话地停在竹曾皮里，密密麻麻，层层叠叠。这时候，他用布带把竹曾皮罩住。到了晚上，他才手持蜂脾，慢慢地凑了上去，引导蜂王到蜂脾，再放回蜂箱。工蜂看到蜂王已回蜂箱，就自然回到蜂桶。

养蜂：这碗饭不好吃

养蜂人不光要靠技术，还要靠运气，看天吃饭。有一年两个多月天天下雨，不仅采不到蜜，没有蜜糖，还买了几百斤白糖喂养蜜蜂，折掉老本。

养蜂这碗饭不好吃，蕴含着许多看不见的风险。有一年夏天，摆在房前屋后的蜜蜂从蜂桶口进进出出，煞是热闹。想不到，有人在稻田里、菜地里喷了农药。不久，看到蜂桶口到处都是因为农药中毒身亡的蜜蜂，他伤心不已。

取蜜：也是一种技术活

取蜜一般在晚上进行。这时汪长成戴着面纱，裹住头部和胸部，看起来有些滑稽。即便如此，他还时常被蜜蜂蜇伤，脸部肿得像馒头发糕一样，眼睛眯得只剩一条缝。他说：“蜜蜂一般不蜇人，因为它一蜇人，自己也死了。”

看他取蜜是一种享受。先把蜂桶翻开朝上，在上面放一个竹曾皮，在竹曾皮的底部涂上少许蜂蜜；用小木棍轻轻地敲打下面的蜂桶，密密麻麻的蜜蜂就会爬进竹曾皮；这时用竹枝叶把剩余的蜜蜂刷干净；然后割下一扇扇蜂蜜，放进桶里掏成蜜糖浆，在竹筛子上放一层白纱布，然后把蜜糖浆瓢上去，黄澄澄的蜂蜜就从白纱布滴在下面的大盆里。

诚信：甜蜜的事业要诚心去做

勤劳的工蜂担负着采蜜、酿蜜、侦察、守卫、清洁、筑巢以及照顾蜂王和饲养幼蜂的工作，甚至还会给蜂王“按摩”，疏松筋骨。蜂王从小吃蜂王浆长大，一辈子养尊处优，至少能活五年；而一辈子勤勤恳恳、辛勤采蜜的工蜂，寿命只有两三个月，如果在盛花期，因为劳累过度，往往只能活十来天。难怪唐代诗人罗隐这样咏蜂：“采得百花成蜜后，为谁辛苦为谁甜？”

汪长成养蜜蜂卖蜜糖，从不弄虚作假，掺白糖进去；取过蜜糖的糖渣从不下锅熬第二次糖，以次充好。他家的蜜糖是黄澄澄的，用玻璃瓶装好，放在阴凉的地方 5 年都不会变质。他儿子在新疆当兵，退伍后留在新疆工作。他每次去探望儿子，都要带上几瓶蜜糖，因为他儿子最喜欢自家的蜜糖。他儿子说：“吃了自家的蜜糖，在新疆工作虽然艰苦但也感觉到甜了。”

【匠人心语】

“养蜜蜂不是为了赚钱，主要是为了甜蜜快乐。”

“养蜜蜂的人，要对得起勤劳的蜜蜂，它们给世界带来甜蜜，我们不能让甜蜜的事业变味。”

“蜂蜜、蜂王浆、蜂胶、蜂蜡，蜜蜂吐出来的都是宝，养蜂是一种甜蜜的事业，我愿意一直坚守下去。”

（汪春荣撰文 / 摄影）

Wang Changcheng, a Beekeeper: Attentively Caressing the Sweet Cause—Bee Keeping

The Ancient Craft: Keeping Bees

Beekeeping just refers to the business of feeding bees and taking the products of the bees: honey, royal jelly, propolis, pollen, bee wax, bee pupa and bee venom, etc. It belongs to the animal industry, so broadly speaking, the bee is a kind of livestock. Beekeeping has a history of thousands of years. And the use of honey began in the age of fishing and hunting.

The Brief Biography of the Craftsman

Wang Changcheng, the sixty-one-year-old beekeeper, loved eating honey since childhood. As a child, what pleased him most was to watch the bees flying in and out of the bee buckets in his brother's home. It was by accident that he took up this business of keeping bees. In 2000, his brother was too old for this career, and saw that he was so fond of the bees, he sold to Wang Changcheng all his 10 buckets of bees. Now Wang Changcheng has more than 30 buckets of bees, and becomes a locally famous beekeeper.

The Growth of the Craftsman

Exploration: Gathering Rich Experience in Beekeeping

After taking over his brother's 10 buckets of bees, Wang treated them like a treasure. Apart from eating and sleeping, all that he thought about was how to keep bees. A long period later, Wang has accumulated rich experience in beekeeping. He could tell the next day's weather by watching the bees. If the bees stop working when the sun goes down, the next day will be a fine day; if it gets dark and the bees are still busy with their work, then it will rain in the next day.

As the time goes on, Wang has gradually got familiar with the noisy swarm. A bee swarm consists of thousands to tens of thousands of bees, with only one queen bee and a small number of drones and a large number of worker bees. The queen bee, though called "queen", has no actual leading power. Her function is just breeding. Most of the bees in the swarm are her descendants. During breeding season in spring, the queen bee could spawn more than 2000 eggs a day, of which the weight is even greater than the queen bee's weight. The worker bees will always surround the queen, like a "waiter", taking care of her needs, such as serving the food or cleaning up garbage. The queen bee is a fully developed female bee, developed from a zygote. Normally, there is only one in each swarm. Its body is one third longer than that of the worker bee, and its abdomen is longer and at its one end there is a sting. In different physiological state, the queen bee may release different information with different content. The feet are not as strong as those of the worker bees, and the hind legs have no pollen frame which can atract the honey. The queen bee has a life span of 4 to 6 years, while the average bee has a life of 60 days.

Bees are very industrious little creatures. As long as flowers bloom and the weather is fine, they go out every day to gather their honey. During the rush hour, the bees may be buzzing around in the flowers before people get up. Every time the bees fill their stomachs with nectar, they fly back to the hive and spit out the nectar in the hexagonal aperture of the honeycomb. In the evening, the bees use their wings to fan the wind, and make the moisture in the honey evaporate and make the honey slowly thicken. When the honey in the hive is full, the bee will seal it with wax for the winter, which is called capped sugar. At this point, the experienced beekeeper will not wait for the bee to seal the honey, and begin to get the honey.

In order to speed up the metabolism, Wang will develop new queen bee to replace the old one. On sunny days, he will get his newly cultivated queen fly to the sky. Then a large number of drones will follow her. Only the fastest flying drones can catch up with the queen and mate with her at an altitude of 30 meters from the ground, which is a quite romantic wedding. After mating, the drone completes its mission and dies within minutes. And the queen lays eggs, and become the new king to replace the old king who has little to spawn. The queen has devoted her whole life to spawning and breeding. During peak times, the eggs she lays one night may outweigh the queen bee herself.

March and april are the seasons for building new bee colonies. At this time, the bees will all fly out of the bucket, which is the happiest thing for them. Wang will then take out his previously prepared bamboo skin board, and walk to the swarm without any haste. After the dark brown swarm is all on the board obediently, densely and thickly, he will cover the bamboo skin board with a cloth belt. In the evening, he will hold the honeycomb and go to them slowly and guide the queen bee to the beehive. Seeing the queen in the hive, the worker bees will follow it into the hive.

Beekeeping: A Not Easy Business

The beekeeper relies not only on technology, but also on luck. If it rains continuously for more than two months, the beekeeper not only could not harvest honey, but also may lose his original capital, because he has to buy a few hundred kilos of white sugar to feed the bees.

This bowl of rice (the business of keeping bees) doesn't taste good. It contains many unexpected risks. One summer, the bees in front of the house came in and out of the mouth of the beehive. Surprisingly, some people sprayed pesticides in the rice fields and vegetable fields. Not long later, he was devastated to found the mouths of the hive were filled with the bees died from the pesticides.

Nectar Gathering: A Skilled Task

Honey gathering is usually performed at night. At this time, Wang will veil his face and wrap the head and chest all up, and may look funny with this. But even so, he would often be stung by the bees. Sometimes, his face might be swollen like a steamed bun, with only one slit in his eyes. "Usually, bees don' t sting," he said. "because if they sting, they will die."

It is a pleasure to watch him taking honey. First, open the bee bucket and put a bamboo cover on it; second, daub a little honey on the bottom of the bamboo cover; third, gently tap the bucket with a small stick. Then a large number of bees will crawl into the bamboo cover. If there are still some bees in the bee bucket, get them leave the bucket with the bamboo leaves. And then you can cut the honey in the bucket. Put the honey cut from the bucket into a barrel and give a good stirring until it becomes a solution, and then pour it onto a bamboo sieve with a layer of white gauze. With all this done, the yellow honey will drop adown into the big bowl from the white gauze.

Integrity: Sweet Business Demands Sincerity

The duty of the industrious worker bees is gathering nectar, making honey, spying, guarding, cleaning, building nests and taking care of the queen and keeping young bees. Sometimes, they may even give the queen a "massage" and help her loose her muscles and bones. Growing up on the royal jelly and without the duty of working, the queen may live for more than five years. The worker bee, by contrast, could only live for two or three months, though diligent throughout in her life. What' s more, if overworked during the blooming period, she usually can only live for ten days.No wonder the poet of the Tang Dynasty, Luo Yin, described the bees this way: "Gathering honey from hundreds of flowers, for whom it is the so hard work?"

Wang keeps bees and sells honey. He never cheats in his business with sugar. The residue of the honey will never be cooked again for the low quality honey. So his honey is always glisteningly yellow and will not spoil in the glass bottles kept in the shade. His son was a soldier in Xinjiang and found a job in Xinjiang after his retirement from the military service. Every time he visits his son, he brings a few bottles of honey, because his son likes his honey best. His son said, "When eating the honey produced by his own family, the life, though hard in Xinjiang, will taste sweet."

The Innermost Words of the Craftsman

"The major intention of my keeping bees is not to make money, but for fun and happiness."

"The beekeepers must be worthy of the industrious bees; they bring sweet to the world; we cannot let the sweet business taste different."

"Honey, royal jelly, propolis, beeswax—all that the bees spit out is treasure. Beekeeping is a kind of sweet business, and I am willing to stick to it."

(Written and photographed by Wang Chunrong)

打爆米的闵会庆：
香飘了几代人的记忆

【老手艺项目】打爆米花

打爆米花始于宋代，为古老的民间传统手艺。史书记载，爆米花松脆易消化，可作为可口的零食。爆米花的发明折射出中国饮食的丰富多彩，其深刻的含义就是开创了一种食物的加工方式——膨化食品。其制作原理就是通过物理的高温高压作用来改变事物的状态和口感，使普通的大米变成可口有特色的小吃。可以说，具有千百年历史的爆米花是近现代各种五花八门膨化零食小吃的“祖先”。

【匠人小传】

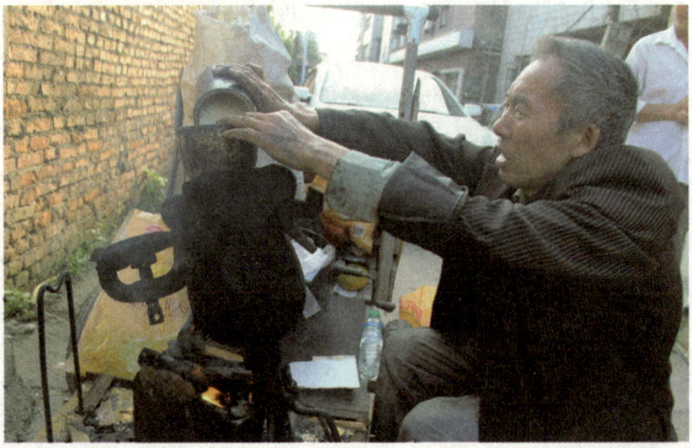

66岁的闵会庆老人，从18岁就开始在景德镇的莲花山附近打爆米。据闵会庆老人回忆，在物资匮乏的年代，拿大米去打爆米花就是最好

的零食。那时候，几乎家家户户都去打爆米花，而如今，这种老式爆米花行业远没有以前那么吃香了，但由于打爆米花的手艺人越来越少，这样的传统手艺也成了稀罕物。

【匠心之路】

坚守：打了一辈子的爆米花

打了近50年爆米花的闵会庆老人先后换了10多口锅。他说，自己打了一辈子的爆米花，走遍了景德镇的大街小巷，那个时候五分钱一锅，而现在是10块钱。

“价钱是上去了，可是成本也上去了。”闵会庆老人告诉笔者，现在买一台打爆米花的锅要1000多块，大米也涨到了3块多一斤，而且并不是每个季节可以打爆米，一年当中能打爆米的时间就是两三个月，天气太热或者太冷是不能打爆米的。“气压不行，压力要到10公斤才能开炮，要不就容易出事。”闵会庆老人的神情很严肃。

工艺：简单而原始的技术

笔者现场“观摩”了闵会庆老人打爆米花的过程。

先是生炉火，架好工具，等待着人们来打爆米花。爆米花锅有五六十厘米长，肚大，口小，底尖，浑身圆溜溜的，锅长期在炉火上炙烤，全身漆黑。锅盖呈圆形，上面连接着一根转轴和一个压力表，在压力表与盖子之间有一小段圆柱形，和底部连着的那一小截钢管，都是用来搁在铁支架上以便于打爆米花机器转动的。

炉火烧好后，闵师傅拿着空锅在火上摇几分钟，这样做是让锅有恒温。他量上一小碗米再拌上一点儿糖精，倒进锅里，盖上盖子，把锅横放在支架上，让锅身正对着炉火。闵师傅左手匀速摇动转轴，右手拉着风箱。

锅身旋转，柴火燃烧时“噼里啪啦”地响，像一首动人的童谣。

过了10分钟左右，闵师傅就开始边摇边看压力表，再把锅身从支架上端起，向旁边一个横放着的箩筐走去。箩筐里早就放好了一条长形麻布袋，把锅身放入

箩筐里，大家赶紧把两只耳朵捂住。他用麻布袋子盖住锅身，在里边把锅盖打开。

“响了！”听到打爆米花的闵师傅的提醒，围观的人立马散开，并用手捂住耳朵。

“嘣”的一声巨响过后，网兜中是一锅白生生的爆米花，空气中立即弥漫着爆米花的香气。

【匠人心语】

“打爆米花看似很简单其实是技术活，控制火候和气压表的温度很关键，还要会修理这些工具，老式爆米花机的很多零部件都不再生产了，厂家也倒闭了。”闵会庆老人说，“干这行社会地位低，又脏又累，看来以后我这手艺要失传了！”

吃爆米花，与其说想念童年的味道，倒不如说怀念童年优哉游哉的快乐时光。

（黄辉撰文 / 摄影）

Min Huiqing, a Popcorn Maker: A Fragrance Floating in the Memory of Generations

The Ancient Craft: Making Popcorn

As an ancient traditional craft in the folks, the popcorn could be dated from Song Dynasty. Based on the historical record, the popcorn is a delicious snack which is crisp in taste and easy for digestion. The invention of the popcorn also reflects the abundance of the chinese diets and hints a new creation of food processing method—puffed food. The theory of making popcorns is to change status and taste of the food under the physical high temperature and pressure, and convert the ordinary rice into the delicious distinctive snack. In another word, the popcorn with thousands of history is actually the ancestor of the various puffed snacks in modern times.

The Brief Biography of the Craftsman

The 66 years old craftsman, Min Huiqing, started to make the popcorn near Lotus Hill in Jingdezhen at the age of 18. According to Min' s recall, the popcorn was once the best snack in the period lack of material. At that time, almost every family ate the popcorns, but the old industry for making the popcorn is not that popular nowadays. And the traditional crafts turn to be rare as the number of craftsmen is becoming less and less.

The Growth of the Craftsman

Perseverance in Making Popcorns

Min Huiqing changed more than 10 pots in the past 50 years when making popcorns. He said he has been making popcorns for his whole life and walked on all streets of Jingdezhen. A pot of popcorns was priced at 5 cents in the past, but now it' s at 10 yuan.

"The price is higher, but its cost also is more." The old master Min said. He told the writer that the pot of making the popcorns was priced at more than 1000 yuan, and the price of the rice was also increased into over 1.5 yuan per kilo. Meantime, he couldn' t make the popcorns all the time but in around two to three months of a year as the temperature condition matters too much. "The pot can' t be opened unless pressure reaches the degree as high as 10 kilos, otherwise, it will be dangerous." Min said seriously.

Popcorn Making Craft: the Simple and Primitive Skill

The writer watched the whole process when Min Huiqing made popcorns.

At first, he lit the fire in the oven, set up the tools and then waited for the client to buy the popcorns. The popcorn pot is around 50cm to 60cm in length with big chamber, small mouth, acuate bottom and round body. The pot is black from head to toe as it' s fired for long. The lid is round with a spindle and a pressure gage connected to its top, and in between the lid and the gage it is a short length of cylinder, the cylinder and the steel pipe connected to the bottom are put onto the stands for rotation of the corn popper.

After the fire was ready, Master Min rotated the empty pot for a few minutes to warm it up. Then he filled the pot with a small bowl of rice and a little saccharin, and lidded it. Next, the pot was horizontally put onto the stands with its chamber against the fire, and Min rotated the spindle evenly by his left hand and pulled the air bellows by the right hand.

The pot rotated, and wood fire crackled, which sounded as melodic as a nursery rhyme.

About 10 minutes later, Min started to watch the pressure gage when rotating the pot. Then he took the pot off the stands and walked to a wicker basket lain aside, in which there was a long sack in readiness. The people around all rushed to cover up the ears when Min put the body of the pot into the basket, and he was about to open the lid inside the sack.

"Watch Out!" Min yelled before opening the pot, and onlookers either dismissed or put their hands onto the ears upon hearing the reminder.

Bang! After the tremendous sound, the net bag was full of white popcorns, and the fragrance diffused in the air right away.

The Innermost Words of the Craftsman

"It looks simple to make popcorns but it' s actually a skill to control the heat of the fire and temperature on the pressure gage on one hand, and to mend tools on the other hand, especially under the circumstance that most of the components for the old-styled popcorn pot are not produced any more and even the factories are closed down." Min Huiqing continued, "It looks as if my craft is going to die out because the craftsmen in this industry are underprivileged and the work is always tiring and dirty."

In fact, eating popcorns is not so much a missing of the taste in childhood as a recalling of the carefree and leisurely time in childhood.

(Written and photographed by Huang Hui)

做棉花糖的万愈丰：云卷云舒走四方

【老手艺项目】棉花糖

棉花糖疏松多孔，具有一定的弹性和韧性，因口感和质地与棉花相似而得名。将白糖倒入棉花糖机中制出糖丝，再用棒子将糖丝缠绕起来而成，入口即溶，因糖丝跟棉花絮十分相似，故得其名。

【匠人小传】

万愈丰，江西都昌人，52岁，来景德镇以棉花糖手艺为生近30年。30年来，他推着一辆棉花糖机子走街串巷，以苦为乐，为镇上的孩子们

从事着甜蜜的事业，积累了丰富的经验。一勺子普普通通的蔗糖，经他用机器一搅和，瞬间就开出洁白的花朵，仿佛盛开的棉花，也仿佛舒卷的云彩。在这种走街串巷的营生中，万师傅打发着自己的平凡岁月，也增添着镇上孩子们的甜美与欢笑。

【匠心之路】

做棉花糖的奥秘

棉花糖制作机是台像个大碗的机器，机器的中心部位是一个温度很高的加热腔，热量打破了晶体的结构，将糖变成了糖浆。加热腔中有一些比颗粒蔗糖尺寸还小的孔，当糖在加热腔中高速旋转的时候，离心运动将糖浆从小孔中喷射到“大碗”的周围。由于液态物质遇冷凝固的速度和它的体积有关，体积越小，凝固得越快。因此，加热腔中的小孔直径很小，从小孔中喷射出来的糖浆马上就凝结成固态的糖丝，不会黏在一起。

唇齿留芳的风味小吃

这天是国庆节，景德镇人民公园人山人海，笑语盈盈。在公园花坛一隅，万师傅给我们演示了花式棉花糖的做法，令人为其精湛技艺赞不绝口。

首先，将准备好的红色砂糖10克和黄色砂糖10克放于盆中，准备好小勺一把，竹签两根，做好操作前的用料准备工作。

用小勺盛取 10 克黄色砂糖，倒入机器出糖器内，待糖丝飞出后，手拿一根竹签顺时针旋转，将糖丝缠绕到竹签上。缠绕过程中保持手持竹签的平衡度，并且保持前后移动的状态，均匀地将糖丝全部缠绕到竹签上。

将糖丝缠绕完成后，做成圆球状，长约 20 厘米，直径 15 厘米，即可完成花式棉花糖的花芯制作。花式棉花糖花芯完成后，接着用小勺盛取红色糖 20 克，倒入出糖器内，为了做出更好的效果，第二次放糖要比花芯增加一倍更好。

等放入糖糖丝飞出后，将已缠绕好的花芯向上倾斜 30 度角，并顺时针旋转竹签，将糖丝均匀缠绕到花芯上，并且在缠绕的过程中保持手法稳定，并向后移动，以达到更好的花边效果。

【匠人心语】

健康是人的第一财富，尽管我是一个做棉花糖的人，但还是提醒大家：孩子吃多了糖，损害牙齿；大人吃糖过量，更是有百害而无一利。

（芷琳 / 撰文　丰月 / 摄影）

Wan Yufeng, a Cotton Candy Maker: Travelling Extensively with the "Swirling Clouds"

The Ancient Craft: Cotton Candy Making

Cotton candy is loose and porous, which has a certain degree of elasticity and toughness, and it is named after its taste and texture similar to cotton.The white sugar is poured into a cotton candy machine to produce sugar wire, and the sugar wire is wound by a rod, with its inlet being dissolved. As the sugar wire is very similar to the cotton batting, therefore the name is created.

The Brief Biography of the Craftsman

Wan Yufeng, is 52 years old and comes from Duchang, Jiangxi Province.He has made a living on the skill of making cotton candy for about 30 years.For 30 years, he pushed a cotton candy machine to go round the streets and took the pain for a pleasure. He engaged in the sweet career for the children who come from town, and acquired a lot of experience. Mixed by the machine, a spoonful of sucrose instantly changes into pure white flowers, some of which are like blooming cotton, while others like swirling clouds. In such living of going round the streets, Mr.Wan spent his own ordinary years and brought sweetness and laughter to the town' s children.

The Growth of the Craftsman

The Tricks of Making Cotton Candy

The cotton candy machine looks like a big bowl. The central part of the machine is a heating chamber with high temperature. The heat breaks the crystal structure and turns the sucrose into syrup.There are holes in the heating chamber that are smaller than the size of the granule sucrose.As the sucrose rotates at a high speed in the heating chamber, the centrifuge moves the syrup from the hole to the "large bowl" .The smaller the volume is, the faster it solidifies, because the speed of the solidification of the liquid substance is related to its volume. Therefore, the diameter of the small holes in the heating chamber is small, and the syrup, which is ejected from the small hole, immediately condenses into solid sugar wire, and it will not stick together.

A Local Snack with Lingering Aroma

This day is the National Day, the People' s Park in Jingdezhen is overcrowded with people, and the laughter could be heard everywhere. In a corner of the garden, Master Wan showed us the method of making cotton candy, which is full of exquisite skills that deserve high praise.

First of all, 10 grams of red granulated sugar and 10 grams of yellow granulated sugar will be prepared and poured into the basin, and then get a small spoon and two bamboo sticks ready to be used in operation.

Using a small spoon to hold 10 grams of yellow sugar and then pour it into the machine, after the sugar wires fly out, hold a bamboo stick and rotate clockwise, the sugar wires wind around stick; keep the bamboo stick balanced during the winding process, and keep it moving back and forth; then the sugar wires will be twined tightly around the bamboo stick.

After winding the sugar wire, make it a roll ball which is about 20 centimeters long and 15 centimeters in diameter.Then, the making of flower core of floral marshmallow is finished. After finishing it, take a small spoon of red sugar about 20 grams and pour it into the sugar machine. In order to make a better effect, the sugar poured the second time should be two times the weight of the sugar used the first time.

When the sugar wire flys out, uptilt the flower core at 30 degrees, and rotate the bamboo stick clockwise then the sugar wires may twine to the stick evenly. During the course, maintain stability of the technique, and move the stick backward, then a better effect may be achieved with a good lace along the outline of the candy.

The Innermost Words of the Craftsman

Health is the most important wealth of a man, although I am a worker of making cotton candy, I' m still reminding you: Too much sugar will damage children' s teeth; Similarly, too much sugar is always destructive to the adults' health.

(Written by Zhi Lin, photographed by Feng Yue)

记住乡愁
（跋）

谢玮

景德镇不仅是举世闻名的瓷都，也是国务院公布的首批中国历史文化名城之一。景德镇历经两千多年的城市发展史，形成了异彩纷呈而特色鲜明的老城文化。其形形色色的老城文化既是构成景德镇地域文化主体的重要因素，也是呈现景德镇历史文化的重要符号。曾几何时，它们与这座城市的发展和繁荣息息相关。

现代城市发展日新月异，随着老城面貌的飞速变迁，许多老街区、老建筑、老物件、老行当乃至老风俗正在逐渐消失或者已经消失，景德镇人的故土印记和家园感也在不可避免地缺失。乡愁淡漠，使许多年轻人对本土本乡的历史文化知之甚少。毋庸置疑，对家园厚土的记忆丧失，是一座城市不容忽视的文化损失。对这些弥足珍贵的老城文化记忆进行抢救性的挖掘和保护，已经成为传承和弘扬传统文化中的当务之急。

记得住乡愁，是关系到一代人精神家园的时代命题。讲好老城故事，弘扬老城文化，留下文化记忆，使老城文化传承、延续、发展下去，是亟待专家学者、文化工作者和各相关部门共同承担的社会责任。正是在这样一种文化情怀和历史使命的驱使下，我们景德镇古镇投资管理有限公司携手景德镇学院老城文化研究课题组的同仁们，以撰写和出版《景德镇匠人志》为切入点，开启了“景德镇老城文化记忆”保护工程的合作计划。

作为一座历史悠久的手工业城市，景德镇不仅拥有以“工匠八方来，器成天下走”为行业背景的陶瓷工匠文化，其五行八作的非陶瓷类匠人文化也颇具独特的历史价值。今天，在课题组和古镇公司同仁们共同努力下拿出的这部分量不轻的“老城文化记忆”专著《景德镇匠人志：匠心无迹》，正是景德镇“非陶瓷类”匠人文化的集中展现。

一方水土养一方人。景德镇自古以来就是一座没有围墙的城市，具有海纳百川、兼收并蓄的包容性。两千多年五方杂厝、商贾云集的城市化历史进程，赋予其老城文化以丰富多彩的人文内涵。本书从“雅艺”“手艺”“食艺”三个板块，多角度多层面地向人们展示了50余个具有代表性的老行当的历史风情或时代风貌。

这些文章以生动鲜活的细节、点面结合的表现手法、张弛有度的叙事风格，在读者面前呈现出一幅幅摇曳多姿的古镇老城文化画卷，写出了人们对景德镇传统文化及社会风情的心灵眷恋；这些绘声绘色的时代记忆，是来自历史长河的美妙回响。

著书立说总是一项充满遗憾的工作。毋庸讳言，本书还有诸多不尽如人意之处：因为一时找不到代表性传人，一些本该纳入本书视线的老行当最终只能成为遗珠之憾；因为课题组摄影专业人员的欠缺，书中一些图片质量也差强人意；少数文章因为采访不够深入也缺乏可读性。但是，瑕不掩瑜，课题组和古镇公司同仁们在此书历时将近一年的采访和撰写过程中体现出来的踏破铁鞋的毅力和煎精熬血的意志是值得称道的——毫无疑问，这也是一种难能可贵的工匠精神。

文化是一座城市的血脉和灵魂，是城市的内核、实力和形象；城市是文化的凝结和积淀，是文化的容器、载体和舞台；城市与文化是与生俱来、密不可分的统一体。一座城市，离开了文化就失去了灵魂。

城市的文化根脉来自历史深处，它是城市的基因、灵魂和特质所在。我们只有知道自己从哪里来，才能明白未来往何处去，否则就会迷失方向、忘记初心、失去灵魂。城市作为文化的生命体亦同此理，它沿着历史根脉走到当下，再走向未来。

对于一座城市而言，经济决定地位，文化决定品位；文化多么发达，城市就多么发达；文化能够走多远，城市就能够走多远。文化，深刻影响着一座城市发展的进程，改变着一座城市的命运。文化，也是城市发展中的新资源要素。

从这一意义上说，景德镇老城文化保护使命光荣，任重道远。《景德镇匠人志：匠心无迹》的出版，只是一个抛砖引玉的开端。

Evoking Nostalgia (Postscript)

Xie Wei

Jingdezhen, known as the famous "porcelain capital" in the world, was listed among the first batch of historical and cultural cities approved by the State Council of the People's Republic of China. With the history of urban development extending for more than two thousand years, Jingdezhen has gradually formed a colorful and unique old town culture. Its varied old town culture, which contributed greatly to the prosperity and development of the city for a long period of time, is not only an important factor constituting a mainstream of the local culture, but also an important symbol for the history and culture in Jingdezhen.

China's modern cities have developed rapidly and Jingdezhen's old town has witnessed many changes. For example, many old streets, old buildings, old artifacts, old trades and even old customs have been vanishing gradually or have virtually disappeared, which will inevitably leads to lack of impression of hometown and sensations of homestead for people living in Jingdezhen. Thus, a lack of nostalgia makes many young people know little about its local history and culture. Without doubt, the loss of memory of their hometown is an innegligible cultural loss for a city. To excavate and protect the precious cultural memories of the old town has become an urgent priority for inheritance and promotion of traditional culture.

Remembering nostalgia is a proposition of the times related to the spiritual home of a whole generation. Therefore, it is an urgent social responsibility for experts, scholars, cultural workers and relevant departments to inherit, continue and promote the culture of the old town by telling the stories of the old town, promoting the culture of the old town, and maintaining the memory of culture. Driven by the cultural feelings and historical mission, Jingdezhen Ancient Town Investment Management Co., Ltd., together with the Research Team for Old Town Culture of Jingdezhen University, takes the editing and publishing of the book The Craftsmen of Jingdezhen & Its Vanishing Folk Craftsmanship as a breakthrough point, launched a cooperation plan for protecting the cultural memory of Jingdezhen old town.

As a handicraft city with a long history, Jingdezhen not only has a ceramic craftsman culture based on its industrial background, where people used to say: "craftsmen come from all directions; vessels go to all parts of the world", but also forms a wide range of non-ceramic craftsman culture with unique historical value. At present, the publication of the book The Craftsmen of Jingdezhen & Its Vanishing Folk

Craftsmanship, a valuable monograph of old town cultural memories, is a concentrated expression of "non-ceramic" craftsman culture of Jingdezhen.

It is said that human beings are shaped by land and water around them. Since ancient times, the city, not encircled by any wall, symbolizes openness and inclusiveness. With more than two thousands of history of urbanization, the historical town where all kinds of people lived and merchants gathered has created its abundant cultural connotation. This book, starting from the description of "elegant art", "handicraft art", "food processing art", depicts the historical charm and styles to readers with over 50 typical old trades through different perspectives.

The essays in the book, with vivid details, skilled expressing methods and balanced narrative style, presents to the readers with colorful pictures of the ancient town and reveals a deep affection for the traditional culture and custom of Jingdezhen. The vivid memory of the times is a wonderful echo from our long history.

Editing books is often regarded as a job full of regret. Undoubtedly, the book leaves much to be desired in some aspects. It is a pity that some old trades have not been included in the book, because representative inheritors are hard to find in a very short time. In addition, due to the lack of professional photographers, the quality of some pictures in the book is barely satisfactory. Moreover, the readability of few articles needs to be improved due to lack of an in-depth interview. However, as an old saying goes, "defects cannot obscure the splendor". The most remarkable thing about the book is that the team members from Jingdezhen University and Jingdezhen Ancient Town Investment Management Co., Ltd demonstrate their pertinacious perseverance and resolute mind during nearly one years' interviewing and editing. With no doubt, it can also be regarded as a valuable craftsman spirit.

Culture is the main bloodline and soul of the city as well as its core strengths and images. City is the cultural crystallization and accumulation, it is also the container, the carrier of culture as well as the cultural arena. Hence, city and culture are born as an inseparable unity. A city without culture is just like a person who has lost soul.

The cultural root of a city comes from the depths of history, which bears the gene, soul and character of the city. Only when we know where we are from, can we understand where we are going in the future. Otherwise, we will get lost, forget where we started and lose our identity. It is for the same reason that a city, which acts as the cultural life entity, goes through a certain development stage to the present and will step into the future along its historical roots.

For a city, economy determines its status, and culture has the reaction to its style; the more its culture advances, the more developed it will be; how long its culture continues, and how long it survives. It is culture that has a deep impact on the process of development of a city and changes its destiny. Besides, it may sever as a new resource element in the process of development of the city.

In this sense, our duty and mission are glorious but arduous.Thus, the publication of this work could only serve as a modest spur to induce more valuable studies and get people more involved.